chasing the wind:
A QUADROPHENIA ANTHOLOGY

gary wharton

lushington **PUBLISHING**

lushington **PUBLISHING**

© 2009 gary wharton
All Rights Reserved.
ISBN 0954218701
http://members.tripod.com/chasing_book.tripod/

No part of this book may be
reproduced, stored in a
retrieval system, or
transmitted in any form
or by any means,
electronic, photocopying,
recorded or otherwise,
without the permission
of the copyright holder.

for m + e, xxx

originally published 2002
by lushington publishing.
reprinted 2004.revised
and third print in 2006.
this edition 2009.

typography + page design:
gary wharton

quadmodbook@yahoo.co.uk
0776 123 9130

printed + bound by
*Paper Tiger Printing
Wells, Somerset, UK*

readers comments 04
introduction 06
cast / crew details 07
cast and crew credits 08
story synopsis 9
a to z anthology 60
brighton locations / anthology 71
general anthology part ii 101
goofs 135
slang usage / definition used in the film 219
general anthology part iii 222
scene by scene detailing 260
bibliography 284

contents

> Some comments about Chasing the Wind: A Quadrophenia Anthology

"The ultimate guide to Quadrophenia."
the brighton argus

"Everything you ever wanted to know and more about Mods, Rockers, the music, the fashion, the scooters, the politics even the haircuts: this book has it all. Written by an author that must have eaten, drink and breathed the whole genre for a long time, it gives a wealth of interesting, often funny insights into this seminal film."
amazon.co.uk

"Believe me when I say that this book really goes into every detail about the film. I can't see that anything else could be added. All in all Chasing the Wind: A Quadrophenia Anthology does exactly what it says on the cover. An A-Z of all things relating to The Who film Quadrophenia. Everything is explained in detail and is complete. A definitely worthy addition to anyones collection."
http://www.thewho.fsnet.co.uk/standard/quad_anth.htm

"He writes with the passion of a true fan."
buzz magazine

"To say he has had a brush with Mod lore is an understatement - he has an in-depth knowledge of the movement, everything from attitudes of mind to how to sit on a scooter."
the brighton argus

"Obviously a labour of love. I've never been to Brighton myself so the biggest compliment I can pay you is you've finally given me the incentive to go....It's a book I will return to on a regular basis."
sean kilminster, tyne & wear

"...Wharton's enthusiasm and love for the film is catching, and he obviously had a hell of a lot of fun putting this book together. This is the ultimate expression of fandom...it is certainly the ideal book for all you Modspotters out there."
andrew corbin, ugly things american fanzine

"It's nice to have someone such as yourself commit to print what you believe in and found out. The book will not only serve me in remembering my youth as a Mod (and today to some extent!) but my children as well; for they are interested in what their dad got up to when he was young(er).
mark gillespie, middlesex

"Just to say many thanks for the book. I'd heard quite a bit about it but have to say its even better than I expected so far I've failed in all attempts to put it down!!!
ian edmonds, waterlooville, hants

What can I say about this book?
To say that I am delighted is somewhat of an understatement!
The book is absolutely amazing!
I think a visit to brighton is on the cards very soon...
I'll be sure to recommend it. Well done on such a superb book.
gary leeke, via email.

En toute chose il faut considerer la fin.
Jean De La Fontaine

Introduction

One of the prevailing strength's of the film Quadrophenia is that each actor and their screen character has his or her part to play in making the movie what it is. Consequently, by watching it over again, the viewer warms to the faces presented, whether it be the asinine Chalky or the bruised Monkey, forever seeking the attention of a distant Jimmy. Evoking that essential quest to seek to define one's true self, Jimmy's experiences presented on screen are of a kind that will always be relatable. Not only that, as well as a cult film, it succeeds in being genuinely accessible as a piece of drama. Chasing the Wind takes the film as its central focal point rather than the original 1973 Who album. The two are inextricably linked but there are marked differences, many of which are revealed throughout the text. Today's mod enthusiast may not care too much for the sensationalist, drug-enhanced lifestyle portrayed somewhat on screen, as mod today is an attitude: crisp, clean and neat. Conversely, the film succeeds in highlighting an all too brief period of genuine idealism: with the life of a mod equal to the carousal ride at a fun fair, pure enjoyment in an ocean of colour, pace, spectacle, movement and élan.

Divided into separate elements, *Chasing the Wind* includes an extensive A to Z anthology of all things relating to the film, from extensive cast biographies, music and fashion summaries to locations and associated connections. Containing as much information as I could muster, there will of course, be things that I have missed but it is as concise as I could manage without anxiety attacks palpable by faceless scooterists zooming by informing me that I forgot to include this or that proving habitual. Now thirty years since its release, Quadrophenia continues to enthral audiences both familiar and fresh, revealing a little more upon each viewing due to a resonance of energy and vigour that flows through it. Special thanks to cast members Kate Williams, John Altman and Phil Davis for their thoughts and recollections collected during the early part of the development of this project. Finally, a big thanks to everyone that has taken the time to contact me from all over the world since the original publication of this work; your enthusiasm has proven invigorating. gw / 2009

QUADROPHENIA (1979)

Directed by FRANC RODDAM.

A Who Films/ Polytel Films release. The January 1997 re-issue was from Polygram Filmed Entertainment and released by Feature Film Company.

THE CAST:

Jimmy Cooper PHIL DANIELS
Steph LESLIE ASH
Dave MARK WINGETT
Chalky PHILIP DAVIS
The Brighton Ace Face STING
Kevin RAY WINSTONE
Spider GARY SHAIL
Pete GARRY COOPER
Monkey TOYAH WILLCOX
Ferdy TREVOR LAIRD
Mr Cooper MICHAEL ELPHICK
Dan DANIEL PEACOCK
Mrs Cooper KATE WILLIAMS
Yvonne Cooper KIM NEVE
Mr Fulford BENJAMIN WHITROW
Michael JEREMY CHILD

Des PATRICK MURRAY
Tailor OLIVER PIERRE
John JOHN ALTMAN
Alfredo's cafe owner GEORGE INNES
Mr Cale HUGH LLOYD
Harry North JOHN BINDON
Hostile Rocker #1 GARY HOLTON
Hostile Rocker #2 JESSE BIRDSALL
Barman at villains pub P.H MORIARTY
Magistrate JOHN PHILLIPS
Harry TIMOTHY SPALL
Des PERRY BENSON

THE CREDITS

Director FRANC RODDAM *Executive Producers* ROGER DALTREY, JOHN ENTWISTLE, KEITH MOON, PETE TOWNSHEND *Executive Producer (Polytel)* DAVID GIDEON THOMSON *Producers* ROY BAIRD, BILL CURBISHLEY *Associate Producer* JOHN PEVERALL *Unit Manager* DAVID ANDERSON *Location Managers* REDMOND MORRIS, BRYAN COATES *Production Assistant* CAROLINE HAGEN *First Assistant Director* RAY CORBETT *Second Assistant Director* MICHAEL FLYNN *Second Assistant Director* KIERON PHIPPS *Continuity* MELINDA REES *Casting Director* PATSY POLLOCK *Story Consultants* ALAN FLETCHER, PETE TOWNSHEND, CHRIS STAMP *Screenplay* DAVE HUMPHRIES, MARTIN STELLMAN, FRANC RODDAM *Screenplay [Un-credited]* PETE TOWNSHEND *Director of Photography* BRIAN TUFANO *Camera Operator* DEWI HUMPHRIES *Film Editor* SEAN BARTON, MIKE TAYLOR *Camera Operator* DEWI HUMPHRIES *Production Designer* SIMON HOLLAND *Assistant Art Director* ANDREW SANDERS *Set Decorator* KEN WHEATLEY *Wardrobe Supervisor* JOYCE STONEMAN *Make-up* GILLI WAKEFORD *Clapper Loader* DEREK SUTER *Property Master* TERRY WELLS *Hairdresser* SIMON THOMPSON *Music Director* ROGER DALTREY, JOHN ENTWISTLE, PETE TOWNSHEND *Music Co-ordinator* MIKE SHAW *Music Producer* JOHN ENTWISTLE *Sound Mixer* CHRISTIAN WRANGLER *Sound Re-recording* BILL ROWE *Sound Engineer* JOHN ASTLEY *Sound Editor* JOHN IRELAND *Stunt Arranger* PETER BRAYHAM *Public Relations* DENNIS DAVIDSON ASSOCIATES.

Processed by Rank Laboratories and recorded on Dolby Stereo.
Re-Recorded at EMI Studios, Elstree.
Made by The Who Films Ltd at Lee International Studios, Wembley and on location in London and Brighton.

AFTER TURNING AWAY FROM THE CLIFF-TOP, an ashen-faced Jimmy walks towards the camera and out of the frame as the soundtrack loops the lines taken from the four themes allocated to the members of The Who in the form of a concise I Am the Sea: Roger Daltrey has Helpless Dancer, Keith Moon has Bell Boy, John Entwistle, Dr Jimmy and Pete Townshend the glittering Love Reign O'er Me. The roar of the sea is a dominant factor in a beautifully sumptuous opening scene, soaked as it is in a rich orange and yellow hue. Interspersed with the introduction of The Real Me, indicative of Jimmy's multi-personality related through the four disparate members of The Who. Cloaked in his army green parka, the imagery seems fitting, as for Jimmy, the exhausting battle is over in his own personal war.

Many people when asked about Quadrophenia will usually say that Jimmy kills himself in the end of the film and are surprised upon being informed that the end of the film is actually the start of his development. A death in a way but not in a literal sense. Director Franc Roddam recently revealed that Jimmy was supposed to throw himself off the cliff but the script was changed during the shooting (as it often was). With the opening credits then appearing on screen, we see the sheer unadulterated bliss of what it is to be a young Mod shining forth from the face of a parka-enveloped Jimmy Cooper as he swirls his way along with the sound of Keith Moon's rumbling, tumbling drumming on The Real Me almost pushing him along the darkened streets. Heading towards the Goldhawk Social Club, a popular dance venue frequented by Mods in the early Sixties, Jimmy rides a 1961 LI Lambretta scooter, his green ex-U.S. army-issue coat helps protect his own particular uniform underneath, consisting of grey shirt and tie, black suit jacket and trousers. Accessorized with two lamps at the front, Capital L and I stickers, six wing mirrors either side of his crossbar and foxtail on the tip of a lengthy aerial attached to the rear of the bike. He also has an added back support for a pillion passenger and a carrier attachment for containing a bag as well as being handy for stuffing your parka into.

Two yellow stars mark either side of his windshield with the registration number KRU 251 on the side of the front mudguard. Never regarded as anything other than functional by the mobile modernist, with the commercial peak of the exploitation of all things Mod, a 1965 advertisement in the New Musical Express [the 'NME'] offered the parkas for sale at thirty-five shillings. Regaled as being 'ideal for outdoor people, cyclists, farmers, football fans or just for strollers.' Those involved in the embryonic days of Mod chose to distance themselves from this preferring to be known as 'stylists' rather than 'Mod' which by then had become a term widely abused in the media and popular fashion circles.

Returning once more to Jimmy, his scooter, not to be mistaken for a motorbike, as his mother [perfectly played by Kate Williams] boorishly labels it, has other customised extras, including a Lambretta windshield purchased for £4 15/-, front and rear carriers costing £3 5/- and £2 19/6 respectively. Whilst each of his mirrors would have set him back £1 2/6. There was also a specific method of riding a scooter if you were a Mod, involving the positioning of the feet to supplement the overall geometry of the machine. All are presented as indicative of a statement of intent; a clarification of a shared identity shown through an individual Mod. However, mishaps did occur amongst inexperienced riders who soon discovered the importance of putting your feet down whilst at traffic lights to counter balance the weight of the scooter and thus avoid it toppling over on you. The sleeker body shape of the Lambretta proved more popular amongst teen-aged riders of the period although many Vespas are seen in the film too. The availability of the scooter was generally facilitated by the ease of monthly repayments through Hire Purchase [HP] or the 'never-never' as it soon became termed. This was not to last as by the mid-Sixties both Vespa and Lambretta had come to be a more expensive purchase. Mods like Jimmy and his mates in Quadrophenia were not the first to discover the joys of scootering, as from 1945 to 1960 the Italian scooter outshone the traditional motorcycle in terms of sales, totalling 160,000 in Britain by 1959. Rally enthusiasts had been scooting down to Brighton in 1958 and 1959, a decade before its reputation was to be placed in a far more menacing significance.

STORY SYNOPSIS   A QUADROPHENIA ANTHOLOGY

"Darlin! Oi!" Jimmy calls out to a girl off-screen, quickly regaining the steering after swerving a little bit. "Look at me, love: ain't I the one! Huh!" He might as well have added. Roger Daltrey's vocal for The Real Me revs itself up as an accompaniment. Meanwhile a posse of leather-clad bikers suddenly comes all about him on their faster and heavier machines, questioning his mode of transport. After much debate and winding-up they disappear as swiftly as they had arrived and Jimmy reverts to his own state of well-being and contentment at being a Mod. A fraction later he regains his composure and continues along with his head held high somewhat aping Kenneth Williams' trademark facial disdain used so succinctly in many a Carry On film. It is such a slight movement yet observing it makes Jimmy seem human and thus easier to relate to.

"'Ere, you got something nice for me?" Jimmy to local dealer Ferdy. Parking up outside the club and in amongst a corral of similar thoroughbreds Jimmy immediately seeks out the sharply-attired, sticky-brimmed hat wearing Ferdy [Trevor Laird]; the spinach provider to most of the Popeyed Mods. As if by magic, Ferdy reveals his stash of goods from under his hat. *"Keep your brain warm, do they?"* spurts an anxious to score Jimmy as the two proceed to barter over the price.

Eventually agreeing Jimmy steps inside, content in the knowledge of being sufficiently equip for the ensuing evening. But not before making the first of a succession of dubious racist remarks towards Ferdy, a further couple coming from Chalky [Phil Davis] and Pete [Garry Cooper]. We know that it is the Goldhawk thanks to the American-style vertical signage outside acknowledging it as such. Management at the club, in keeping with most other venues, had a membership scheme to which youngsters would have to contribute five shillings and an additional five upon each visit. In actuality, the real Goldhawk bared no resemblance to its on-screen portrait as can be revealed by a photograph of its exterior found on Jack Lyons's website. 'Irish' Jack as he came to be nicknamed by Who manager Kit Lambert, was one of the leading Mods down there in the early days and on his site he gives a sharp view of what the atmosphere at the club was like, "What a place!" he recounts in one of his anecdotal stories, "It

11

chasing the wind STORY SYNOPSIS

looks like a Woman's Institute private residence from the outside but that place [could] take off like nowhere else on a Friday and Saturday night." This story, A Day in the Night of a Goldhawk Mod, is one of a dozen to be enjoyed on the site enhancing the connection to those who were not born during the period described. Pete Townshend, writing in his foreword to the absorbing and extensively well-illustrated book The Who Concert File [co-authored by Lyons with Joe McMichael] credits him as being partly responsible for inspiring the character of Jimmy for the original 1973 Who album. The Goldhawk was a place often frequented by Mod idealists and fledgling High Numbers/ Who manager Pete Meaden, would often go there to soak up the latest fashions which changed weekly. It was a frenzied environment overflowing with ideas nigh on impossible not to be swept along with such was its vitality. Faintly heard from within the club in this scene is Hi Heel Sneakers being performed by Cross Section. Always found at Mod hangouts, never once is any comprehensive piece of information discovered about perennial hat wearing Ferdy other than when Jimmy and his mates meekly go looking for him later in an unspecified part of London. And this only because of their need to gather further supplies for the forthcoming Brighton weekender. Otherwise, Laird's character is given a cliched role in parallel to the vacuous one of the contemporary dealer. Ferdy's look is a very fine one, all-dark toned suits fittingly topped off by a trim, pork-pie hat. He and Jim's best pal Dave [played by Mark Wingett] are the only ones seen sporting them in the film, embracing a fashion that saw a resurgence amongst many youngsters in the late-Fifties and on in to the next colourful decade.

Where the suit had been seen as an appropriation by the young working class, so to it was for the hat. Its image was shifted away from the middle class respectability of old and reintroduced as a fashion accessory. In a 1964 advertisement for the Modique Co. found in music paper Disc, 'Hats for Mods' were being sold in tones of midnight blue, brown and slate grey at 69/6 individually. The headwear trend would return in the late-Seventies where it was widely associated with the Two-Tone record label with its emerging bands The Specials and Selecter adopting the Jamaican Rude Boy look. Suite up and wearing wraparound dark sunglasses, just as Ferdy does, the London-based band Madness also had a similar styling with their Nutty Boy persona. Entering the club and clutching his bag of synthesis as if a trophy, Jimmy displays his treasure to a fellow mod who dashes off to speak with Ferdy. Is this the same boy slouched on the floor in the gents toilet later on? A relaxed and youthful-looking band called Cross Section blast out the first slice of non-Who music [following on from I Am The Sea and The Real Me] from a podium positioned very near to the audience seen dancing in front of them. Their jaunty take on Hi Heel Sneakers goes down well as we pick out some of Jimmy's mates including Monkey [Toyah Willcox with a harsh cut of hair that makes her look almost hawk-like in appearance], Spider [Gary Shail] and the rest, dancing about in such an infectious manner. Accredited to Rob Higginbotham, Sneakers is a catchy tune that has seen covers by Jerry Lee Lewis, Stevie Wonder and Tom Jones. American singer Tommy Tucker had a British hit with it in 1964. Dimples, the second cover performed by the band finds Jimmy dogging Steph [Leslie Ash] grooving with her boyfriend Pete, wearing a white striped jacket coupled with the naffest haircut amongst the male Mod contingent. Dave approaches and proves all-encouraging whilst smoking a cigarette. Adopting a look consisting of a mustard jacket, green-striped shirt and tie with his ever-present pork pie hat Wingett projects a Technicolor delight of male adolescence. It is ironic that once the film was released theatrically in late 1979, its certification as an 'X' [prohibiting admission to anyone under eighteen] meant that at seventeen he was too young to see it. However, director Franc Roddam did arrange a private screening for the cast sometime after, which he did attend. All the while Jimmy, eyes-a-popping, outfitted in a black and purple stripe jacket with a burgundy tie looks strangely camp, what with finely combed hair and side-parting coupled with his eyeliner unflatteringly creates the impression of lengthening his nose. In keeping with many Mods, Jimmy is slightly built in a physical sense. Spider and Chalky both of whom we will get to know more of soon, share a similar kind of physicality whereas the height of both Dave and the Brighton ace Face [Sting] is rather noticeable next to them. Looking at Jimmy burning his eyes into the long-haired Miss Ash, Dave knows precisely

chasing the wind   STORY SYNOPSIS

what his friend is thinking because he has the same carnal thoughts towards the svelte-like Steph dressed as she is in a sleeveless dress in what looks like grey or off-white, her hair lengthy and brushed over the forehead.

Dave encourages him to go up and talk to her even though she is with somebody else, he jokes that if he fails to do so then he himself might just go for it. It is an indication and a typical one at that, of how the friends tease each other only in this instance its reverb for future trouble proves ominous. With its opening line of "I love the way you walk..." Dimples, begins and it is fun to see the two mates having such a good time. Giggling together and jigging to and forth in a style popularised in the Seventies by Status Quo fans, from which it seemed that all movement had to generate from the groin. Neither of the two Cross Section tracks saw a release as a single and the group seems to have slipped back in to anonymity after their foray in Quadrophenia.

Ending an eventful evening Jimmy returns home, methodically repeating the daily task of steering his Lambretta along the narrow alleyway at the side of the house leading to the rear of the property. It just about allows enough space through to where he can garage it safely in the shed. Creeping up stairs and on to the landing he cringes upon hearing his mother's feelings of conjugal neglect, agrivated by his father [Michael Elphick], spoken from within their darkened bedroom. Jimmy moves on and in to his sister Yvonne's room. Here he is startled to discover her in a blue-tinged space sitting in the lotus position clad only in her bra and pants tanning herself under a sunlamp. Clumsily knocking over a bottle of nail varnish on the dressing table, he has a bit of fun in teasing her about the perils of artificial light before grabbing a pair of scissors and leaving. Played by Kim Neve, as her brother comes in the pictures upon her walls are few, photos of The Beatles are glimpsed [in the accompanying photo booklet to the Who's original double-album Jimmy's bedroom also has the Fab Four on his walls but this is not the case in the film]. Annoyed by his clumsiness and tales of horror she does a double take once he has left so at least they do communicate. She is never seen again only heard about when Jimmy's mother draws a disparaging comparison of her two children following his delayed return home from Brighton in a later scene. Interestingly, in the novelization of the film

14

STORY SYNOPSIS   A QUADROPHENIA ANTHOLOGY

[see bibliography] Alan Fletcher fleshes out her character a lot more.

At first glance the Cooper household has a weathered feel to it apparent even in the darkness; palm patterned wallpaper in the living room and Jimmy's room is just as appalling. Only the vertically lined paper covering his walls evokes the 'tuppenny rush' arcade amusement game, the one where you have to position the coin perfectly between the lines to win. Brighton pier still has one, however; it is a twenty pence piece that is needed to play today. In the familiarity of his bedroom Jimmy cuts out another newspaper article and adds it to his collection covering part of the awful vertical patterned wallpaper. Satisfied with the evening's pleasantries he relaxes on his leopard-skin print bedspread, on a Mod high and thinking of Steph. The clipping, titled "On The Run" is a Daily Mirror headline [Monday, 3 August 1964] reporting upon the Easter non-violence at Hastings involving fellow Mod youngsters. Adding it alongside the others on his wall we see the "Riot Police Fly to Seaside" a subsequent Mirror feature telling of the new mobilisation of Scotland Yard's Flying Squad and its ability to swiftly assist local police forces at any seaside resorts. From a purely chronological perspective the collected scriptwriters have extended a great deal of artistic licence and as an historical document it can best be defined as anomalous. The events described at Hastings occurred in August and Chalky [Phil Davis] will later mention that prior to the Brighton visit he had been prevented from going out since 'Margate'. Trouble there took place after those that arose in Brighton that May. Returning to Jimmy, a rogue's gallery of topless and nude women fill the space next to the Mod cuttings, reminding us of the Who's Pictures of Lily and Sixties playwright Joe Orton's similar collage seen in the film biography Prick Up Your Ears. A black and white portrait of a Union Jacketed Pete Townshend peers over Jim's shoulder, whilst a photograph of a heavily accessorized scooter is seen to his left. The first two verses from Cut My Hair, the third Who track on the soundtrack, plays over the scene.

In a very revealing moment, Jimmy is next shown enjoying a bath in a cubicle at what seems to be a public bathhouse. Filmed in Porchester, west London, it

15

chasing the wind   STORY SYNOPSIS

is a bit baffling to comprehend such a place nowadays but presumably the alternative of a cold tin bath in the front parlour was not very appealing. If there had been bubbles in the tub then they would have soon popped by the noise coming from the cubicle next to his, where somebody is singing a Gene Vincent song. *"Don't sing all that old rubbish!"* bemoans a perplexed Jimmy. *"That isn't rubbish pal, that's Gene Vincent, alright."* Replies the unseen protagonist as a childish battle ensues with Jimmy hollering back You Really Got Me by The Kinks. Me was a number one hit for The Kinks in August 1964 whilst lead singer and songwriter Ray Davies was also a product of art school just like Who guitarist Pete Townshend. The similarities between them continue in the way that both songwriters used humour to express social commentary in the guise of a splendid pop tune: Dead End Street and Dedicated Follower of Fashion prime examples from the Davies portfolio. As an aside, the debut Kinks single flopped [as did The Who's High Numbers debut] and the song, Long Tall Sally, shares its name with a clothing shop located next to the Brighton alleyway where Steph and Jimmy find refuge during the running battles with the police in nearby East Street. The influence of the Kinks upon Townshend presented itself on the Who's first hit I Can't Explain, a favourite live track by fans with a similar arrangement to You Really Got Me. Explain was produced by Shel Talmy, an American producer resident in Britain whom had previously worked with the Kinks. For teenagers like Jimmy there was no specific Mod band to follow, rather groups that Mods liked such as The Who, The Yardbirds and The Small Faces. Highlighting the polarization in music tastes between Kevin and Jimmy presents the latter being interested in the sounds of now aligned with the formers inclination for what had already passed. *"What do you think this is the bloody Eurovision Song Contest!"* bellows a burly male assistant banging on their locked doors. Finally confronting each other, it turns out that Jimmy recognises the other lad as his old school friend Kevin Herriott. They chat and 'Kev' tells him that he has been away serving in the Forces.

    Following on from baths we now find Jimmy at a greasy café relishing his ritual feasting upon eating mushy peas, pie and mash laced with an extra request for liquor poured on top. As he begins to eat, a distilled roar of a heavier type of

STORY SYNOPSIS   A QUADROPHENIA ANTHOLOGY

motorcycle is heard spluttering to a halt outside. Dressed in full riding leathers, Kevin comes sauntering in and his fashion sense causes Jimmy to do a double take. *"Am I black or summit?"* puzzles the coarse, lumberjack shirted, chunky-booted, 'DA'quiffed greaser. *"Well you isn't exactly white in that sort of get-up!"* returns Jimmy, dressed casually in a burgundy jacket with its bottom button un-done, three-button long-sleeved pale blue sports shirt and blue Levi's with a one inch turn-up [Kevin also wears the same brand of jeans] their contrasting appearance could not be more acute. Their conversation is coarse in its use of language however; we do learn that Kevin has returned home for good following a complete discharge from the army after the cigarette-smoking biker saw action in Aden where independence had been sought back in the mid-Sixties. A deadpan case of irony or simply demonstrative of his thickness ensues as he says that he left military life because he could not stomach the discipline. With the maintenance of appearance of paramount importance, the arrival of two mod associates causes Jimmy to beat a hasty retreat from a dejected Kev. He evidently cannot be seen fraternising with a *"fuckin' Rocker."* As one of the Mods describes him; that face belongs to John Altman, an actor who would go on to achieve notoriety as Nasty Nick in EastEnders *[see picture above]*. Having been introduced by the distinctly softer tones of a scooter engine arriving outside, accompanied by a nameless mate, John wears blue jeans, white sports shirt and a cotton jacket. The realignment of the suit, collar and tie was slyly reapplied by teenagers in the Sixties into empty fetishes, to be desired, fussed over and enjoyed in Mod circles. Of course, not all could afford to buy them and perhaps this explains John's scruffiness when viewed alongside the peacock styling of Chalky, Spider or Pete. Advancing to 1979, Quadrophenia generated a momentary Mod revival complimented by the emergence of enthusiasts and commercially successful bands like The Jam and those on Coventry's Two-Tone record label. The demand for related items such as 'Mod suits' could be purchased for £40 through mail order in music magazines. Back in the early-Sixties some Mods would visit tailors to have suits personally fitted in the days

17

chasing the wind   STORY SYNOPSIS

before off-the-peg combinations were readily available on the high street.

Jimmy pays a thirty shillings cash advancement to a female assistant at a local outfitters for his latest suit in preparation for the Brighton trip. Meanwhile fellow number Dan [Daniel Peacock] and Lou struggle to be accommodated by a bald-headed, bespectacled tailor, Oliver Pierre, confounded by Dan's finicky stylising demands. He asks his co-hort what he thinks about the suggested cut of the cloth, *"Fuckin' rent-a-tent, innit."* comes the laconic response. It is a funny moment at which Peacock like Timothy Spall [Harry] later on, is adept at raising a laugh. He handles the scene beautifully, drawing further smiles from the audience at his own expense in another shared meeting with Jimmy at a barber shop on the day before the Brighton weekender. Away from the alternate state of evenings, lunch times and weekends spent at coffee bars and dancehalls, everyday life for young Mods was often drab and stifling. A fact painfully evident in Steph, whom Jimmy next pops in to see at the supermarket where she works on the checkout. Robot-like, even her voice betrays her contempt for the job, until the arrival of the little Mod enthusing about his *'handsome'* new suit, *"...three-button, side vents, sixteen inch bottoms."* goes down well. *"Gonna be one of the faces, are you?"* teases the cardigan and overall-wearing Steph with her hair pulled back in to a functional ponytail. *"Whadda you mean, gonna be?"* Proclaims Daniels in full sway, *"I AM one of the faces!"* A debatable point now, it is said that the Cadbury's hot chocolate drink bought by a customer there is said to have been a 1970s design and not circa 1964 [which the film is supposedly emulating: although a specific dateline is never eluded to] Next to her, the other characters in the story are also employed in menial jobs, including a post room clerk, chemist shop assistant, and council waste worker but it is never revealed what either Spider or Chalky do to sustain their positions within the Mod circle.

Proper preparation being endemic to the Mod, Jimmy is next found grooming himself in front of a three-mirrored dresser in his bedroom accompanied by the buzz of Zoot Suit playing in the background. Performed by the High Numbers AKA The Who, he removes the stash of pills from underneath his mattress and opting for a burgundy suit and a yellow button-up sweater, Cinderella is ready for the ball. His room contains a small wardrobe, wretched leopard-skin print bedspread with multi-coloured striped sheets underneath, yellow/ green vertical lined wallpaper print and his most important piece of furniture: a mirror. The High Numbers went back to being The Who following the departure of Pete Meaden and Helmut Gorden, an early management union up until the introduction of Kit Lambert and Chris Stamp in mid-1964. Meaden reshaped the band in to a mod package and after being consumed by the scene he wrote I'm the Face and Zoot Suit, which was the first recorded record by the group. Filling its lyrics with the latest lingo it was put out as a single in July of that year but in spite of gaining the pre-requisite airplay, it flopped. Re-released some sixteen years later, Who fans led it to enter the lower reaches of the Top 50. In essence the Zoot Suit was an early definition of youth culture that evolved in and around the clubs of Harlem in Thirties America. Its reputation aligned itself to the criminal classes and the sight of such a bizarre look; all extra large jackets and baggy hips, provoked violence amongst those unable to be confronted by such an evocation. American modern jazz musicians and the original Mods would later promote the form here but in the States, it faded amidst the austerity of the war years. Meaden composed the songs whilst blocked on amphetamines and confessed to lifting elements from a dusky southern jazz number by The Snowmen called Country Fool.

During possibly the most invigorating group scene in the film, our introduction to Dave, Chalky and Spider, the main cliché of Mods in Quadrophenia occurs in front of the mirrors above the washbasins in a gent's pub toilet. Each preening themselves unselfconsciously, a cigarette-lipped Phil Davis, is introduced as the *"ponce"* by an eyelined Jimmy after having not been seen around the local scene since the scuffles at Margate. Immediately the smartly set fellow Mod wearing a suit set off by a lime green shirt and glistening cufflinks, tries to bum some drugs of Jimmy demonstrating a slyness symptomatic of his character. His swift appropriation of a bottle of booze at the coming party adds to his predisposed nature. Chalky wears his hair a little longer than most of the others and is similar in physique to Jimmy. Comments have been made that he is a bit of a Roger Daltrey clone.

It transpires that Chalky was not involved in any violence but his vanishing was caused by his worried father padlocking his scooter thus preventing him journeying to Margate. This small seaside town of limited social amenities back in the Sixties saw clashes between local youths and day tripping Mods during Whit sun 1964, adding to Bournemouth and Brighton and coming after Clacton. Margate heralded the legendary 'Sawdust Caesars' diatribe by local Magistrate Dr George Simpson. His speech hit the front pages of the printed media and was adapted in Quadrophenia although transferred to fit in with the Brighton phase of its story. Chalky does not come across as being too bright yet he has a good relationship with the others whereas Spider consistently succeeds in irritating. Smoking away, as is Jimmy, Dave, dressed in a dark pin striped suit and lined shirt, says to the others that he would have sorted his own father out if he had dared do that to him. Dan, resplendent in a blue button-down shirt with matching tie, suit and cufflinks, tells them of house party in Kitchener Road (since acknowledged as being a real location in Clarendon Gardens, Wembley) which they all shortly zoom off in pursuit of on their scooters. John and Jimmy exchange some smutty banter about the physical attributes of Steph, prior to the latter's attempt at inviting her along being quashed by the return of Pete from the bar. All the while Dave, coated in mascara, gently teases Jimmy to deflect his obvious disappointment at not being able to get her to come with him.

Noite sem fin – The endless night:
The subdued melody of the Supremes' Baby Love is heard as the lads arrive on their scooters whilst fellow Mod John re-joins them as they re-group next to a battalion of scooters parked-up outside of a decent-sized house before making their way up to the front door. The arrival of this rowdy bunch ruffles the feathers of the host's snooty boyfriend who bars their entrance, *"you didn't even have the decency to bring a bottle!"* he snorts. Dave, Jimmy, Ferdy, Spider and Chalky fill the doorway in what is a great scene offering up the vivacity of those involved and with Spider [Gary Shail] very much coming in to his own. He gives the other boy quite a verbal lashing before John's pragmatism paves their way inside. In the midst of much frowning by the lads waiting at the door, Jimmy takes a cigarette from his pack of Senior Service, the same brand that Steph is seen

smoking at Alfredo's coffee bar towards the end of the film. Be My Baby by the Ronettes is in full flow as the group separate and Jimmy looks around the place packed with as it is with people talking, smoking, drinking and dancing. Ferdy is observed mingling but still wearing his wraparound shades even though its nighttime. Between a mouth full of food, Dan tells Jimmy to go and look in the lounge. Within which a mass of dancing and chatting boys and girls the horrid patterned wallpaper, more Seventies than Sixties, is broken up by a few art prints, one of which is a piece by Lowry seen behind Jimmy and Monkey when they smooch on the couch. Dave vies for the charms of Monkey but is dismissed as she spots Jimmy, and tempts him with her bag of amphetamines, in exchange for a snog that she has to almost beg for! He forgets that she works at a chemist and is able to pinch 'Blues' as and when she can. Jimmy and his mates, in the quest for some pep fuel will visit the same chemist for the proposed Brighton weekend. Chalky goes straight for the alcohol and swigs slyly from the bottle. The soft tones of Rhythm of the Rain whisper as Jim sees a deeply alluring Steph, and she sees him, dancing closely with Pete. Pulling away from the grasp of a dejected Monkey, cigarette still in his hand, Jimmy abruptly puts on the Who single My Generation, anathema to cosy couples, which he happily notes its success as Steph and Pete quietly leave and the male Mods begin to jump about the room. Just as Jimmy sets about putting the Who single on the record player, the cover to the double Who album The Who Sell Out / A Quick One, first seen on its side above as Rhythm of the Rain clicks into play yet when Jimmy sees Steph, it has miraculously turned upright and is clearly displayed. As an album, it was in all actuality not released until 1974. Monkey's presence in the film is especially heartened when Jimmy, upon spotting Steph with Pete, discards her. The audience feels the expression upon her face: one of rejection. Watch out for Peter McNamara, whom many will remember as the skinhead always harassing Tucker Jenkins in the Eighties kids telly drama Tucker's Luck. He can be spotted looking rather uncomfortable behind Jimmy's mates as they dance to My Generation. Watch how Peter curses at someone off-screen after they ruffle his tie, an object that causes him a great of discomfort throughout the time he is on view. Watching the cliché of

chasing the wind   STORY SYNOPSIS

male Mods gathered together screaming the lyrics whilst head banging along to its verve their camaraderie draws forth the same response from the viewer. When Daltrey stutters the 'Why don't you all f-f-f-fade away...' its impossible not to join with them in their acerbic reply. Sing-a-long Townshend if you will. The dum-dum-dum- guitar riff has been heard a thousand times and is still, frequently played during the encore to many a Who gig. Keith Moon's tumbling, rumbling drumming detonates perfectly next to Roger's hollering intonation, the phrasing of 'talkin' bout my gen-er-a-tion' by Pete whilst Entwistle's nimble fingers gel to make impassive listening a non-option. The Townshend exposition on his psychological state at the time of writing My Generation and the other early singles is one centred around struggle, "[It was] about trying to find a place in society." Offers the composer in The Guitar Greats. "I was very, very lost." From an opposing perspective, author Peter Wicke saw its significance as specific, "To the self-perception of a small selection of British working-class teenagers to whom involvement with rock music had become a cultural process of a quite particular kind." It is indisputable that The Who sound and performance was synchronization betwixt the band and its live audience. To which punk was to follow on as an approximation of and is equally representative of what The Who means to many. Three minutes and fifteen seconds of exquisitely arranged angst expertly loaded up and sprayed out at machine gun speed, My Generation flew up the Hit Parade landing on the number two spot in 1965. The original high camp Mod is, I feel, relevant in its connection to Generation with the Oscar Wilde tale The Picture of Dorian Grey. In the novel, a portrait ages but Gray himself does not, a point articulated by Jim Curtis in Rock Eras – Interpretation of Music and Society,"...both groups felt a similar alienation from the British Establishment." Artists as diverse as Brian Eno acknowledged the wealth endemic in My Generation and the emergence of The Who, "[They] made it possible to occupy an area between fine art and popular art," begins the soundtrack producer of Dune, a film starring the Brighton Ace Face Sting, "and have the ambiguity work." Back at the house party, Jimmy walks out of the lounge, flicking the light switch off, and wanders off in search of Steph. Pete casually pushes a be suited fella out of his and Steph's way as they leave the house whilst Jimmy does the same moments later. A closer look at the unfortunate youngster will reveal the identity of the extra as future comic novelist Ben Elton. Jimmy's frustration is not tempered by seeing Steph scoot off into the night on the back of Pete's scooter, accompanied by the subdued din of the anthemic Who single expending its energy back in the lounge. Peculiarly, it is Jimmy's scooter that somehow seems the most visible in amongst a mass of others during the time Pete, following Mod etiquette, starts the engine of his bike then allows Steph to climb aboard before joining her. However much Pete is disliked by most of the others, Jimmy and Dave particularly, he does know how to treat a girl as we see here. He is also seen picking-up an American girl, to the contempt or should that be jealousy of the others whilst at the ballroom in Brighton. Wearing what looks like a considerable amount of make-up on his face Jimmy swallows more pills as he stands outside. *"Get in there!"* What would be some time later on Jimmy returns inside only to discover everyone seemingly paired off in one of the upstairs bedrooms and bathroom areas. John and Dave, the latter still resplendent in his hat and tie but wearing nothing else, are both seen enjoying themselves as a refuelled Jimmy passes through the room. The sound of Jimmy's scooter takes Dave away from his partner on the bed in the overcrowded bedroom and opening the window he spots Jim circling the front lawn. For Jimmy there is not much else to do other than disappear not however before concluding his Elvis, circa Roustabout, impersonation manifest in ploughing around and around in the front garden. As he zooms off, smashing the white picket fence, an image of respectability, and to the alarm of his semi-naked pal, he just misses colliding with the expensive-looking car containing the hosts' returning parents. *"Look at my plants!"* hollers an unseen female voice from within the car. Arriving at the stillness of the canal side in a beautifully composed scene a reflective Jimmy sits alone and motionless on his parked scooter. Townshend's gentle vocal lilt from I'm One builds on the gloom of the youngster's mood, with a sort of melancholic numbness prevailing.

The themes echoed in the song relate to Jimmy being aware of his mod identity if uncertain about anything else that he has to confront in his life. He arches one of his side mirrors to reflect a light on a middle-aged couple canoodling under a

chasing the wind   STORY SYNOPSIS

nearby bridge before vindictively showing his envy by riding straight at them and off once more in to the night, a reflex that he will repeat often as events unfold.

After the disaster that was the night before, a knackered Jimmy acknowledging his employee responsibilities, distributes post to the various departments within the advertising agency where he has a position as a mailroom clerk. Maintaining his immaculate appearance, he delivers the internal mail with a dissipated expression after feeling the effects of his behaviour from the house party and frustration over Steph. The unrecognised empathy with the 'licking boots' lyric from Bell Boy rings true as the young Mod performs the same kind of fetching and carrying menial work. Within such a pressurised environment most people that he comes in to contact with are unwelcoming and aggressive.

The wittiest moment is again set in a gents toilet only this time at the anonymous ad agency. Mr Fulford [Benjamin Whitrow] and Michael [Jeremy Child], two frightfully posh executives, are seen discussing the latest branding campaign for the People Like You cigarette advertisement whilst sprucing themselves up. *"Gorgeous tart."* Concedes the younger executive absently. A coughing and spluttering Jimmy is heard in one of the off-screen cubicles before coming out and retching into the sink between them. Looking down with some disdain at Jimmy during these moments does either verbally acknowledge the other. Meanwhile Michael, the younger of the two men, but cut from the same cloth, questions the health issues against tobacco. Concluding his electronic shave, Fulford waves away such considerations dismissing the issue as one of no importance to the younger generation. Satisfied with their grooming both leave whilst Jimmy, now alone, strikes up a cigarette and barks wildly as a result. It is a terrifically timed moment and its dryness gushes through the first-rate playing by all three actors. The only query here is why is a lowly clerk using the facilities of management executives such as Fulford and Simon?

Jimmy comes in to the kitchen, which resembles something like the Fowlers' used to in East Enders, after falling asleep on the train home and missing his stop, following his exhaustive time at the party is in no mood to eat. Seen in amongst the bare necessities is a bottle of HP brown sauce. Poking his head into the lounge where his redheaded mother sits transfixed by the menacing grey telly, the white vested Mr Cooper, still clutching a bottle of beer, snoozes in the chair next to her. She enquires about his lateness whilst keeping her eyes on the screen, again challenging him about his behaviour with the ignorant cry of his abnormality. *"Oh yeah!"* growls her son, barely disguising his contempt as he glances at her before leaving the room, *"What's normal, then?"* His father momentarily stirs but is instantly dismissed by his goggle-eyed wife.

In an image directly replicated from the Who's own Quadrophenia album cover, four reflections of Jimmy are presented in the wing mirrors of his scooter within the sanctity of the garden shed. The difference being that within the Who photo the four faces are that of the separate band members. Within the unravelling of the story presented through the album, Jimmy scrambles upon a rock where the four aspects of his personality picture themselves to him in the falling water. It is a neat touch giving the clearest visual connotation its origins in Townshend's story thus far. Jimmy tinkers with his scooter as the roar of a motorbike in the evening air is heard coming down the alleyway outside. Armed with a spanner, he relaxes upon recognising the would-be aggressor is his old mate Kevin. Jimmy appears quite small in contrast to the bulky, be-goggled and very R.A.F-looking Ray Winstone. Dressed casually in a sweatshirt and jeans, Jimmy seems more vulnerable as himself, and without the mod pretence. They discuss the intrinsic differences between bikes and scooters and Jimmy gives his spirited mod speech reiterating his Mod ideology. *"It isn't about the bikes, is it?* He begins, *"It's the people…"* Kev reasons that beyond the visual aesthetics so important to the Mods and against the more practical apparel worn by Rockers, that they are basically similar. The little mod has none of it. *"I don't wanna be the same as everybody else – that's why I'm a mod, see?"*

The average age of people working at the ad agency is a little above the teen-aged Jimmy, all apart from Harry the projectionist characterised by an expletive-laden Tim Spall and his youthful assistant Des, played by Patrick Murray. Although meant to be elsewhere Jimmy is playing cards with the podgy Spall and the shy Des. The advertising campaign for the Private Blend "People Like You" cigarette commercial is about to be screened for Mr Fulford and clients in the viewing theatre next door and shutting down something to do with

chasing the wind   STORY SYNOPSIS

the projector, the model in the film catches Jimmy's eye as she had with Michael previously. *"I was late...she was waiting in the wrong place..."'"* wafts the velvet hued tones of voice-over actor Ray Brooks overheard by Jimmy from in the projection booth. Accompanied by a black and white, cliché-ridden liaison between lovers meeting in a park, an Onedin Line soundtrack drowns any sense of restraint. Conversely, the trio have a laugh together and seem to have an on-going working relationship fuelled by a similar taste for French Blues and such like. It is impossible to talk about Quadrophenia without commenting upon the drugs commonly used or abused by the Mods to enable the necessary sustenance for their weekend adventures. Calling My Generation up as an example, Roger Daltrey's stuttering was said to be adopted to represent a side effect of an amphetamine user in that they made it physically impossible for the brain to convey as much as it so desperately wanted when blocked and consequently, frustration crept in. As a bonus, users also experienced paranoia, anxiety, violent thoughts and depression. Amphetamines gave confidence, an ability to talk to anyone or at least seek to communicate, and the strength to dance all night. The heightened aggression from using speed, the most common form of the substance, meant that the male Mod did not have much of a libido afterwards but boy could he groove. Fashion-wise, Jimmy looks smart in a brown and black boater jacket accompanied by a white and red striped tie with grey shirt. The maxim of clothes as ammunition reigning over him. The other two, both wear tank-top jumpers and are clearly not the type of people that he would socialise with outside of work. [There exists a photograph taken of a young Mod during the summer of 1964 wearing exactly the same item of clothing. In the picture he not only has the same pullover but in addition has the Continental helmet-like hair cut, parka with a Who patch and Union jack on it and with desert boots on one assumes had a scooter to boot.] Jimmy can be seen in a similar pair whilst at the greasy spoon café early on in the film. Compliant with the requisition for lined jackets and shirts by Mods, Jimmy and Harry are closely aligned in this respect, the former favouring a thin pin-striped equally preferred by Pete, Steph's boyfriend, seen at the house party. Harry's can be spotted hidden a bit under his blue tank top. Oddly, Jimmy calls Spall's projec-

STORY SYNOPSIS   A QUADROPHENIA ANTHOLOGY

tionist character 'Des' three times but when he motions to leave after giving a mountain of small change as payment for the money he owes him quips, *"...we'll make a mod outta you yet Harry. Only I don't think they make Levi's in your size!"*

Making off to collect some photographs from the art department, upon arriving he is chastised for being late. An older man with what can only be described as a Paul McCartney moustache, circa Sgt.Peppers, castigates Jimmy for casually taking a peak at the black and white shots inside consisting of a bikini-clad model. *"Watch the cloth, moth!"* returns the sharp Mod before making his way out of the office. *"Tacky herbert!"* sighs the designer from within, all the while Jimmy replies beautifully by gesturing a non-verbal 'wanker' farewell. Teen-aged Mods employed in positions such as clerks could not be criticised for their appearance, infact, they often were better dressed than anybody else but a difference was there: hinted at by the feeling that there was an underlying deviation. This vexed some of those excluded from the culture of being young in the Sixties, which in itself was a force to be reckoned with, fashions developing as shorthand to highlight the generation gap. More often than not he is supposed to be elsewhere delivering this or that, nevertheless, Jimmy is next discovered in a record store. Selecting the catchy Who single Anyway, Anyhow, Anywhere, Jimmy takes refuge in a listening booth where he sets about gawping at the photos of the model; a second features her in a studio shot with an umbrella used as a prop. A version of Wishin and Hopin, performed by The Merseybeats, written by Bacharach and David, can be heard in the booth next to him within which a young GPO worker is eyeing the saucy pictures too. Remembered more for its version by Dusty Springfield the band was managed in the mid-Sixties by Who man Kit Lambert resulting in their enjoying of a couple of minor hits. Peculiarly androgynous up until this point, the young man in the white crash helmet resembling the type once worn by police motorcyclists [very Fifties, high on the head with straps on either side] shyly nods his approval to a grinning Jimmy Cooper.

Perched on his parked scooter preening himself in anticipation of seeing Steph after she finishes work at the supermarket, Jimmy, sporting a suit with vertical

chasing the wind   STORY SYNOPSIS

printed lines running through the material combs his hair in the moments before. Amongst the ads in the shop window is the recognisable red and white Findus frozen food logo, "Findus. Success on a plate for you" as their old ad used to go. With the day's work done and resembling a young Jane Asher, Steph looks more like her self in a long black leather coat and brown top as she and a mate come out from inside the store. Accepting his offer of a lift home they sound each other out about Pete and how they feel about each other. Evidently filmed on the streets unannounced, they drive under a railway bridge that advertises over its side the London Goldhawk Building Society. Listen out for the sound of a passer-by calling out as the couple glide past on Jimmy's Lambretta. It looks as if Phil Daniels is not actually riding the scooter due to the close proximity of the camera, which crops the lower half of the front of the vehicle. Toying with each other, Jimmy asks his pillion passenger what it is she sees in Pete as a boyfriend, *"Bit flash though, in he?"* Teases the driver. *"I wouldn't be with him otherwise, would I!"* admits Steph in a typically candid answer. *"You jealous?"* she quizzes. *"Nah."* Responds Jimmy coolly but without much conviction. *"That's a pity, I thought you was!"* Concludes Steph making her intent quite transparent. The little Mod grins away knowingly, with the wheels for their romance firmly set in motion.

Night Train by James Brown plays on an unseen jukebox at Alfredo's coffee bar and espresso place, as Chalky, Dave and a black sunglasses-wearing Jimmy discuss the forthcoming Brighton escapade whilst gathered around a Buckaroo pinball machine. *"I wanna get out of me head."* Interjects Spider, wearing a chequered suit in mixed colours, inviting himself into the discussion. *"Well it wouldn't be too difficult with your monkey brain!"* Dismisses Dave, barely hiding his irritation of the straw sucking but neatly turned out Spider. Jimmy and Dave are dressed alike, casually in v-necks and Fred Perry type sports shirts. Alfredo's cafe is comparable to the photograph of the one included in the Quadrophenia booklet of the Who album; very plain and functional, with its walls coated in magnolia. Noticeable around the place is a Pepsi logo, photos of Elvis Presley, wrestling and Buddy Holly posters. Volubly but without malice the boys leave the café after being ordered to by the owner. Jumping on to their scooters parked outside the Art Deco-fronted coffee bar, their next port of call is revealed as the Goldhawk club. For the moment, watch John Altman, in amongst the Mod faces, clearly seen carrying a fur-lined parka whilst leaving the café.

On the road towards their favoured location Spider's scooter stalls in front of a pub called the Bramley Arms, and he motions to the others that he and his girlfriend will catch up with everyone inside the club. Whilst the couple moan to each other about the technical problems encompassed by riding a scooter Da Doo Ron Ron sets the tone of the evening over at the club as we observe Jimmy and Dave crouched on the floor opposite those that are dancing away to energised tune from The Crystals. The floor is full of girls and Toyah is seen grooving away in amongst them. Jimmy, continuing to sport sunglasses even though he is indoors, after wearing them at Alfredo's too, completes his look with a pair of brown lace up shoes favoured by mobile Mods and known as Desert boots, as does Dave. *"Oh shit!"* Tinkering away with the scooter, Spider curses his luck as a motley crew of bikers pulls up in front of his scooter. Led by Gary Holton and Jesse Birdsall in amongst a dozen others who circle like a pack of hyenas, they clamber off their bikes to see what the problem is. The duo in the black leathers and white scarves are seeking the slightest opportunity to attack, *"Which one are you,"* begins Holton, cross-examining Spider, *"the boy or the girl? Cos it's hard to tell with you lot!"* Spider takes the bait and pushes at Lenny [Birdsall] after he manhandles his girlfriend and violence ensues with the sharp mod taking a thrashing *and* getting his scooter kicked over. Observe how it takes a second or two for Gary Holton to get his heavy motorcycle off and moving following the attack. Meanwhile back at the Goldhawk, Chalky rushes up to Jimmy and Dave enjoying the music and watching the others dancing, informing them that Spider has taken a beating. Monkey and the other girls at the club all appear to have bleached blond hair and bobby socks in a seemingly Fifties style. Dashing outside on to the steps of the basement exit of the club, the boys chat to Spider and his girlfriend before zooming off, enmasse, onto their scooters in pursuit of those who inflicted the attack. Pay particular attention to the pale blue jacketed John and watch as he squeezes past Jimmy and takes a seat on one of the other scooters. Chalky and Jimmy seem especially keen to find those

29

chasing the wind STORY SYNOPSIS

responsible and as is revealed later, Chalky needs little encouragement to seek a confrontation. Others come thick and fast, in Brighton he believes that he recognises one of the Rockers that forced him off the road whilst on the way to the south coast and in his very first introduction, with Jimmy and the others in a pub toilet, his aspirations are made clear. Posters on the sidewalls of where the Mods are gathered advertise forthcoming gigs by the Yardbirds at the Crawdaddy club and The Pretty Things and Zoot Money at the Marquee. Da Doo Ron Ron continues playing back inside as the mainly female crowd dance along. To the right of our view can be seen John, one of the Mods that had just zoomed off on one of the scooters in the previous scene!

A group of eight scooter-helmed Mods, led by Jimmy with Dave as a pillion passenger, cruise the night time streets passing Shepherd's Bush tube station and market before spotting what they had been looking for: two Rockers at a nearby mobile snack bar. Rightly startled by the sight of the oncoming scooter gang, wise to the fact of what is likely to happen and they make a dash for it. Unfortunately, Jimmy's newly rediscovered mate Kev is one of them. Outnumbered, the lads flee towards the market place where Kevin falls from his motorbike and is set upon by the Mods. One of the scooters is a Lambretta with a Union Jack flag painted on to its frame, this particular bike was also seen at the start of the story when Jimmy buys drugs from Ferdy outside the Goldhawk club. To his horror, Jim discovers that he and his mates are giving a hiding to his old mate, and he screams at them to stop. Unaware of his identity, they continue the beating all the while Jimmy, still wearing sunglasses, zooms away screaming on his scooter. Having finished their misguided attack, the Mods scarper whilst the listless and bloodied Kevin lies amongst the market debris. Shepherd's Bush market positively glistens as its closed-up stalls with sundry exterior coloured lights in yellow, blue and red add to a displaced seaside ambience. The sound of a synthesizer slithers across the scene and into the next. Back in the familiarity of the alleyway at the side of his house, a distraught Jimmy vents his anger by aimlessly snaps his shades in two. Shrouded in a Fred Perry sports top and a blue v-neck sweater with a strip on its collar just as Dave has, a disconcerted Jimmy then comes in through the front door, moves into the hallway and up the stairs where his inebriated father confronts him. With the time shortly before midnight, and disgusted with himself from earlier, Jimmy cannot look at himself in the mirror in the hallway: a resounding declaration for a nihilistic Mod. Accidentally knocking his son back down the barren-looking stairwell, covered with nothing but a piece of carpet in the middle to walk upon, the two square up to each other in the lounge. Breathing heavily, George Cooper [Michael Elphick], in direct contrast to his screen son is quite a presence physically, with his white vest revealing a rugged frame. *"You're barmy, that's what you are...dressing up like a freak."* Barks his father as Jimmy motions from side to side, in a style similar to the way that Who front man Roger Daltrey does on stage. *"You've got to be part of a gang, haven't you?"* continues the insightful but misguided Cooper senior, *"Got to be a mod or 'this or that': Haven't you got a mind of your own?"* In a change from the Who album, it is his father who openly discusses the chequered family mental health problems to a bemused Jimmy. Contained within the lyrics of The Real Me on the album it is Jimmy's mother that reiterates the familiarities of such struggles. *"Bloody split personality."* Declares his dad. Thankfully the tension between them is expunged with the sense of the ridiculous enjoyed by the two and after his son skips of to bed, Mr Cooper slumps in to his chair and takes a stale swig from a bottle of Guinness beside him. In the sanctity of his room and coming directly after the tête-à-tête with his father, a fully clothed Jimmy finds pleasure by masturbating on his bed whilst looking at the model photographs which he was supposed to have delivered previously.

The next morning Mrs Cooper barges in to his room only to discover her son still in his clothes from the night before, asleep on top of his bed. A packet of Senior Service cigarettes are glimpsed on the bedside cabinet where an alarm clock reads 8:45 a.m. Pleading sickness so that he will be left alone, she still persists in loudly barracking him about obtaining a sick note from the doctor. Again, her lack of understating towards him is aired only this time with his behaviour questioned by that familiar statement appertaining to normality. Later that same day, dressed in an informal white Fred Perry sports shirt, Jimmy discusses with Dave the best possible source for drugs that are needed for

chasing the wind   STORY SYNOPSIS

Brighton. Wearing a black donkey-jacket [just as Jim's dad does in a later scene] whilst working at the council tip, a fag puffing Dave, minus his pork pie hat, suggests that Jimmy goes to ask Pete for a possible contact. Neither appears to like Pete, Jimmy for obvious reasons and Dave because he regards the him as being a *"flash cunt"*. Interesting in as much as Steph had earlier acquiesced a similar definition.

    Agreeing to pay Pete a visit at the scrap yard where he works for his uncle, Jimmy turns off the main road and drives in through the main entrance of the yard. Pete soon spots him after his two-guard dogs, Butch and Jenny, bark away at the already uncomfortable Mod. [The scrap yard used was said to be in near to the Bramley Arms pub location of earlier]. Fenton fails to offer any assistance in locating a supply, weary of any come back. Jimmy leaves but not before a display of how the two fail to communicate in any way whatsoever is presented. Puzzled at Jim's dismissive attitude to fancying a day off work, Pete articulates his profound grasp of capitalism; *"...you don't work, you don't get any money. And I like money."* In addition, he shows his true colours by voicing his dislike of *'beatniks'* and manages to put in a dubious comment about the imminent reappearance of Ferdy from whom he suggests they get their supply from. Continuity wise, some of the cars lying around and observed in a number of shots an Austin 1100 for example, are bloopers. Launched in 1964 and seen behind Pete, are wrecks dating from the Sixties, surely unlikely to have been junked that very same year? Jimmy, Chalky and Dave next gather beneath the steps outside Ferdy's house but fail to locate him from questioning either of the two middle-aged residents. Ska man Derek Morgan's Burnin' Fire features as the barely audible background music. Again it is left to Jimmy to ask for information or to get something done whilst Chalky is the most uncomfortable of the three lads. He makes a throwaway racist remark about the kind of faces seen around the neighbourhood and provides a hugely funny summing up of his innocent ignorance through an observation that the place reminds him of somewhere like Calcutta. *"Calcutta's in India."* Replies Dave. *"Yeah. West India."* Shoots back a deadpan Chalky.

    Enjoying a drink whilst out with a mate, Pete is next called to the bar to receive

STORY SYNOPSIS   A QUADROPHENIA ANTHOLOGY

a phone call from a belligerent Dave who sums up what most of the others think of Pete in one word. His response is juxtaposed with Chalky, Jimmy and Dave squashed in to an old red telephone box. Dave's aggressive manner succeeds in his being given an address at which they can score some drugs. Gliding across one of London's historic bridges to the sound of a section of music taken from The Rock, the trio scoot off towards their destination. Preparing himself outside, Jimmy takes off his parka coat before heading in to the pub alone whilst the others wait next to their scooters. The exact name of the pub is not clearly identifiable but looks like the 'Wellington' from a darkened sign on its exterior [seen briefly when Jimmy and the boys decide to seek retribution for being conned only moments earlier].

In the time before they make the deal, looking ill at ease and juvenile, Jimmy asks the barman if he can see a Harry North. Ignoring the momentary curiosity of a middle-aged woman standing next to him we notice the décor of the lounge has a slant towards photos of boxers on the walls coupled with a dimly lit nuance. Moments later he is led behind the scenes by way of a sliding door revealing a boxing gymnasium. Jimmy mistakenly gives North the impression that he is the nephew of Charlie Fenton [Pete's uncle] before asking him for a tenner's worth of amphetamines. We see that having disrobed of his parka, Jimmy is wearing a white Fred Perry sports shirt, crisp new Levi jeans and incredulously a snake belt, just like Spider and surely a faux pas for a Mod? Passing his mates, Jimmy follows Harry's honcho to the back of a Jaguar where he is handed a plastic bag full of drugs in exchange for his banknote. Rejoining the others, Chalky is the first to discover that they have been duped, the drugs are merely paraffin. After contributing £3 each, with Jimmy chipping in the rest, the furious threesome led by Jimmy move to attack the car in revenge before speeding away as those from inside come dashing out. *"Do we have to do this?"* Remonstrates Chalky to Dave and Jimmy as they force open the flimsy bars of the window at the rear of a high street chemist shop [the one used for the scene was in King street, Hammersmith]. Comedy ensues as the shoeless threesome clamber inside whilst Jimmy adopts a serious tone in his quest for prescription drugs that they can use or rather abuse, for the eagerly-anticipated Brighton

33

chasing the wind   STORY SYNOPSIS

weekender. All the while the others generally mess around. Perhaps not seemingly held as the brightest light on the Christmas tree, Chalky enquires to no one in particular about the risk of their footprints being identifiable, decreeing ala Stan Laurel that if you have fingerprints why then you have footprints. Each wearing gloves and shoeless, they set about searching but Chalky is again the first to be side-tracked following a discovery of some condoms by Dave, *"Can't be too careful!"* giggles the little Mod as the others turn to see him with unrolled 'rubbers' on each of his fingers and thumbs. There is a great deal of fun in the scene especially when they manage to knock over a prominent display of boxed sanitary products. A ringing telephone or is it an alarm causes them to panic and flee but not before locating some 'Blues.' In the haste to get away, Chalky takes an extra moment to collect a little something for his mother, the identity of which is not made apparent as they scramble back out of the window from whence they came. Back at Alfredo's that same night, the boys join some of the others including John, Dan and Spider, where they tell everyone about the robbery of the chemist where Monkey works. Chalky and Dave break away and tell the other's sitting nearby of their cache. Dan and John are seen floating about in the busy café as Chalky reveals, by lobbing half of it over Spider, that it was a bottle of talcum powder that he took for his mother in the raid whilst Jimmy pays for a couple of bottles of Pepsi after briefly telling Monkey about the events of the night he cuts her dead by offering Steph one along with some of the pills. Steph, not especially interested in them, appears preoccupied with what she has planned, suggesting that he see her home at the end of the evening. At the side of Steph's house they kiss and agree to see each other although she says not to tell anyone about it as she is still planning on travelling down to Brighton with Pete, as previously arranged.

The mailroom at the ad agency next finds a joyful Jimmy singing the Kinks' You Really Got Me to the rhythm of the mail franking machine on what turns out to be Friday: pay day. The plaintive Mr Cale, as portrayed by Hugh Lloyd, warns him about missing work and his general behaviour possibly leading to him being sent to see the boss, the prattish Mr Fulford. Cale looks on wistfully as he wishes Jimmy and another young lad, a good weekend as the camera leaves him where he stands: alone.

In a traditional gent's hairdressers, with the male stylists wearing white, buttoned-up jackets it seems the kind of place that young men would be asked if they required 'something for the weekend'. Jimmy finishes his turn following a trim whilst refusing the barber's suggestion of using lacquer to hold his fringe in place. *"Poofs wear lacquer, don't they!"* puffs Jimmy, whom we had seen at work earlier that day with a touch of make up upon his face. *"I wear lacquer!"* responds Dan naively, taking the vacated seat. *"Usual miracle?"* asks the same barber as the audience giggle gently at Dan's slowness. *"You know how the hair falls?"* inquires Dan, oblivious to any put-downs.

In what appears to be a different kitchen from the one seen earlier Jimmy's parents are busy doing what they always do; his dad sits reading a paper whilst his mother dashes about. *"Gordon Bennett! What have you got on?"* gasps Mr Cooper looking up at his son from behind the Daily Mirror with its front-page headline of 'Fear of another weekend of violence.' [forewarning of the precipitated confrontations between warring youths at seaside resorts]. Jimmy comes in wearing a new pair of wet Levi's, which he is shrinking to fit the contours of his body all the while searching for old papers to scan for any reports of seaside skirmishes. This vision causes a great deal of mirth in the mind of his father but none at all from his mother who preoccupied in organising her cleaning duties to notice. Levi's instigated a 1979 press campaign using a photograph of Jimmy on his scooter from the scene where he visits Dave at the council tip, with a by-line of 'Some things never go out of fashion'. As Jimmy's dad, Michael Elphick demonstrates a lot of interest in his screen son and he is such a fine actor able to convey a dozen emotions in that rough, durable face. Mrs Cooper offers no such enthusiasm, real or not, when he asks her to come in to the lounge to see The Who a moment or two later. The beginnings of the popular mod music television show Ready Steady Go! is overheard, with the sound of Manfred Mann's 5-4-3-2-1 playing on the set in the lounge, which Jimmy dashes away to see. A throbbing screen uncovers The Who performing with Pete Townshend playing the opening riff to Anyway, Anyhow, Anywhere. *"I s'pose they wear wet jeans too, do they?"* smirks his dad to his son, so captivated by the site of the

chasing the wind   STORY SYNOPSIS

Who launching their Pop Art explosion complete with drummer Keith Moon wearing a white target sweatshirt. George, Mr Cooper Senior, joins him and ribs him on their appearance and the level of noise that they are generating. Not such an over reaction when the truth is revealed detailing many viewers actually complained to the station about the band. That happened as a result of The Who being given a segment of the show to play a succession of songs culminating in the release of the Ready, Steady, Who! EP. His dad leaves but not before informing Jimmy, transfixed by the flickering dynamism of the band blasting forth, that listening to this kind of music will make him deaf. Achingly true in that Pete Townshend is a suffer of tinitus following years of exposure to the mighty sound systems so favoured by The Who.

Revealing his new suit freshly purchased from Dave Wax tailoring, Jimmy prepares for the visit to Brighton by searching for his stash of pills hidden under his lurid leopard skin bedspread. A transistor radio echoes the fears of violence by Brighton shopkeepers for the oncoming weekend from Big Al on *"266: Wonderful Radio London. Whoopee!"* A jingle from R.L, one of the emerging commercial stations in the early Sixties, was used in The Who Sell Out concept album from 1967. Set at a fictitious pirate radio station the album features commercials and various links and mock advertisements in between tracks. But back in 1964, where our story is set, Radio One had not yet been launched, however, pirate stations such as Caroline and Luxemburg offered up a serving of the latest pop tunes to a hungry teenaged audience. The Florida Room at Brighton, played many times by The Who, provided regular 'Record Nites' for teenagers to go and dance along to in an age before the music video. Also reported on the radio news was the quest for independence by African nation Aden, later to become Yemen, at the time a British colony. Sometime that same morning Jimmy and his mates are seen in battalion-like formation sounding like a squadron of fighter planes on the road down to the south coast. Interspersed with a similar group of bikers also on their way down there. Chalky rides on ahead of the other Mods after jousting with Dave about who has the quicker bike but is cut off the road by a huge posse of bikers that come up behind him. His scooter is similar to Jimmy's, with a blue windshield, red and white coloured frame admonished with more than a dozen mirrors and consequently resulting in be exceedingly slow and weighty. *"Thinks he's Davy Crockett!"* roars one of the Greasers with more than a passing resemblance to American comedian Bobcat Goldthwaite seen in the Police Academy films; the American contemporaries of the old Carry On films, but nowhere near as endearing. Chalky does a forward summersault when his scooter comes to an abrupt halt at the side of the road whilst Jimmy and Dave subsequently catch up and check to see if he is hurt. *"It looked good from back there!"* puffs Jimmy, barely able to contain himself. *"Dirty bastard fucking grease monkeys!"* growls a dishevelled Chalky from the ground to his mates. Discovering that nothing apart from his pride, has been hurt, they go on ahead without him. Get Out And Stay Out one of the new tracks purposely written by Pete Townshend for the film plays over the moment, presupposed by a hatless Dave. The same bikers are again seen moving ever closer to Brighton on the same stretch of road. The film gives us our first look at the Brighton seafront as Get Out And Stay Out continues to play over this and the preceding scene whilst the seaside town begins to prepare for its oncoming visitors with deckchairs being set out on the beach. The first Mod arrivals can be spotted on the water's edge, set off by the Palace Pier [now Brighton Pier] in the background. Police officers mill about on the corner of the promenade-facing end of East Street whilst two morning swimmers exercise in the water. Jimmy halts the scooter posse to inform them of the distant view below them belongs to Brighton. In actuality, it is the coastline at Eastbourne.

The eye of the camera pans from one end of the pillared walkway along Madeira Drive, Brighton, revealing a sea of parked scooters in front of the terrace of shops presented in advance of our initial sight of Jimmy. Observe the two old ladies in mackintosh coats standing in front of the public toilets, which have remained, the conveniences not the old girls. They look directly at the camera seemingly oblivious to the predesigned scene taking place. The gift shop with Kodak logos outside contained within a row of a half-dozen businesses selling food and seaside souvenirs, are all still in place today. All the concessions are much the same as they were, changing in name only. The pavement where the scooters are parked has now been broadened and huge concrete moulded

chasing the wind   STORY SYNOPSIS

spheres prevent any such positioning today in an area freshly cleaned and packaged up as Madeira Colonnade. Seafood restaurants use the space to put out tables and chairs in the summertime. Madeira Drive, next to the Palace Pier, from the Aquarium down, has received a mass of investment resulting in its stonework being cleaned and giving the impression that its all just been erected. Still, visitors are rarely seen strolling any further than this spot unless attending a gig at the Concorde 2, a former meeting place for visiting bikers in the days when it was a café. Lots of Vespas and Lambrettas are seen as the young male and female enthusiasts sit, stand and chat away. One guy with his back to the screen has a large white arrowed 'O' Who logo on the back of his parka like the one seen on the Who's Quadrophenia album cover which shows Jimmy with his face turned away from view. Another lad has a Union Jack on the back of his seen just before the introduction of the Ace Face. Jimmy and Dave walk along the pathway behind the other Mods surveying the crowd in the moments before Steph arrives on the back of Pete's scooter. Looking fine in a cream blouse, three-quarter length skirt and cream heeled slip on shoes they chat inanely until the sight of the local Ace Face causes her to gasp, *"Phew! Look at him! Don't 'e look smart?"* Sting arrives on his chrome Vespa scooter with a troop of a half-dozen others, briefly glancing at the visitors before pulling away, off towards the pier. One of his mob has a red and white Danish flag flying on the rear of his seat a sight that we again see later on, opposite the Grand Hotel, where Jimmy discovers a thoroughly different looking Ace than the paragon that is seen here. Jimmy loses sight of Steph, motioned as she is away by Pete whilst a flabber-gasted Chalky turns up a short time later on his battered scooter now with a wrecked headlamp and minus its collection of wing mirrors. With the evening activities in full flow, Green Onions performed by Booker T and the MG's, fills the dance floor of the Brighton ballroom visited by the London Mods as we see Chalky, Spider, Dave and Jimmy mingling amongst a mass of others. Pete chats with an attractive young American girl whilst the Brighton Ace Face dominates the floor with his idiosyncratic, robotic dancing. Even Spider, Chalky and Dave all want to be close to him and make a move to get a closer look. Dan is seen sitting at a table after also making the trip down. Chalky offers his comments upon the appearance of an *"out of his head"* Jimmy, speeding away and dancing wildly to the beat of the infectious music. By the by, we see that Chalky is holding a pint of beer, an inaccuracy in that many ballroom/ dance halls were not licensed for the sale of alcohol in 1964. Louie Louie from The Kingsmen sustains the groove as the Ace captivates not only those around him on the darkened dancefloor but also the camera. We catch a glimpse of Ferdy in the crowd along with one of the local Shepherd's Bush faces, John. Jimmy and Steph fall out as she seeks to dance closer to the silver-haired Ace; whilst he would rather she danced with him, a "Face" but not the "Ace Face" so blankly portrayed by Sting. Moment's later Jim is spotted jigging away on the edge of the balcony above, in stylised chicken motion. Egged on by the others below he dives in to the crowd before bouncers grab him and kick him out. Monkey, always anxious for his well-being, protests furiously. Observe the arched eyebrow of the Ace used to demonstrate his annoyance at having the attention taken away from him by the youngster. He resembles an eagle, very bird-like. Wah Watusi by The Orlons begins and plays through the next scenes. Ejected from the ballroom, Jimmy wanders off under the walkway next to the Aquarium that flows out on to the beach. In large blue capital letters we see the word 'Ballroom' illuminated above the main entrance of what in fact is the Aquarium itself. Wah Whatusi continues to permeate on the sound system as we see Steph now dancing with Ace. Conversely, a friendless Jimmy smoking a cigarette, stares out at the sea in one of the many beautifully composed shots of the Brighton seafront seen in the film. The Orlons' hit is just about audible in the background.

The Mod crowd begins to leave the ballroom mainly pairing off together, Dave with Chalky and Steph with a girlfriend. Much to the disgust, read envy, of the others, Pete retains the company of the American girl. After asking Spider and his friend if they had seen Jimmy, Dave and Chalky also pass through the tunnel leading under the pier in search of somewhere free to sleep. Whereas Dave has the mentality to view Steph purely as a sexual object, it does not appear to have registered in the mind of his mate, who simply agrees with him about her appeal following his request to accompany them after their night out. Having turned left

chasing the wind   STORY SYNOPSIS

from under the Aquarium walkway the two amble along the dimly lit underside of the pier debating whether to enter one of the unlocked storerooms.

  Startled in to action by formless voices demand that they make up their minds, they choose to stay setting the stage for an amusing morning. Interesting in that Alan Fletcher, one of the writers of the screenplay, based the sequence upon true events experienced by some of his friends back in the sixties. The final shape to be seen that night is one of a solitary Jimmy on the beach near to what looks like the marina area. Meanwhile the Brighton Ace Face and his crew complete a loop formation before slowly driving away on their scooters in the semi-darkness of an area on Madeira Drive known as Peter Pan's [once located past the Concore II music venue but now since demolished].

  The opening keyboards from Quadrophenia, an instrumental track by The Who, flow on in to the next scene. Wonderfully framed within the landscape that absorbs his ego, the paltry-sized form of Jimmy is set against the forceful sea as the vastness of the beach gradually reveals the sight of the pier in the distance. A section from the piece plays in synch with the morning sea as a fishing boat crashes on to the shore. The beach today finds virtually no fishing vessels on its shoreline poignant when being aware of Brighton's past as a small fishing village from which local people made their living and sold their wares at a former fish market on the front. *"Come on. Get a move on. I've heard there's a few Mods about."* Beckons one of the Rockers, giving Chalky and Dave a rude awakening. They discover that they shared their space with a set of fornicating rockers who fortunately do not realise their mod allegiance, made obvious from Dave's v neck sweater, pork pie hat and cream-coloured trousers next to Chalky's plaid jacket. The duo say that they'll catch up with them later and sink back under their covers astounded by their good fortune.

  Arriving together at the Beach café situated to the west of the Palace Pier, Dave and Chaly greet the others including a chewing and smoking Monkey congregated on a table near the service counter. Jimmy is revealed to be sitting alone a little away from them. The two lads order some food and relish in re-telling their tale of the amorous greasers. Thereafter Dave approaches his mate whom, not in the best of moods, is soon agitated by his friendliness. He asks

STORY SYNOPSIS   A QUADROPHENIA ANTHOLOGY

what happened to him last night and is told that he missed out on catching Steph without Pete in tow. Tucking in to a sandwich oozing with a drippy egg, Dave is told to take his feet of the seats by a passing waitress to whom he replies, *"Piss off!"* before complying with a disarming grin that proves to be a great asset. Chalky, Spider and Ferdy join them after after having had their path warmed by Dave and they all have a good laugh at his teasing of Jimmy's interest in Steph. Spider is revealed wearing his own snake belt as he stands in front of the table.

The scruffiest looking air [or are they sea cadets?] troop ever seen parade along East Street and the neighbouring Bartholemews, dressed in service-issue jumpers, a exclusively Seventies adaptation as in the Sixties they would have been given battledress tunics to wear. Nonetheless, the Ace Face, Chalky, Jimmy and Monkey and others, one lad is seen sporting a Pop Art target t-shirt whilst another has a Manchester United scarf wrapped around his neck, sheepishly mingle in with the band as it passes the corner of Bartholemews, halfway on its way down to the seafront end of East Street. They arrive next to the ABC cinema where one of the films presented is Heaven Can Wait on Screen 2 advertised alongside Grease. Both released in 1978, this goof is would be in parallel to the disappearing scooter windshield at Beachy Head, only that Franc Roddam has acknowledged the fact of the error but for artistic reasons he felt the shot was valid. They continue to march, passing in front of the New Heart and Hand public house painted as it once was in a garish blue tone. The pub has, like the cinema, two entrances, one on East Street and a second on to the seafront. Jimmy and the others Mod youngsters regroup on the promenade immediately parallel to Madeira Drive just after the Volks railway pick-up point, opposite to where we had caught a first glimpse of the scooters. The scene then purports to be the same sequence but it is not, its cut as the impetus now moves on to the east of the Palace Pier. Steph, still minus Pete, surprises Jimmy by catching up with him. Dave is also in amongst the front faces of the crowd, as will Chalky be soon. A press cameraman wrapped in a sheepskin coat appears in front of them, and proceeds to photograph them whilst walking backwards ahead a group substantial in numbers. Spider initiates a *"We are the Mods...we*

41

chasing the wind STORY SYNOPSIS

are the Mods, we are, we are, we are the Mods!" chant as everyone seems to enjoy the moment of attention. Watch when Dave comes between Jimmy and Steph, gently hugging her only for a moment later to slip off the kerb. As the mantra gathers momentum he disappears from view and is not seen in the next sequence that presents Chalky standing next to Steph and Jimmy. A male Rocker and his female pillion passenger, whom for no apparent reason wears an ill-fitting blond wig, speed past the seafront entrance to the ABC cinema which is itself virtually opposite to the animated Mods on the promenade. Chaos is about to erupt as Chalky thinks that the driver is one of the group that forced him off the road earlier that day. A small way from the pier finds the same biker parking up alongside a half-dozen other bikes of a similar ilk outside of a café at the top end of East Street. Oblivious to the fact that a couple of hundred Mods are storming across the main road towards him, we can clearly see the East Street signage above a Lyons Maid ice cream logo over a small, canopy-style corner entrance. Visible to the left of the screen is the Queens Hotel, its own signage now removed from the front of its seafront face. What is confusing is that if you look for the café today you will not find it. It has long since gone. The Queens Hotel on the front remains but what was the café/ snack bar seen in the film is presently called Character's Restaurant. Locally, it has been said that the snack bar used in the film was actually a shop on the esplanade-end of Ship Street, a little way up from here. The filmmakers used the alternate premises, presently a fish and chip shop, to generate the impression that it was in East Street. Speaking to the non-co operative management there, it was confirmed that this was where 'Jimmy smashes the café window.' With memories having faded, in the filmed sequence he actually dives out of the way as another lad throws an item through the window and on to the road, which categorically *is* recognisable as East Street. To confirm the solution to the puzzle, observed opposite the café in the scene is the blue painted exterior of the former New Heart and Hand pub [which curves around on to the seafront and next to Brill's Lane and fomer cinema]. There is another café on East Street glimpsed briefly in Quadrophenia when Jimmy and Steph run past it following Sting's smashing of a shop front window called The Gravy Train. *"Let's fuckin' have 'em!"* spews

STORY SYNOPSIS   A QUADROPHENIA ANTHOLOGY

Chalky as the battle cry goes out to attack the Rockers. Watch the look of surprise on Steph's face as it begins with hundreds of Mods flying across the King's Road with the Palace Pier behind them towards the half-dozen Rockers milling around the small entrance to the café. In a poor piece of non-acting one of the black leather and white scarf-wearing lads feebly attempts to close one half of the narrow wooden doors to prohibit the attack. He can clearly be seen gurning at them. "The noise was very frightening indeed," remembers East Street trader Hugo Barclay to the author, "the roar as these groups of people decided to move was astonishing." Whilst the others scramble inside, one lad tries to escape by running through the clusters of Mods but his audacity is confounded by Chalky and Dave. This set's the scene for a moment or two later. With the p.o.v taken from inside the café looking out, the place is blitzkreiged by the marauding Mods who set about piling in to the horrendously outnumbered occupants therein. Quite a terrifying sight with many youngsters chanting the mantra of *"Mods! Mods! Mods!"* Meanwhile back on Madeira Drive, Pete, set off in his sunglasses and ox blood coloured leather jacket blocks the path of a Rocker by inflicting what looks like a very severe kicking. The middle-aged café assistant makes a frantic phone call to the police as Jimmy lobs an egg at him. He protects himself by utilizing a tray as a shield as his brylcream-retained hair erupts within the mayhem! Jimmy moves hastily away as another lad picks up a table and throws it through a window, shattering out on to the road outside. *"Over the edge!"* returning to that terribly authentic-looking thumping, lots of knees go in to the chest of the unfortunate Rockers who are then forced over the top of the terrace by Pete and the others. Whilst on their way scrambling down what looks like at least a 20 ft drop of a curved wall, Dave smacks one of those fleeing with the remnants of a deckchair as we see the initials CMCC printed next to a Confederate flag on the back of the leather jacketed Rocker. The scenario enacted is a direct reference to the actual events of the summer of 1964 when youngsters resembling Rockers were forced over the edge of the Aquarium terrace. Newspaper photograper Colin Jones captured its image for the Brighton and Hove Gazette. The action shown in the film is not on the same part of the terrace but

43

chasing the wind STORY SYNOPSIS

further along the Drive where the walkway is steeper and consequently the drop down greater. *"Jimmy! Jimmy!"* cries out Steph grabbing him as he rushes out of the café with many others. Notice the fact that she is wearing woollen gloves in a scene that is supposedly set in summer. With the violence curtailed many of the youngsters regroup outside the entrance of the besieged eaterie. A final glance inside reveals the bruised and battered, post-battle Rockers sprawled about the tables and broken chairs. A girl curses the Mods as she tends to a male friend. *"I was there! Am I alive?"* wheezes Jimmy feeling the rush of adrenaline next to the mass of other Mods and it is all Steph can do to stop him bouncing away as he tells her of his involvement inside. The siren from the top of a police vehicle seen immediately behind them causes the group to disperse by running back across the promenade towards the beach.

Jimmy and Steph are next seen contained amongst the others hastily sprinting down the walkway leading to beach and along a terrace of small concession outlets. A couple sitting on deckchairs get the shock of their lives as one, a woman wearing a pretty, yellow coat gets knocked over by the force of the crowd as they rush on to the beach. But just like the Rockers beaten up and forced over the edge of the terrace before the female victim here was said to have been a stunt performer. The *"We are the Mods!"* chanting continues a pace on the beach as the youngsters face a stand off with the many white-helmeted police officers arranged opposite. Dressed in a pale blue suit, local Brighton author and presenter, the late Pete McCarthy can be viewed standing at the front of the crowd. The discernible order of 'come forward carefully' is audible as the crowd does exactly that. The attention marginally turns to a team of police vehicles with their sirens wailing travelling along the road towards the trouble spot. One of them is recognizable as an old, boxy black Mariah van. Having been on the beach a moment ago, the spotlight now transfers to the Aquarium steps which the many male and female Mods dash down making the area appear a great deal larger than it actually is. Pete grabs a nearby flower pot and lobs it through the window of a palmistry reader called Madam Victoria, almost hitting the poor woman who had been sitting there looking out a second ago. Her premises used to be situated to the right of the bottom of the steps alongside the main entrance to the Aquarium. In the film, Jimmy and the others are seen coming out from here during the scenes set at the 'ballroom' inside. Not stopping for more than a fraction, Pete and the others move past her window and take a right passing underneath the road above through a tunnel that as we already know, flows out to the Beach café and the underside of the Palace Pier. It is the very same thoroughfare that Jimmy, Steph and her friend and Chalky and Dave all pass through following their evening at the ballroom.

Immediately following this the Mods regroup on the beach beneath the side of the Palace Pier where Chalky and Dave join Monkey, Jimmy and Steph amongst the throng of gathered faces. Watch as the petite Toyah gets jostled by the keyed up crowd but gives an elbow in response. Chalky tells his mates that he and Dave have just beaten a few Rockers utilizing their knuckle dusters brandished by both of them on their fists, the sighting of which Steph seems shocked by. Like a calvary arriving too late, a cry of *"Let's get the bastards!"* is heralded by one of the Rockers that dash down the steps from the promenade above the Mods. Again adroit editing has meant that where they would have rushed down the Aquarium steps and out on to the beach, the Mods would have come out on the other side of the pier and not to where this scene takes place. Gary Shail, Daniel Peacock and John Altman all get in to the thick of the violence with the latter two ending up scrapping with others in the water itself. Labelled by the media as 'The Battle of Brighton' a young man in a brown suit, not discernably Mod, takes a horrific beating first of all from the Rockers equipped with pieces of wood and chains as the ensuing aggro, stunningly orchestrated even after repeated viewing retains an almost balletic rhythm. The Palace Shell Fish bar signage at the end of the row of concessions seen as the Rockers confront the others, has since been removed and the premises now houses a mini-amusement arcade and fish and chip outlet. Many of the extras on the Rockers side would seem to have been recruited from the same club as it was well documented that groups and Mod/ scooter enthusiasts from clubs like the Barnsley 5:15ers travelled from around the country upon hearing that the filmmakers were looking for extras. In amongst the many Mod faces mixed within a wash of blue denim, Dan kicks a lot of Rockers whilst John takes much of a beating in the overspill of the sea beneath the side of the pier during a moment which finds the camera recording events from the sea back onto the shore. At one point Spider ends up fighting with two Rockers, a male and female and Dave proves himself an able scrapper venturing forth in a succession of 1:1 combat as well as beating up an old chap in a black leather cap! In the Sixties followers of the Rocker look did wear such things since adapted in Brighton as a particularly queer look. Significantly, Roddam keeps Jimmy and Steph together throughout these moments as masses of people are seen rushing past and impeding the view of the camera in the course of the frenetic energy given out from the scene. With the girls shown fighting as well as boys, especially the Rockers, Steph and her slip on shoe is seen kicking out at one guy's bottom at about the time Jimmy pulls her away as events turn frightening with the arrival of horseback police. They rush past the camera at one point, very, very close to it. Throughout the violence, Jimmy is only ever seen to throw pebbles at unseen assailants on the water's edge but Chalky is observed really going for it and later on in East Street we hear him on the soundtrack saying, *"Leave it out!"* as Jimmy is nabbed by police, and Dave calls out for his other friend. Two middle-aged mounted police officers, one on a black and the other on a white skinned horse seen in the film were both said to have been genuine officers. The former strikes out at the camera with a truncheon, very Henry V-like and just about avoids knocking over a woman dressed in a red polka-dot skirt that gets caught up in the skirmishes.

During the Sixties, Brighton had a real white skinned horse on duty in the area called Kim. New proposals have been advocated to bring back mounted police patrols in Brighton for their visual deterrent effect after their withdrawal in 1984.

A view of police vans getting closer to the beach is interspersed with the sight of the Ace Face in action outside of the entrance to a gents toilet, still open today. Sting adeptly assaults two policemen using the fractured remains of a deckchair, wearing his elegant three-quarter length leather coat and charcoal grey trousers the look of glee on his face permeates beyond acting. If played back on slow mode you will see him conclude his scrapping and turning to run up the slope with the others, and look directly in to the camera lens displaying a demonic, satiated grin. No wonder he was later cast by Franc Roddam in gothic horror The Bride. On regular playback the scene passes very quickly with nothing presented as not being what it seems. Exquisitely photographed, the moments when viewed on slow-mode appear balletic. An ocean of parka and blue jeaned youngsters dash back up from the beach after being corralled by the horse riding police in a successful attempt to break up the fighting. Out on to King's Road, two cars, both I think Triumph models, get caught up in the chaos. One of them, a dark blue convertible, presently heading towards the Palace Pier appears to knock over one of them; however, it looks like he gets back to his feet a second or two later! After this, the male and female contingencies make a beeline for the nearby East Street, which had earlier seen the attack at the café. Passing the Pickwick steak house [now reopenwd as the Santa Fe bar and restaurant], New Heart and Hand pub and the ABC Cinema they rush down from the top end of the street. Opening with a long shot of hundreds of Mods sprinting along an empty East Street their roar is the only sound heard as they move towards the Wimpy bar before hastily turning on their heels and sprinting back from whence they came as the police cut off their escape by Bartholemews [where the marching band had been seen earlier]. Bartholemews is located about halfway down East Street, severing it into two and taking the one-way traffic out on to the Kings road. A glimpse of a black wooden framed shop front window is seen as they run past. Today it is painted white and houses a premises called Metal Guru, formerly a gents clothing store, dress hire business and pet store. It seems that the marauding Mods are finally contained by the police after they block off the other end of East Street. We see the Ace wearing black leather gloves, next to Jimmy and Steph and a mass of others all springing up and down to a mod chant as the authorities attempt containment. Ace soon becomes annoyed at being penned in and pushes some of those nearest away to enable himself to lob a crate through a clothes store window. Notice one youngster in a Union Jack t-shirt, another in a Union Jack blazer and a further with patches on his parka and a Who logo with Union Jack on the back. John, Monkey and Ferdy can all be glimpsed in amongst the sardined crowd prior to the diversion. Jimmy and Steph rush pass a store called the Gravy Train which

chasing the wind   STORY SYNOPSIS

is now the Time Out café, following the window being smashed and the penned-in Mods scattering. Ace really does seem a menacing presence and you can almost hear his brain ticking over as he cultivates his plan. In the midst of the two youngsters running down the narrow alleyway, the eye of the camera is set from above the fire escape of the building housing Choy's Chinese restaurant which flows through to Little East Street. As they reach the depths of the alley, they hear the approach of an irate police dog barking furiously. Jimmy manages to open the back door of the restaurant and pulls Steph to safety behind it. She looks lovely in a long black leather coat, blouse and shoulder-long hair generating a plain but pretty appearance. [The Choy's yellow sign to the left of the doorway, glimpsed momentarily, has rusted away and has recently been removed]. The white painted door with its old-fashioned flip-up metal handle has remained, only now it is painted red [depending upon when you visit] and a Yale lock means it is sealed most of the time. Amidst a high decibel count, parka-clad Mods continue to resist the police around the exterior of the Wimpy burger bar and the bookshop next to it [now in business as Pine Secrets]. Steph pulls Jimmy towards her and they begin to kiss as she sits on the floor in the corner immediately behind the door. Jimmy gives it some serious French kissing as the camera pans down. There is no noise heard from the violence in East Street but it is far from tranquil. The Ace Face, such a menacing presence amidst these scenes, pulls a police officer down from his horse in front of the Pickwick that resulted in a local extra being bitten by an Alsatian dog! The kicks reigning down on the policeman on the floor and elsewhere the violence storms on a pace as does the momentum between the lovers. An unseen police voice amplified through a loud hailer orders officers to *"get in there – turn them over!"* along with *"Control those Kids!"* which far from sounding authoritative is simply limp. Typically in a middle-class accent more indicative of an old B movie shown on a wet Saturday afternoon by posh actors portraying the working classes of Forties/ Fifties Britain. During the actual 1964 skirmishes a police loudhailer attached to a van ordered youngsters to disperse but only succeeded in being stoned by youths using pebbles from the beach. The presence of a mounted police officer is seen in amongst the bedlam which features Dan having a crack at another officer. The battle between the uniformed blackness of the police and the greenness prevalent on the backs of many modly parkas persists. In what can only be described as the swiftest on-screen 'quickie,' the lovers finish their union with a whimper from Jimmy. Tidying herself up, Steph and Jimmy rush back down the alleyway and turn right, back out on to East Street once more. Notice the yellow signage belonging to Choy's restaurant on the back of the door and the 'Crafts' lettering seen opposite the alleyway which belonged to art shop Celtic Crafts, now the Sun Bo Seng Chinese restaurant. Picking their way lightly through the aftermath of the an innocent Jimmy is forced in to the rear of a Black Mariah van by two officers only to find himself in amongst three battered-looking Rockers and a solitary constable. Dave turns Steph away from the incident which takes place next to the corner entrance of the cinema and the Fishbowl pub parallel. Now renamed The Greyhound, it could be found on the corner of a pathway that leads down to Pool Valley, the main coach terminus for travel to and from Brighton. Somewhat perplexed by being nabbed, Jimmy's anxiety is increased after he is accidentally jolted forward and on to the lap of one of the others. The young Greaser, resembling actor John Hannah from Four Weddings and a Funeral, slams him back into his seat. The reason as to why the police van shunted to a halt a moment earlier is revealed as being to accommodate one more occupant: the Brighton Ace Face. Sting, all kicking and cursing, struggles furiously with the trio of officers outside the vehicle before relenting and taking a seat. Its doors are slammed shut and it moves away, hastily turning left and on to the Grand Junction and on towards the Palace Pier. The line "I see a man without a problem," from Is It In my Head plays along with the sequence following on with further lyrics from the aforementioned Who song prior to concluding with the same opening line after the scene we see Dave and the others returning to London on the coastal road. The arrival of the Ace raises Jimmy's spirits. Ace motions an offer of a cigarette to the Hannah look-a-like from the confines of his elegant cigarette case but as he attempts to take one Sting childishly snaps the case shut. Seated opposite Jimmy, all overwhelmed by his presence, the allies each enjoy a smoke and even the police officer next to them gets offered one. In the aftermath of the events in East Street, a view of

chasing the wind   STORY SYNOPSIS

a number of Mods arm-locked to the ground by police officers or else standing around in a state of suspended animation, almost as if none of them know what happens next is not one to savour. Ferdy and Chalky are highlighted in amongst the war-torn faces now well-contained at the top end of the street next to the Pickwick. The police van containing Jimmy and the Ace Face is fleetingly glimpsed motoring along the nearby streets. Steph travels on the back of Dave's scooter in what looks like the start of a fledgling relationship between the two. Here, Dave does not have his hat glued to his head, the only other time being when a Rocker knocks it off during the fighting on the beach or whilst at work. For those arrested at Brighton, an appearance in court is imminent, *"It is strange to see this procession of miserable specimens, so different from the strutting hooligans of yesterday."* Begins a snippet of the commentary voiced by Dr. Simpson on the second day of hearings at Margate Magistrates after the Whit sun bank holiday of 1964. Much of his speech is used in the courtroom sequence in Quadrophenia [actually shot at nearby Lewes Magistrates] where we see the Ace Face, Jimmy, and John in amongst a crowded courtroom. Dressed immaculately in a leather coat, shirt and tie with his arms folded across his chest betraying his sense of tedium Ace manages to retain his sense of humour even after the events on his manor are curtailed. The Magistrate decrees that he will be subject to a fine totalling a not insubstantial £75, remembering that this is meant to be 1964. To the roar of approval from the youngsters alongside, Ace asks if he can pay immediately and asks if he can borrow a pen to write out a cheque. In actuality it was a seventeen-year-old called James Brunton who cheekily enquired to magistrate Dr Simpson, if he could pay his fine by way of a cheque. The young lad was not even in possession of a bank account! John is seen wearing a white Fred Perry sports shirt within a motley crew of battered Rockers in their leather jackets, many with those awful white scarves. The actual speech took place at Margate magistrate court, not Brighton, but its use of language had a significant influence on the reporting media. Dr Simpson had a huge effect, whereby reporters were heavily influenced by what he was saying rather than by what actually might have taken place. "It is not likely that the air of this town had ever been polluted by the

STORY SYNOPSIS A QUADROPHENIA ANTHOLOGY

hordes of hooligans, male and female, such as we have seen this weekend and of whom you are an example. These longhaired, mentally unstable, petty little hoodlums, these sawdust Caesars who can only find courage like rats, in hunting in packs, came to Margate with the avowed intent of interfering with the life and property of its inhabitants. In so far as the law gives us power, this court will not fail to use the prescribed penalties. It will, perhaps, discourage you and others of your kidney who are infected with this vicious virus that you will go to prison for three months." After the frivolity of the comments made by the Ace, the colour drains from Jimmy's face as the ominous formality of his full name, *"James Michael Cooper"* is called by a member of the court.

Exhausted after the Brighton experience life for Jim gets even worse as he steps inside the family home back in London. *"You're a little animal...a little savage...you're sister's not like this!"* shrieks his mother, pouncing on the unsuspecting youngster as she immediately berates him about the stash of amphetamines found under his mattress [on the Who album track Cut My Hair she finds his box of 'Blues']. Brandishing an edition of the Daily Mail with its front page headline of 'The Reckoning' directly reporting on the Mod vs Rockers bank holiday violence as proof of her son's intangible involvement he stands no chance. Kate Williams as Mrs Cooper, is outstanding in what was an improvised scene between the two actors who had literally just been introduced by Franc Roddam. "I was very impressed that Phil, a young actor, should be that trusting with someone he had just met." Recounts Miss Williams in a letter to the author. Reminiscent of the green-faced wicked witch from The Wizard of Oz Kate smothers both Jimmy and the whole scene with her presence before forcing him to leave. Later that same day a distraught and dishevelled Jimmy hastily parks his scooter up inside the shed in a clever scene that appears to present him as if he is inside a train compartment rather than a shed with its window having a train pass along the tracks at the bottom of the garden. Over this and the previous confrontation with his mother, Get Out And Stay Out, one of the new Who tracks written especially for the film supplements the action on screen.

Probably the most heralded scene from Quadrophenia takes place in the office of Jimmy's boss, Mr Fulford. Called there to explain his lateness at returning to

chasing the wind   STORY SYNOPSIS

work, Jimmy is forced to remain standing in front of his seated, suit-wearing boss, who has two telephones upon his desk seemingly demonstrative of his importance. He also displays a handkerchief in his left breast pocket just like the magistrate at Brighton does. Jimmy admits to being in Brighton and Fulford does ask him to concede that he was not involved in the violence there. Significantly, the young Mod admits only to being present at the time. Jimmy is given the usual discourse about his having the good fortune to have a job that many others would be grateful of. Unfortunately for him, this has quite the opposite effect upon Jimmy who snaps,*"I'll tell you what you can do with your 'igh teeth and your job: you can take that mail and that franking machine and you can shuff 'em right up your arse!"* Such a perfectly played moment with both characters frowning at each other in a state of mutual confounding of each others nature. All the boss can muster is a ineffectual, *"I beg your pardon!"*

This next scene is the last instance that we see Ferdy, Dave, Chalky and Monkey coming as it does after Jimmy's delayed return to London following his £50 fine in Sussex. In a crowded Alfredo's he informs the others there that he decided to quit his job and proceeds to buy a load of drugs off of Ferdy using his £5 'golden handshake' severance pay. *"What you gonna do with that lot?"* laughs a blasé Dave not aware of how pertinent this observation is, *"Start a one man riot!"* "Yeah. Of self-destruction!" Steph should have added but she she initiates no attempt to talk with her one-time lover. Smoking Senior Service cigarettes, the same as Jimmy's from at the house party, her harshly curled hair gives her face a pert appearance as she sits close by Dave making it obvious that they are now together. Dave wears a brown collared top with two vertical lines running down its front with two horizontal ones on the breast pocket, rounded off with a pair of Levi's. Jimmy no longer maintains his crispness of appearance now dressed only in his blue v-neck with neither a shirt nor tie underneath. A despairing Mr Cooper gets treated shoddily by a cold Dave and distant Steph, and observe how his face betrays his inner anger. Where were his mates in Brighton? None of them came looking for him after his arrest and it is left to a condescending Dave to explain that they had their jobs to get back to. He seems to forget that Jimmy did not choose to get arrested. Marvin Gaye's

STORY SYNOPSIS   A QUADROPHENIA ANTHOLOGY

Baby Don't You Do It and He's So Fine from The Chiffons permeate forth from the jukebox throughout these moments. With the evening growing late, the group including Chalky, Spider and Ferdy, start to make their way outside as the coffee bar closes for the day. *"See you found yourself another little boy, then?"* growls Jimmy to Steph. *"I can always get you a job..."* counters Dave in the brief moments before his goading goes beyond the point of no return, *"she says you're good at going up-and-down in alleyways!"* He indubitably deserves the head butt that Jimmy launches at him causing a nosebleed. As a scuffle begins Chalky and Ferdy come between the two warring Mods meanwhile Monkey, shows whose side she is on, *"Forget her Jimmy. She's a cow!"* summarises the young woman. Jimmy ignores her concern and as a passing shot throws out a curse,*"You're all wankers and cunts!"* He roars away on his scooter in to the darkness and out of their lives.

Presumably in the midst of that same evening, he journeys home before being ordered to stay away by his irate mother earlier (The exterior of the property being in Wells House Road, Acton in west London). He seems to be almost crying for help from his dad. Nevertheless, kicking the front door and calling him an *"Old spunker"* is perhaps not the most appropriate form of address. Still, we really feel for him. As ever, his vest-wearing father comes sprinting out of the house and almost grabs his son from the frame of a hastily departing scooter. The viewer almost yearns for him to catch a hold in more than a literal sense. Alas, he fails. The exterior of the house resembles a stage set in its minimalist appearance; three windows and a front door similar to the cover of the Quadrophenia Who album. Kate Williams mentioned that the hallway scene from the film was shot in a terraced block that was shortly due for demolition and one presumes that the exterior of the house may well have been the same property. Finding solace again by the canalside, Jimmy sits alone on his scooter whilst a barge passes behind as the rain lashes down. A segment not dissimilar to that heard in Cut My Hair, is also heard, I think it is a piece from The Punk And The Godfather, used here and in the previous scene where Jimmy badgers his parents. It sounds like Pete's voice has been sampled to play as if it is an extra instrument.

The next morning reveals Mr Cooper senior coming out from the house wearing a black donkey jacket similar to the one worn by Dave at the council tip. Collecting his pushbike positioned next to the shed he sets off for work. The display of railtracks in the distance becomes heightened in its adoption as a cipher symptomatic of an escape route to take Jimmy back down to Brighton. Following his father's departure, a wet and soggy Jimmy surfaces from having slept in the shed and opens the back door to the house. In silence he visits his room for the last time, tearing down the articles and nude photos upon his wall. Grabbing a tie from its resting place on the top of the mirrored chest of draws he puts it in his bag which does not appear to have much else contained within it other than a spare shirt. He will subsequently discard the bag by lobbing it out of a train window on the way down to the coast but not before his perception of one last hope remains: Steph.

Waiting for her to pass by in a neighbouring street as she sets off for work, in a vain attempt at reconciliation or conciliation, depending upon your view, an unhinged-looking Jimmy in black v neck jumper, blue jeans and unkempt hair, endeavours to talk to her. Remembering what happened at Alfredo's, she is in no mood for reconciliation and her hostility presents itself in chastising his behaviour. The moment is a painful one for Jimmy and its poignancy succeeds through the naturalism of his speech, punctuated by pauses and broken sentences as he desperately tries to communicate: full of questions, he receives no reassurance. *"Look, I ain't mad you know!"* he scowls, forced to push his scooter as she walks on. *"What is wrong with you then?"* returns Steph. *"I dunno...it's just...it's just it seems that everything's going backwards, I can't think straight, nothing seems right apart from Brighton. I was a Mod there, you know. I mean, that's something..."* Steph is unsympathetic, it is as if because he can no longer stay within the perimeters upheld by the group, in look and pretence, then the result is expurgation. Finally destroying any hope that the little Mod had left for them, Steph summarises their liaison as *"...a giggle...we fancied each other and had it off."* Poor Jim, realisng that he and Steph never really made a connection he, blurts, *"Fuckin' meant something to me!"* Screaming at him to *"Fuck Off!"* he takes his frustration out verbally and physically on his beloved Lambretta, kicking it furiously as she walks away.

"*You killed me scooter!*" Coming after that soul-destroying encounter, a scooter-riding Jimmy collides with an on-coming Royal Mail van in an accident that could have been far more serious. Jimmy clings on to his bag removed from the back of the bike in a serious state of mental fatigue. All the while the two uniformed G.P.O workers' efforts to placate him succeed in making it worse when one attempts to move his scooter from the road up on to the pavement only for it to topple over. Filmed in Wembley, watch as a male passer-by hastily moves out of the way as this happens. These events, of course prove to be the last straw; symbolising his castration from all things Mod. All that remains with him are the clothes he stands in as he abandons it on the side of the road. Standing on a platform at Waterloo train station the solitary Jimmy Cooper pops some pills washed down with a swig from a bottle of gin as Pete Townshend's gentle questioning of "Why Should I Care?" introduces the next Who track, 5:15, to the film as he prepares for the journey back to east Sussex.

To the sounds of Roger Daltrey's gruff vocals at the start of 5:15, a middle-aged woman walks along the carriageway and opens the toilet door to find a startled-looking Jimmy in the midst of applying some eyeliner. He stares at her with a gaze that is reminiscent of a child's guilt at being discovered doing something wrong by an adult. Pushing past the speechless female he again barges beyond two men standing in the narrow walkway next to the old compartments of trainstock now phased out by most networks. Vexed by his incumbent bag Jimmy throws it out of a pull-down window much to the delight of two uniformed public school girls adorned in straw hats. Recognising Fulford in a separate carriage he mouths 'wanker' to himself and continues on past to find another seat in what turns out to be a First Class compartment. Why his former boss should be on a train down to Brighton is not disclosed. Sliding open one of the glass-panelled doors young Mister Cooper sits himself down in an empty seat between two city gents. Barely able to contain their mutual displeasure and apprehension, the two men, dressed in matching suits and bowler hats, ignore the arrival of the eye popping teenager. One or both busy themselves with reading The Times. The chap seated to Jimmy's left has a moustache redolent

chasing the wind STORY SYNOPSIS

of Windsor Davis' in It Ain't Half Hot Mum. Handkerchiefs are firmly positioned in breast pockets also. Jimmy wears a suit with a shirt and tie and whilst there outward appearance may be conducive, there is little else shared in this compartment. His tie is loosened to about an inch or so, exactly as the Ace in court and Spider in another scene.

A glimpse of railtracks and the sea at Brighton are juxtaposed as the final essence of the song concludes with the waves breaking on the shore. Back in Brighton things are very different from before as the camera is positioned outside of the window at the Beach Café, then it moves inside as we find him seated at a window seat. Jimmy now sits near to a pillar, the second in from the entrance as you turn left. Popping yet more pills, the Palace Pier opposite is reflected in the glass and he almost motions to talk to the female assistant but finally says nothing. After all, what could he possibly have to say to her? Smoking on a cigarette it is painful to sense his isolation in the deserted eaterie. Love Reign O'er Me plays as a lone male swimmer is observed exercising in the water. Its slightly abstract imagery as the figure moves in the water and the stroke of his movement makes his arm rise up evokes the symbolism of Excalibur rising forth from the water and disappearing again. It also brings to mind the Stevie Smith poem with its misunderstood plea of 'drowning not waving' being aligned to Jimmy's plight in that he is losing everything that he believed meaningful.

As the phosphorescent, the surf left after the initial channel of energy of a wave remains, wearing tassled, slip-on loafers and not the desert boots that we have seen him in before, a very sharp cut now finds Jimmy crouching on the shingle as the beauty of Townshend's lyric and Daltrey's voice combine to enrich the moment. The incoming tide laps at his feet and dangling parka which seems to please Jimmy in a pose that was to be used to promote the re-issued film release in 1997. His parka comes in practical as it is wrapped around him whilst he looks briefly towards the figure in the water. The connection to water flows throughout the film, from the moment we see Jimmy practicing being underwater at the baths to his theatrical dive off of the balcony in to the crowd below at the Brighton ballroom. Motioning to his feet, he generates the impression of being

STORY SYNOPSIS   A QUADROPHENIA ANTHOLOGY

small in stature as he moves away from the shoreline leaving the swimmer behind. The Palace Pier with its lurid signage and Union Jack beneath it, is observed in the distance as Jimmy comes off the beach, its Eastern-shaped domes on the pier building, influenced by the similarly-attired Brighton Pavilion, remain its most quixotic characteristic.

Ambling alone along the promenade in his burgundy suit with not a Mod in sight [only the frail and middle-aged are glimpsed], he makes his way towards East Street as the song continues. A tender smile blows across his face in the time it takes him to walk up the alleyway once more. Such are the dimensions there that only a single person at a time can pass along it. Leaning against the rutted stonewall, plastered over with a smooth skin of concrete by 2001, his lament immediately surges forth. *"Fuck it!"* he roars and kicks at the closed doorway as Love finishes. Along with the repeated *"Bell Boy!"* and *"ME!"* these are the only words uttered by the lonely soul throughout his return to the town. Dejected, a wonderous sight next meets his eyes; Sting's chromed Vespa scooter with its VCB 160 registration, eight lights and dozen mirrors with tassles attached to its handlebars sitting glistening in the sunshine parked along the side of the Grand Hotel. Both Jimmy and the camera greet its appearance like an old friend until his dreamlike state turns in to something distinctively nightmarish as the Ace Face emerges from the main entrance a hundred yards away. Uniformed in full bellboy regalia, Sting follows the tail of an affluently attired male guest into the lobby after picking up his three suitcases outside. Dropping one and hastily picking it up again he looks deflated, in his expression, at having to cow-tow to the moneyed guests but that's nothing to the shock that it has upon Jimmy. Daltrey relates Jimmy's memory of previously being in Brighton with the Ace until making way for Keith Moon's mockney vocal styling erupts with the line, "I work in a hotel all guilt and flash…" as an apoplectic Jimmy cannot believe his eyes as he rushes up the steps after the Ace screaming out with a clenched fist, *"Bell boy! Bell boy!"* In total disarray at what this signifies, The Ace does not acknowledge him as Bell Boy plays out in full, summarising the moment as Jimmy's fragile world comes tumbling down before him. The song stops then restarts with the "you were under the impression..."

57

chasing the wind   STORY SYNOPSIS

refrain from I've Had Enough. Bell Boy fades just as it is about to reach its most pertinent lyric relatable to them both…"always running at someone's heel. You know how I feel…" Running back down the steps of the hotel and away towards the scooter, he somehow manages to start its ignition with what would imaginably have been the key to his Lambretta. Bearing in mind that the Ace rides a Vespa, why should it fit? It was commonly known that Vespa keys were interchangeable on many models but would they really have worked with a completely different manufacturer? Sill, Jimmy starts the scooter and rightly nicks it. Two men jump out of his way by a concrete pillar that is in truth a part of the Brighton Centre immediately to the left of the Grand's main entrance.

"But things ain't quite that simple."

Bumping up off of the road that leads to Beachy Head, a succession of scenes are very sharply cut starting with Jimmy coming off the road as we see Belle Toute, a well-known local landmark used as the location for The Lives and Loves of a She Devil, in the background. Various close-ups and long shots of the scooter-riding Mod follow to the strains of I've Had Enough as Jimmy makes his way along the lush green clifftop, synchronising with the Townshend lyrics relating to Jimmy's former adherences [scooter, parka, fashion] contrasting with the dominance of Daltrey's sumptuous vocals outlining the young man's disdain of such a lifestyle. The vocals to the song are suggestive of two separate tales, Roger offers up an articulation of Jimmy's anger and lament whilst Townshed defines the essence of his lifestyle. The repetitive use of 'enough' is demonstrative of Jimmy simply coming to a crossroad in his life. Watching the events at Beachy Head, Jimmy cannot go any further, having literally been pushed to the limits, never mind Cagney's 'top of the world, ma' for this young man he has arrived at the edge of his. With the scooter's exhaust billowing heavily, the camera distances itself from Jimmy as the lushness of the song title is cried by Daltrey in such an stirring manner. Although very Seventies sounding now, the way in which the synths act as a pumping heartbeat is perfect. Parallel to this is the effective method in which the director manipulates the scene by the contrast in scale between Jimmy to his surroundings, a tactic used on previous occasssions at the beach, "...where nothing ever goes as plans." With his head bobbling we see a possessed yet vacant, numbed and punchdrunk all at the same time, Jimmy, interspersed with a shot of the famous red and white lighthouse in the water below with the huge expanse of white rockface towering above. Here, the sea takes on its own character in the film, an organism resembling a lime green, plastic sheath of synthetic bubblewrap. Crying out a primordial *"ME!"* Jimmy, with the scooter now stationary with its face projected at the cliff edge, turns the bike around and heads away. However, he stops and turns again, in preparation for what is about to pass. He stands up as he motions the scooter towards its destiny supplemented by the rejection of all things Mod referenced by Pete Townshend through Daltrey's exclamations: ""I've had enough of dancehalls...pills...streetfights...kills...fashions..."The scooter flies over the edge, crashing onto the rocks below. The collected sound effects of a train horn, a train passing over tracks and the sea concur before a dramatic pause is concluded by a single line refrain from Helpless Dancer, "You stop dancing." Utilised as it is in a typical Who way where the energy of a guitar forces its way in to your head and takes the affected to another place. The battered and beleaguered scooter remains on screen viewed forlornly as the closing titles play out to a soundtrack of Dr Jimmy.

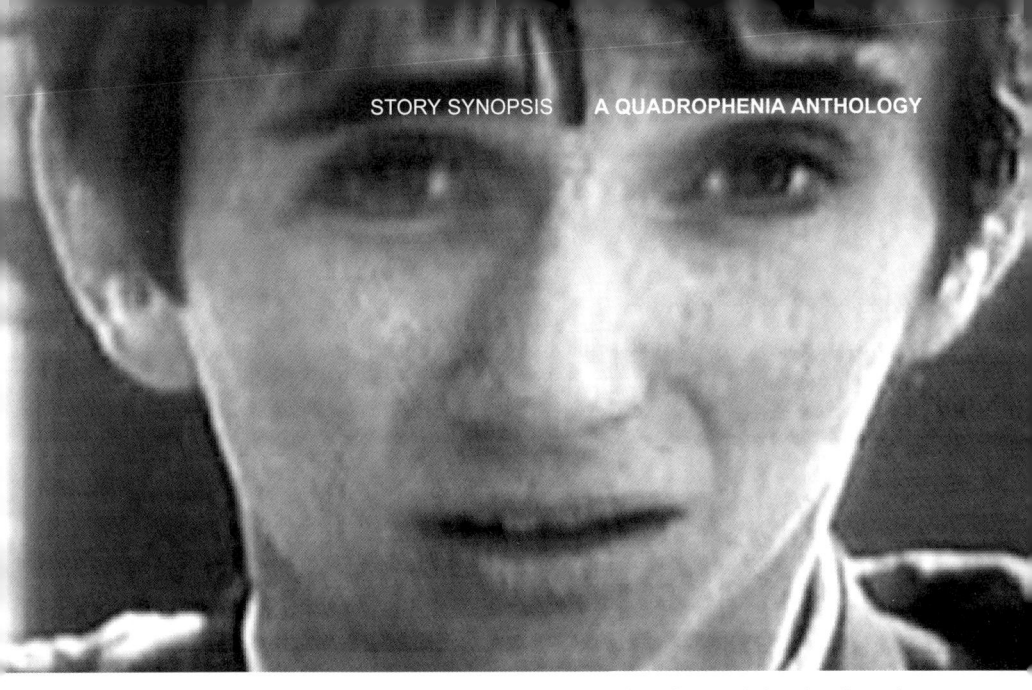

chasing the wind A TO Z ANTHOLOGY

John Altman

"Quadrophenia is one of the best things I have been involved with because it was such fun to film. [Brighton Evening Argus newspaper, 30 January 1997].

Born in Reading in 1952, John plays one of the lads on the periphery of the main core of Mods in the film [namely consisting of Phil Daniels, Mark Wingett and Phil Davis]. Quoted whilst at the Brighton Odeon premiere marking the 1997 re-release of Quadrophenia he is best known for his role of Nick Cotton in East Enders. Initially introduced along with a fellow Mod mate at the greasy spoon cafe where Jimmy had been sharing a table with old pal Kev [Ray Winstone] John asks Jimmy, *"What's this fuckin' Rocker doing here?"* An anxiously departing Jimmy offers no explanation to the leathered-up Kev who merely sits there open mouthed. Unlike the fully suited-up Jimmy, Chalky, Dave, Spider, Ferdy and Pete, John looks out of synch in the fashion stakes. Indeed he seems to wear the same pale blue cotton jacket, sports shirt [not a Fred] and Levi jeans throughout his time in the film except for a white sports shirt and parka in Brighton. Is his character meant to show the development of Mod trends as illustrated by Colin Larkin in his book The Virgin Encyclopedia of Sixties Music? "The sartorial slide of the mid-sixties Mods," states the author, "started when they began to swap their smart suits firstly for casual American college-boy styles and then for trimmed parkas, Op-Art clothes and T-shirts." I think for Mods like the one portrayed by Altman, it was simply lack of funds that limited their acquired attire. For John, it was merely a question of being given the clothes from the wardrobe department even though he himself felt they were a little soft looking. In the midst of the Brighton beach battles, alongside Daniel Peacock, John takes quite a beating from some of the denim and leather wearing rockers culminating with both actors brawling away as the boisterous sea cascades around them. Director Franc Roddam uses the location simply, effectively adding its own energy to an already vigorous scene. It is guaranteed that upon first seeing Quadrophenia that two initial images remain a] that Jimmy does jump off the cliff top and b] the sheer dynamism of the beach fighting moments. "The film achieves a rare thing," enhances Philip French in Cult Movies, "convincing crowd sequences and even more remarkable, realistic riots." Even after many screenings these images retain their machine gun pace in spite of some inept performances from many of the involved extras. What this does is enhance the chaotic naturalism of such events and thus make them authentic. Roddam consciously pushed the envelope in stirring up the haze between those acting in this landscape. "I was with at least 200 kids running down a street and a policeman grabbed me," explains Phil Daniels about the East Street confrontations [within which Altman is featured oddly wearing a parka coat whilst on the earlier beach scenes he has that awful blue sports jacket], "I can remember hitting and kicking the shit out of him." Concludes Daniels in a quote taken from the beautiful photomontage segment located at the end of the 1994 4-Front video of Quadrophenia. "It seemed about as real as you can get." However, that was not to say that the scenes were un-choreographed, bolster wood was used for the wrecked deckchairs utilised by both groups during these moments. But John remembers the action got pretty "close to the knuckle." For Equity-trained actors such as Altman and Danny Peacock, they were called upon to deliver the freshly written Quadrophenia script in and around the main characters and the experience proved a great learning curve. We can surmise that Altman's character, not unlike a number of youngsters that followed the mod movement at some point in the Sixties, did not ride a scooter. In fact, in the midst of the 1964 Whit sun holiday scuffles in Brighton many of those caught up in the violence were frog-marched up to the train station by police. Others attempted to gain a lift out of the town by hitching but only succeeded in creating a twenty-mile queue outside of Brighton. So not all Mods could afford to own and run a sexy Vespa or Lambretta scooter. John can be spotted in a succession of scenes in Quadrophenia including dancing at the Goldhawk club and at the Brighton ballroom, at the house party in Kitchener Road and briefly with Jimmy in the pub gents. After the Brighton visit by the group, which for Jimmy, the Ace Face and John concludes in a courtroom finale, Altman plays no further part in the story. Other work incls: The First Great Train Robbery (1978), An American Werewolf in London (1981). See also: Fashion, goofs, My Generation, Mark Wingett. CONTACT: Roger Carey Associates, 7 St George's Square, London

Anyway Anyhow Anywhere - Jazz musician Charlie Parker was the inspiration behind Pete Townshend's writing of AAA, a visual presentation of which is enjoyed by Jimmy when he watches the band on Ready Steady Go! It is again heard as his record of choice in a listening booth at a music store.

Leslie Ash

"She was terrified because of her over-protective boyfriend at the time. But she wasn't interested in me."

[Phil Daniels, The Sun, February 2006, discussing the famous alleyway scene between Jimmy & Steph during the rioting in Brighton.]

First seen at the Goldhawk club in Shepherd's Bush, dancing with her boyfriend Pete. She shares fourteen scenes with Phil Daniels. The last time that Steph [Ash] sees the cuckold Jimmy turns out to be an abject occasion for him and considerably more so than for her. In the course of the story Steph has been abandoned by the equally bumptious Pete [Garry Cooper], gotten off with Jimmy and then drops him for his best mate Dave [Mark Wingett]. Representative of the times, where casual relations were envogue thanks to the broader availability of the contraceptive pill; [which had gone on sale in 1961 but was rather difficult for young girls to be given without their parents knowledge] "The separation of sex for pleasure from sex for procreation," was how social moralist Malcolm Muggeridge categorised the prevailing mood. Steph's behaviour is undeniably that of a child of the sixties only, in the process, the more conventional Jimmy is devastated by her attitude. Her casual interpretation of Brighton passion as nothing more than *"...a giggle, that's all. We fancied each other and had it off,"* to a by now dishevelled Jimmy towards the end of the film. Steph may look a dish in her three-quarter length leather coat, [both Sting and Garry Cooper wear similar male styles] cream blouse and knee-length skirts, very much in keeping with the mod scene but what she lacks in sensitivity Jimmy oozes. With her final expletive-riddled farewell sending him ballistic, resulting with a torrent of equally vicious depth concluding itself by his kicking the hell out of his beloved scoot, all is lost for Jimmy. pathos. Conversely, Jim after seeing her at the Goldhawk club and visiting her at the supermarket where she sits at the till, her hair pulled rigorously back in to a ponytail, her drabness and boredom is placated by an enthusiastic Jimmy. She asks if he sees himself as one of the leading mods to which he responds, *"Whadda you mean gonna be?"* pipes Daniels growing in confidence each second, *" I AM one of the faces!"* This is a key interaction between the two evident because Jimmy knows exactly how to arouse her interest and it is indicative of her more than casual interest in both him and the question posed. This is reiterated later when Jimmy quizzes Steph about her relationship with the flashy Pete, *"I wouldn't be with him otherwise, would I."* A perfect example of Modness of mind. On a lighter note both these scenes give a glimpse of their mutual attraction and in the beginning their courtship is endearing. However, the fact that Steph and Jimmy become involved does not prevent her travelling down to Brighton with Pete, she does at least make it clear to Jim that she has already accepted Fenton's offer to do so.

Inside the Aquarium ballroom she and Jim fall out over her curiosity towards the local Ace Face (ALA Sting). Steph is not alone in being intrigued by him; Spider drags both Dave and Chalky towards where the Ace is dancing to an enrapt audience. Finding himself unable to compete Jimmy gets the idea of dancing precariously on the edge of the balcony above the main crowd but his action leads to his ejection and separation from everyone from the club. As soon as he allows his mod pretence to slip, that stiff upper lip of attitude, Steph immediately drops him, whilst his so-called friends show themselves as strangers [only Monkey expresses solidarity]. Turning the tables somewhat, he and we, the audience, finds Steph's callousness a bitter pill to swallow. Yet for all this her attitude can be construed as modish: to be a part of the scene, to act casually and to enjoy the hedonistic pleasures of self-autonomy. The difference implicit for mod girls and rocker girls was that the former tended to wade in to the seaside violence whilst the latter did not. The females seen around mod environs were often plainly made-up and minor in the status quo of the predominantly male dominant youth culture of the Mod. The original wave of the movement was exclusively male and rigidly so. It was not until 1964 or so that the term 'mod' had aligned itself to the Carnaby Street commercialisation, which led to genuine converts leaving the scene. The Daily Mail in 1964 reported that the British teenager spent a collected total of £220m pa on clothing items including suits, shoes, jackets, underwear, trousers and shirts. Broadly speaking anything regarded as fashionable by then was given the Mod label, meaning modern in style rather more so than the modernist that we are concerned with. As an eighteen-year-old at the time of filming Ash, with her shoulder-length hair [a hairpiece according to a co-star] covering her ears and accompanied by a low fringe does not strike one as essentially mod. Contrast her look with the styling given to Monkey [Toyah]; all shortly cropped-bleached blonde, little or no make-up and Steph fails to fall in to the same rigid category. Another pronounced mod look is embraced by Spider's nameless girlfriend [perfect hair, boyish yet indelibly feminine] but alas her character remains barely outlined. Caught up with Jimmy amidst the seafront violence, Leslie can be seen kicking one boy up the rear as Jimmy frantically motions her away, *"Leave it out, Steph!"* he pleads, pulling her away from an incoming police horseback charge. With the chaos reigning all about in the nearby East Street the couple remain together throughout, breaking away from the trouble by dashing down an alleyway that leads to Little East Street. They soon find refuge behind a doorway and we all know what happened next. 'Vive le France!' Mr Cooper. Not surprisingly the alleyway has since become a shrine for enthusiasts and its nicknamed "Quadrophenia alley" by local people. Leslie and Phil Daniels blend well together on screen although ironically their fondness for one another shines brightly in the on-set photographs taken by Frank Connor in in the 4Front-video release.

Acting for Leslie crystallised as a four-year-old in a 1964 appearance in a washing-up liquid commercial. A former model, her acting is perhaps not the most abstruse but this has been more to do with the type of parts that she has been cast in. Think of the delectable but vacuous Debs in Men Behaving Badly. Leslie endeavoured to broaden her appeal by acting in the 1999 West End musical The Pyjama Party and, with previously lesser success, as a presenter on the Channel 4 music show The Tube back in 1982. Still on telly, she has worked with Quadrophenia cast and crew members on CATS Eyes [with Mark Wingett], The Bill [ditto], Stay Lucky [with Roger Daltrey co-star Dennis Waterman] and Bugs [with Jesse Birdsall]. Film wise, Birdsall and Oliver Pierre, the latter being the harassed tailor in Quad, were both cast in Shadey (1985), Pierre had acted with Leslie in 1982 on the film Nutcracker; The Curse of the Pink Panther (1983) numbered Ash, Michael Elphick, Patrick Murray and First Assistant Director Ray Corbett amongst its crew. Personal life issues have unwittingly thrust Leslie back into the media spotlight in recent years. She lives in London with her husband and children and is slowly recovering from serious health problems which have been well-documented.

See also: Jeremy Child, Frank Connor, Phil Daniels, Toyah, Mark Wingett.

Albert Bailey Boom Op [Sound] on Quadrophenia. Sound Recordist for My Beautiful Launderette (1985) and My Son the Fanatic (1998) both of which were written by Hanif Kureishi and the former directed by Stephen Frears. It was Frears that directed Gary Holton, P H Moriarty and fellow Quadster Daniel Peacock in Bloody Kids (1980) a TV film given a cinema release. The smarmy Pete, Garry Cooper, has a small role in Launderette to conclude the Quadrophenia connection.

David Bailey One of the leading young artists in the photographic circles of swinging London his shots of Pete Townshend and Quadrophenia actors Toyah and Sting are collected in If We Be Shadows [Thames and Hudson, 1990]. Further Who pictures can be found in David Bailey Archive 1, 1957 - 69 [same pubs, 1999]. In London's East End of 1964, Bailey absorbed what he termed the body dynamism of the strutting Mods and Rockers of the area and he would draw upon what he had seen for future projects. A photograph of The Who standing in front of a huge billboard containing an image of Jean Shrimpton [one of his favourite models] concludes the Mod appropriation. The image can be viewed in The British Century by Brian Moynahan [Weidenfeld and Nicolson, 1997] and is accredited to Decca record photographer Dave Wedgebury, who of course took the famous My Generation album shot of the band standing beneath London's Big Ben.

Roy Baird Acting as a Producer on Quadrophenia Roy sustained a continuous career in the film industry largely as a Producer, Assistant Director and Production Manager. His Quad linkage was exemplified with production duties on McVicar (1980), Buddy's Song (1990) and Listzomania (1974) each providing substantial acting duties for Executive Producer Roger Daltrey. Mr Baird also crewed for Tommy director Ken Russell on cult classics The Devils (1971) and The Music Lovers (1970). Independently, he was employed as Assistant Director on The Leather Boys (1963), regarded as a quick cash-in on the early development of the 'Ton-up' boys later to transpose in to the greaser/ rocker but a decent film nonetheless. He and Bill Curbishley were pivotal in seeing that the film was made shortly after Keith moon had died.

Bands During the filming of Quadrophenia Toyah Willcox won a recording contract with Safari Records and Phil Daniels was regularly performing with his own band, culminating in the release of an album in 1980 titled Phil Daniels and The Cross. The Ace Face, Sting, was then in an up-and-coming band called The Police whilst Gary Shail went on to compose songs for a film starring Roger Daltrey called Pop Pirates.

Bank Holidays It would not be until the bank holiday scuffles of 1964 that the press became broadly aware of the Mod cult. The notoriety for 'Mods versus Rockers' scuffles at resorts predominantly along the South coast, has proven to be placed within its genuine context: generated out of boredom rather than anything at its primary core. "In the end we stopped going," reflected one former mod in BBC documentary You'll Never be Sixteen Again, "because everyone from all over the country used to come down. They weren't real Mods, they were just looking for a fight. It got a bit silly." See also: Brighton, Mods, Rockers,

Sean Barton Film Editor on Quadrophenia who has since worked with Franc Roddam on other projects. Sean's career has developed over three decades, mostly recently with the excellent This Year's Love and the raucous Guest House Paradiso both released in 1999.

Beachy Head "The sun searches out every crevice amongst the grass, nor is there the smallest fragment of surface which is not sweetened by air and light...Discover some reason to be up there always..."
Richard Jefferies, The Breeze of Beachy Head-England in Camera Colour – Sussex [Ian Allen Ltd., 1981]
Used for lots of telly commercials and films which have taken advantage of these chalk headlands situated on the South Downs, three miles from Eastbourne and about forty-five miles from Brighton. With a drop of 534ft down to the sea below and its famous red and white lighthouse at scale of 142ft. a visitor's centre informs the million visitors that travel to the area each year. Ghoulishly, Beachy Head has the dubious honour of being the foremost suicide spot in Great Britain. A front cover for a past video release of Quadrophenia finds a scootered-up Jimmy dominating its imagery. So effectively utilised for the climactic scene in the film, finding Jimmy experiencing his most traumatic moment in his young life, the water appears as if it is a mammoth ream of movable, plastic bubble-wrap.
See also: Beachy Head, John Surtees, [S.B Publications, 1997]

The Beatles Yvonne, Jimmy's sister, has portraits of the band members on her bedroom wall. In the photographs accompanying the 1973 Who album, there is a picture of the group in Jimmy's bedroom whilst in the film there is not.

Beatniks AKA Beats "The thing that amazed me was the number of people who stood around, watching those dirty Beatniks!" [Manager of the Metropole Hotel quoted in the Brighton and Hove Gazette, 7 August 1964]. Interesting in that this group of mainly middle-class youngsters are viewed as a forerunner for Mods. They are mentioned just the once in Quadrophenia, by Steph's ungainly boyfriend Pete who jokingly compares Jimmy's attitude to work with theirs when he visits him at his Uncle Charlie's scrap yard. Back in the Brighton of 1964 there were more of these longhaired, opt-outters than there were rockers and some were unintentionally involved with skirmishes with the visiting Mods.

Bell Boy Keith's Theme. Recorded at the beginning of June 1973 and used so effectively as a narrative device that finally destroys any semblance of truth in the Mod ideology for young Jimmy upon seeing the Ace working at Brighton's Grand Hotel. Roger's vocals kick start the track before Keith sings in a mockneye accent. As the events of Brighton are retold in the lyrics, 1963 is acknowledged as the year that saw the Ace lead those in Brighton during the scuffles. Yet Quadrophenia, the film, is set in 1964.

Perry Benson Played Eric in the mail room at Jimmy's ad agency. Perry is also in This is England (2006) the poster of which is a homage to Quadrophenia.

John Bindon "He had a colourful past," recounts Ken Loach after directing him [and Jimmy's mum Kate Williams] in Poor Cow (1967) "...a great character." Kicknamed 'Biffo,' the 6'3" Bindon acted in a trio of British films in the 1970s: Performance (1970), Get Carter (1971) and Barry Lyndon (1975) all very much indicative of their time. Whilst in Quadrophenia, Harry [Bindon] is visited by an anxious Jimmy after the fun boy three's quest for supplies for their Brighton beano prove fruitless. Jimmy inadvertently gives Harry the impression that he is Pete so as he can score some blues. *"A pill 'ead,"* sighs Bindon to one of his cohorts as the naive young Cooper is led off to lose his, Chalky and Dave's tenner kitty money in exchange for a bag of paraffin coated rubbish. The three lads reek a juvenile revenge by trashing Harry's svelte-looking Jaguar. If the story had covered a longer period of time then no doubt Jimmy would have been paid a visit from Harry's boys in lieu of the damage inflicted upon his motor. The London-born Mr Bindon, aka 'Biffer' died in London in 1993. He was fifty. A book and telly documentaries have since revealed many of the elements in the life of a complicated individual.

Jesse Birdsall Born in north London in 1963 he will forever be remembered as Marcus in the ill-fated soap Eldorado and in another BBC drama, Bugs. However, in Quadrophenia, Jesse and fellow greaser Gary Holton form part of a gang that fortuitously stumbles upon a stranded Spider and his girlfriend after experiencing mechanical problems with his scooter. It is obvious that trouble is brewing and indeed it soon does with the heavily uniformed black leather jacket and trousered Lenny [Birdsall] laying in to the outnumbered couple. This event indirectly leads to the mistaken attack on Kevin [Ray Winstone] as revenge for the assault on Spider. Unfortunately for Kevin, he sports the exact same riding gear as any typical rocker, polished off with the same greased back coiffured hair. Resembling World War II 'Flying Aces', their dapper white scarves provided a rare example of recognisable dandyism even this item has its practical use of giving protection against the wind for the no-nonsense Rocker. Both Holton and Birdsall acted together again in Bloody Kids (1980) released after Quadrophenia. For young bikers like Lenny growing up in the early-Sixties, the wearing of a leather jacket was entirely functional, in direct opposition to the robes adorning the skinny Mod which communicated a statement of intent in a non-verbal manner. Perhaps only the parka army coat provides a similar example of modernist functionality in that its adaptation served in keeping their expensive suits free of grime. Other work incls: Getting it Right (1989). See also: John Altman, Stephen Frears.

Les Blair Perhaps not duly recognised or renowned as a commercial director in keeping with compatriots Ridley Scott, Stephen Frears or Alan Parker, Blair occupies the kooky space in between fellow filmmakers Mike Leigh, Ken Loach and the late Alan Clarke. His relation to Quadrophenia is relatable in that Phil Daniels, P H Moriarty and Ray Winstone all acted in his 1984 film Number One. Individually, Phil Daniels portrayal of twins in the Blair comedy Bad Behaviour (1993) is worth seeing for this added value alone if you are aPhil Daniels fan.

Blur Categorised as a leading force in the Britpop resurgence blossoming in the mid-1990s, they recorded a version of Substitute for an early Who Covers Who album released in 1996. Phil Daniels contributed vocal narration to their Parklife

single and appeared in the jolly video clip to go with its release. The track can be found on their Best Of album and video compilation. Lead singer Damon Albarn acted in Face, a film with Quad actors Ray Winstone and Phil Davis in leading roles. See also: Bibliography, Phil Daniels, The Who.
Booker T and The MG's Made an album and record titled Green Onions, an instrumental track which most will know but not quite be able to say who recorded it or what it's called, features in the ballroom that the London Mods visit whilst in Brighton. The single peaked at number seven on the UK chart in December 1979 after Quadrophenia had been released in cinemas across the country. Having evolved from an improvised jam at the end of a recording session, the song was release as an a-side in 1962, a year after Booker T Jones [the MG's being The Memphis Group] had formed the band and a little over a decade before it was disbanded. Both the band and Onions was a big favourite of Pete Townshend's for its guitar work and consequently played live in their High Numbers days. As a band they were re-united in 1990 and are featured in The Blues Brothers (1979).

David Bowie Played the Marquee club in his formative years and his association with The Who is expressed with his backing vocals on Keith Moon's solo album and Bowie's own versions of Anyway Anyhow Anywhere and I Can't Explain featured on his Pin-Ups album (1973). In addition, Bowie has covered tracks by The Yardbirds, The Merseybeats, The Pretty Things and The Kinks as well as The Who's own Pictures of Lily. A Bowie song featured on the soundtrack of Almost Famous (2000) as are The Who, Sting and Elton John.

Peter Brayham Stunt Arranger and Co-ordinator on Quadrophenia. Peter has a plethora of experience in film and television including arranging the stunts in Listzomania (1975) directed by Ken Russell and starring Who vocalist Roger Daltrey; director and actor would again come together on the Tommy shoot, also a 1975 release.The Ray Winstone thriller Tank Malling (1988) and Life is Sweet (1990), memorably enhanced by a Timothy Spall appearance, further developed the Brayham-Quadrophenia integration. In 1986 Peter worked on a series of Boon starring the lugubrious Michael Elphick.

[Pictured] 'Quadrophenia' Alley in East street, Brighton.

ⒶⒷⒸ ①②③④ East st BRIGHTON 27010

Today until Wed. next
(No. 1 cinema closed Mon. until 7.15 p.m.)
Doors open 1.30 (Mon. 7.15) Last
prog: 7.40
QUADROPHENIA
(X) (2.30, 5.30 not Mon.) 8.30
SUPPORTING PROGRAMME
(1.50, 4.45 not Mon.) 7.40
(Persons under 18 not admitted)

brighton:

its locations

and the part it plays in the film

No unaccompanied children admitted after 7p.m
ALL PROGRAMMES MAY BE SUBJECT TO LATE CHANGE

chasing the wind   BRIGHTON

[Above] The Brighton Ace Face [Sting] about to join Jimmy in the back of a Police van amidst the rioting in Brighton.

"that, my son, is Brighton!"

"We started filming in Brighton with the riot.
Staying in some holiday hotel on the front.
I hardly went to bed for a fortnight.
I last saw the film when they re-released it about six or seven years ago. There was a big reunion in Brighton. Big party. We all looked and felt much older."
[Phil Davis aka Chalky, in a letter to the author].

BRIGHTON   A QUADROPHENIA ANTHOLOGY

LOCATIONS The editing skills of Sean Barton and Mike Taylor shine forth in the clever juxtaposition of Brighton locations cut together to create a discernably different slant. For example, when the Mods rush down the Aquarium steps and turn right under a tunnel thoroughfare, it takes them under the road above and out on to the beach in front with the Palace pier seen to the right. The Beach Café is to the left and opposite takes you under the top end of the pier itself. In the filmed sequence they arrive on the beach with the pier *behind* them, therefore a cut was made, as they would have had to pass under the darkened recess of the pier structure before arriving. In addition, the Mods are seen to dash down the steps after just being on the beach which in turn would have meant going back up from whence they came and looping back under the subway flowing on to the beach.

1 East Street: Jimmy is nabbed by two police officers as he and Steph attempt to move away from the violence there. The black Mariah van points down towards the seafront in what is a one-way street only for Sting to be arrested a second later, in Brill's Lane, parallel to this it would have been an impossible detour.

2 Brill's Lane: A narrow road that is entered into by turning left past the Pickwick pub on East Street. It flows past the side of the old cinema to its left and the New Heart and Hand pub [now open as the Santa Fe restaurant/ bar] to its right. When the Ace Face is arrested following some serious resistance against a group of officers, he clambers in to the rear of the van that has just picked-up Jimmy at the nearby East Street. Nevertheless, the van positioned on Brill's Lane in itself next to the seafront entrance of the ABC cinema would mean that it has miraculously performed a 360 degree turn to achieve such a feat. It then proceeds to head down towards the promenade and turns left as the road meets the main road. Impossible in that it has once again turned itself around from the time Sting is arrested two seconds previously! So three cuts have been incorporated in to what appears to be two sequences.

3 Aquarium and Ballroom: Actually the Brighton Sea Life Centre [formerly known as the Aquarium and pictured above] acknowledged as it is in the film through the 'ballroom' lettering outside its main entrance. The Florida Room, which The Who gigged at a number of times in 1964 and 1965, was entered through a separate point to the left of the Aquarium entrance. The arched walkway is utilized in the film by Jimmy and the others at the end of their first night in Brighton and during the beach battles of the next day.

4 Beach: Predominantly the area on the west side of the Palace Pier was favoured by the filmmakers for the scenes where the Mods v Rockers fighting occurs and as the backdrop for Jimmy's lament sometime later.

5 Beach Café: Located to the left after passing through the Aquarium tunnel / walkway. The premises was a firm favourite for visiting Mods back in the Sixties and it is shown during two sequences shot here, the first when Jimmy and the others have breakfast and the second occasion finds Jimmy sitting alone at the window seat.

6 Promenade: Cleverly used by the filmmakers during the course of the story. Sharply edited scenes mesh as the Mods march on the seafront where two locations [either side of the Palace Pier] are cut together generating the on screen impression of oneness.

7 Madeira Drive: Found past the Brighton Aquarium, with the Palace Pier on the opposite side of the promenade. Presented on screen as the rendezvous point for visiting Mods as they arrive in Brighton for their weekend. Featured as the location where Pete and the others force some Rockers over the edge of its steeped terrace, the Brighton Ace Face and his scooter-riding posse ride around an area further along the Drive known as Peter Pan's Amusements [on the opposite side of the promenade to where the scooters park up upon arrival].

8 Grand Junction / King's Road: The former is found connecting with the seafront end of East Street whilst the latter is the residence for the Grand Hotel.

Film links - *"I ain't mad you know! Nothing seems right apart from Brighton...."*
The Brighton riot scenes were the first to be filmed by Roddam and writing in her auto biography, Toyah Willcox adds her own colour to the period, "Brighton was just buzzing with noise, energy, pent-up anger and nostalgia revisited." Lots of films and television shows have been shot here from Brighton Rock (1947), Carry On At Your Convenience (1971), Carry On Girls (1975), Circus (1999), Mona Lisa (1986), Genevieve (1953), The Fruit Machine (1988), Dirty Weekend (1993), The End of the Affair and Villain (1971).

History
"That most sparkling and delicious of English watering places."
John Betjeman, 1960.
A transitory place with a real spirit, consisting of six miles of seafront, the town dates back to the Norman Conquest and the Doomsday book. The 1740s saw Brighton become a fashionable health resort. Recommended by a Dr Russell was to drink a half-pint of seawater daily at 5am and that breathing in the coastal air was advantageous to good health. The Prince Regent, also the Prince of Wales, was often here and this followed that the resort was hugely popular by the late-1700s. His Royal Pavilion folly remains as a testament to these times. As Brighton its name came in to use in 1818 evolving from Bristelmestune - Brichthelmeston - Bryghteston - Brighthelmstone.
It is the morning that is the best time to hobble on the cobble and to savour gazing at the West Pier and its ugly duckling sibling, the Palace, in the distance. The Brighton of now is a kaleidoscope of many colours and the one consistent essence is its variability. Those that take the decision to come and live here and often leave again, as is often the case, continue to return.
With its sea air, space, openness, diversity and zeal, the town has a magic to it that is only definable through time spent living here. Little wonder that Jimmy is

chasing the wind   BRIGHTON

so perplexed when he does come back again, the place is more than the total of its parts, a state of mind if you will. It has always attracted youngsters from Beatniks to hippies through to New Agers. Aside from these factors and the Mod connection, the town is infamous for a 'dirty weekend.'

London connections
"Dip me in the sea at Brighton, London-by-the-sea - That's the place for me." Sunshine Girl, 1912. Just over 50 miles from the capital, in the mid-Sixties, a train down from London cost 12/-. Brighton has often been called 'London-by-the-sea' but in reality this is a myth. However, the town was awarded city status in December 2000.

The Who and mod connections - BRIGHTON GREETS YOU
A sharp group photo of the band posing on Brighton [then the Palace Pier], finds Roger Daltrey and Pete Townshend looking modish, John wearing a jacket made out of a Union Jack print and Keith wrapped up in a striking target sweatshirt, with the theatre in the background [removed in 1986]. "The whole of the South coast was turning into mods." Recounts Pete Meaden, the former Mod maestro and moulder of The High Numbers immediately before they made their name as The Who. Meaden was to travel down to the coast some time later in a vein attempt to see the band play at the Aquarium but even he could not get in! Many local traders, Brighton youngsters at the time of the holiday invasions, and now in their late-Fifties did not like the events, "It was no enhancement to Brighton." said one to the author. "You stayed away from the promenade if you knew about the bank holidays. It was awful."

THE WHO AT THE FLORIDA EVERY WEDNESDAY
THE WHO MAXIMUM R & B
WEDNESDAY NIGHTS AT THE FLORIDA
ADMISSION 3/- & 4/-

ABC Cinema, Grand Junction Road / East Street
Opened as the Savoy Cinema on 1 Aug 1930 with a capacity of 2567 seats in a single auditorium. The theatre was designed by William R.Glen and is held as a fine example of the architecture of its time, understated and genteel.

Nicknamed the 'white whale' due to its glazed white terracotta tiles on its façade, this was a popular choice for cinema architecture during the construction period. Renamed the ABC by 1963, in the proceeding year the town had little over a dozen cinemas and during the Whit sun episode, the ABC was playing The Nutty Professor starring Jerry Lewis and the 'X' certified The Evil of Frankenstein Nightmare. Now restructured and open as pub, the ABC has a part to play in both the 1979 film and the original 1964 scuffles in the town. Situated at the top of East Street with a corner entrance taking preference over the former seafront one, back in the summer of 1964 one of its set of four glass-fronted windows was cracked by a stone thrown by a youngster from the seafront. Two hundred or so boys and girls ran across the promenade causing traffic to halt whilst fighting broke out in front of the cinema's seafront entrance. Closing in November 1975 for quadrupling it reopened in April 1976. Quadrophenia (X) was presented at the ABC 1 from Thursday 18 October, 1979 at 2.30 / 5.30 / 8.30 with a supporting feature playing at 1.50 / 4.45 / 7.40 respectively. In order, Screen 2, 3 and 4 screened Airport '80 (A), Boulevard Nights (X) / Freebie and The Bean (X) and The In-Laws (A).

Teaser ads appeared in the local press maintaining the "A Way of Life" by-line and target logo only this time supported by photographs of Steph [Leslie Ash] and Ace [Sting]. "I fancy Ace 'cause he's so dead cool. Top mod, you know?" begins the copy beneath Steph; "We had a great day at Brighton – a real bundle with all the Rockers.

They deserved everything they got. I mean, let's face it, they're dead square, ain't they?" Not to be outdone, Sting's speech bubble is equally as embarrassing,

"Sure, they all think I'm cool, cause I am...Mods are cool. I got the best scooter, the tightest Levis, the sharpest mohair jacket. No wonder all the birds fancy me and the rockers at Brighton better watch out."
The excellent Who biography The Kids Are Alright (AA) had already played in Brighton back in August with The Who playing two gigs at the Brighton Centre in November at around the same time as Phil Daniels and Ray Winstone could both be seen in major roles in Scum (X) which was playing at the ABC also that month. Renamed as a Cannon cinema by the Eighties, it reverted to the ABC before closure in 2000.

Arches Coming out and turning right, having passed underneath the Aquarium walkway, Palmist Professor Paul Hughes-Barlow has the premises half in and half outside the shadow of the belly of Brighton Pier. In an area both crummy and battered, initial research led me to believe the archway that Dave and Spider spend the night in was under the top end of the pier foundations but I believe that it was actually further north in one of the arches now utilized as artist quarters. Why? Because the sturdy, aged doorways here are metal and not wooden as seen in the film. See also: Beach Cafe

Bank Holiday traditions
"20th century pantomime"
Nik Cohn.
"Bank Holiday without clashes between police and assorted Mods, skinheads and Rockers would almost be like the seaside without cockles, deckchairs and lettered rock." Ray Miller, Brighton Evening Argus, 2 Sept 1981.

Local commerce was concerned that the gathering of youngsters would prove intimidating to the family visitors of Whit sun 1964 and in a way their concerns found some truth with most trippers enjoying the bank holiday weekends but keeping away from the areas around the pier where the youths congregated [in front of Beach Café].
Some families and older visitors were caught up in the surge of violence.

Beach "A beach is a place that a man can feel that he's the only soul in the world that's real..." The Who's Bell Boy track from Quadrophenia.

"Charming weather and a great deal of company make it really a delightful scene." [March 1857print.] The beach at Brighton is shingle not sand, with glimpses of sand revealed only at low tide. You can visit the smelly toilets outside of which the Brighton Ace Face so succinctly assaults those unfortunate police officers. Then rush back up the walkway that leads on to the promenade, dash across King's Road and on to East Street. The fighting sequences in Quadrophenia [and some incidents from the original tussles] took place on the part of the beach to the west of the Palace Pier, sandwiched in between it and the now-skeletal West Pier. There are still a number of food and amusements concessions filling the long, narrow terrace beneath the promenade, a palmist and a mini-gaming arcade can be found occupying the space where the 'Snack Bar' and 'Palace Shell Fish Bar' signage are seen in the film. The clock tower presently situated above the main entrance to the pier above, observed as the beach fighting moves in to full-on mode, was removed from the top of the Aquarium many years ago. See it as Steph and Jimmy dash away from the horse backed policemen just prior to Sting's hammering of the two constables.
Beach Café 'The cafe was really hairy.' Phil Daniels.
Leslie Ash agreed too.
Found by turning left from under the Aquarium walkway or taking the steps down from in front of the Palace Pier [now renamed the Brighton Pier] this is where the café used by the Mods in the film is located. Look for the concrete Crazy Golf course and you are right there. If continuing on up the walkway back up to the promenade the visitor will arrive opposite the Aquarium and a little further down, Madeira Drive. Established in 1964 and still owned by George, with his wife, nothing has changed much except for the replacement of the original wooden framed windows seen in the film where Jimmy sits looking out. Three weeks were needed for shooting the two scenes set here:
1]. Jimmy sitting alone with others the following morning after his expulsion from the Brighton ballroom in a scene that took a dozen takes for which Mark Wingett had to continu-

CINEMAS
BRIGHTON
BC — (1) Quadrophenia (X)
2.30, 5.30, 8.30 plus support
progs. 1.50, 4.45, 7.40. (2)

79

ously bite in to a runny egg sarnie! Jimmy sat at a bench positioned three pillars to the left of the main entrance and, 2]. Jimmy alone, after returning to Brighton, drinking coffee and popping pills. Director Franc Roddam added something to the first scene that was based upon a real moment that he shared with Maureen, the original co-owner, she demanded that he take his feet of the seats and this is played out in the film by Dave who tells the waitress to *"Piss off!"* as he attempts to cajole a moping Jimmy all the while biting into the slippery sandwich. *[Pictures: Jimmy & Chalky at the Beach Cafe].*

A sign seen in the café during filming prohibiting food being brought into the premises remains. It can be seen when Chalky and Dave come in following their night sleeping under the pier. However, the canopy above the service hatch, where Chalky orders breakfast has gone. The new owners sunk all their capital in to the venture just as the scrapping at seaside resorts was becoming big news. They feared the worst but Mods did frequent the café at the time and even called Maureen 'mum.' During location shooting the cafe proved such a hit with cast and crew that they chose to eat there rather than from the catering van parked above on the prom. Not surprisingly the proprietors made a mint. Closed in over the winter months, visitors continue to ask the affable George about the movie and want to sit in Jimmy's seat. See also: Beachy Head.

The Box A tiny disco owned by Pete Townshend in the Sixties situated above a Wimpy bar on Western Road, the burger bar occasionally made the local press with local residents complaining about its late night opening and congregation of youngsters on motorbikes. Its interior was painted entirely in silver!

Brighton Aquarium aka The Brighton 'Ballroom'
"I was one of the extras in the scene where Jimmy meets Steph and dances with her. I went up to Phil Daniels and offered him some of the chips I was eating. And he took them too! It was a very memorable shoot that day, Phil and Toyah Willcox kept mucking about, the director was pulling his hair out, and we all had a great time." Louise Short.

In actuality the exterior of the Aquarium is known simply as the 'ballroom' in the film. Its green, ornate lamps placed outside the main entrance and on its walls opposite remain. However, its circular nautical architectural accoutrements distinguishable in the film scenes on either side of the main entrance to the venue are today hidden by a couple of plastic Sea Life logos. If visiting the town to explore the locations seen in Quadrophenia then this is somewhere that simply has to be sought out. It is all there like a mini-set but slightly different in a logistics sense. Its twin, green-capped pagoda kiosks mark it out, as they stand proud opposite the tacky pier. The steps that Jimmy and the others dash down and where Pete lobs a flowerpot through the palmist's window is as it appears on screen. Blocked off for a few years, the space is now utilised for storage. However, the three stone arches; to the left an Indian palmist and to the right, the former smashed by Pete, finds its central point a walkway where many of the Mods are seen to pass through in the Brighton segment of the story. The walkway is still open if slightly haggard looking, and leads through to the Beach café, the underside of the pier and on to the beach.The Pagoda towers lead the visitor down its steps to a lovely space that succeeds in subduing the noise of passing traffic from the main road above. It is here that Jimmy and the Mods enter the 'ballroom' and where the Ace Face is found dancing in his own inimitable style, Jimmy falls out with Steph, and then dives off the balcony before being ejected by security! Green Onions plays firstly then Louie Louie. Back in 1881, vaudeville acts included unicyclists; wirewalkers and performing dogs could be enjoyed at the venue, originally built underground so as not to impede the sea front view. In Victorian and Edwardian times, its now displaced terraced gardens housed a roller-skating rink with space for soloists and orchestras to perform. A Concert hall in 1902, by the Sixties dolphins and formerly sea lions, had become the latest attractions. Confined in a pokey tank, its reputation was notorious [see the film The Fruit Machine]. Today finds it totally remodelled and popular once more as the Brighton Sea Life Centre.

Aquarium sun terrace On the May Day Bank Holiday of 1964 Rockers had to scamper down a

chasing the wind   BRIGHTON

The Brighton Aquarium steps seen as the mods run riot in the town.

twenty-ft. slope to escape from deckchair hurling youths loosely defined as Mods. A couple of hundred or so people were caught up in the violence, at what had been such a tranquil spot added to the Aquarium in 1873. Music recitals and a miniature golf course resided on the terrace back in the Thirties. The famous photos of the flying deckchairs was captured by Colin Jones and reproduced a thousand times since, it can be found in Mark Sampson's Brighton History and Guide [Alan Sutton Publishing, 1994]. Today, you can stand where it happened but reconstruction work covers most of the original area and the bandstand has also vanished. Opened in August 1872, rebuilt along modern lines in 1925 and reopening again in 1929, it's beautiful Italian style entrance had an open frontage prior to the erection of its towers on either side of the entrance. Balustrades on either side lead the visitor down shallow granite steps towards what was the 'Ballroom' in Quadrophenia. To its right is an archway that runs under the road above leading to the beach and Palace Pier. Designed by pier engineer and designer Eugenius Birch, he also created Brighton's West Pier [now a skeleton] further along the promenade; the Hippodrome theatre [where The High Number played], and piers at neighbouring resorts like Eastbourne and Southsea [where Tommy was filmed]. The clock tower that was a part of the main entrance to the Aquarium is now a focal point of the pier and glimpsed [in the background] during the beach fighting moments of the film. In actuality, the film 'ballroom', was not as it seems, the true Florida Rooms was to the left of the main entrance and all interior shots for Quadrophenia were filmed at a derelict nightclub in Southgate, north London. Nearly three decades later it is now a fitness and health centre. Presently, the Brighton Sea Life Centre has seen major structural redevelopment in an area called Madeira Drive, where tourists rarely venture much further along unless travelling upon the Volks train that runs the length of the seafront from the pier and in an easterly direction towards the Marina / Black Rock areas.

Madam Victoria's As a part of the Aquarium building and to the right of the main 'Ballroom' entrance in the film, Pete throws a flower pot through her window in a hairy moment that almost looks as if it could have struck because a nanosecond earlier she had been sitting there. Jimmy, Steph and her female friend, Dave and Spider all pass through the archway next to her consultancy room, leading out under the pier and on to the beach. When filming took place, her service was listed in the Brighton phone book of 1978. Watch as she hastily ducks out of the way as a plant pot is thrown at her window during the riots. Looks realistic, doesn't it? that's because she missed her cue when to move and the scene is a piece of uber realism!

See also: newspapers, Florida Rooms, Hippodrome

Brighton Centre Standing immediately next to the Grand Hotel on the King's Road is the Brighton Centre [formerly the Brighton Conference Centre, opened 1977]. Not one of the town's better-looking buildings, it is here that Jimmy rides off on Sting's scooter and narrowly misses the couple walking by. The scene was cleverly shot so as not to reveal the more modern (and rather ugly) appearance of the building.

The Who played the Centre twice in November 1979, on the weekends of the tenth and eleventh. Modster Paul Weller gigged there in a final, ill-received Jam concert in December 1982. Following on to the Brighton Centre is the Odeon multiscreen cinema, the venue for the 1997 re-released Quadrophenia premiere.

Brighton Dome The Who played one of the town's largest live venues on 21 April 1967 as a part of the annual Brighton Festival. Tickets were priced from 17/6 down to 6/- each.

Brighton Rock "Not since the Boulting Bros' Brighton Rock has a British film [Quadrophenia] captured the vulgarity and violence of a bank holiday weekend by the seaside so effectively." Sight and Sound, August 1997. Written by Graham Greene, this pre-world war II novel was set in the town back then that was infamous for its razor gangs and overall seediness. The book was filmed in Brighton back in 1947 starring an excellent Richard Attenborough as archetypal anti-hero Pinkie. Next to Quadrophenia it is the most well-known film shot in and around the town. See also: Ecclesiastics.

East Street "It is one of the musts in any first visit to the town." [Brighton Evening Argus 1971].

Originally Great East Street, it developed as a boundary marker after French invades had annihilated Brighton, with its resembling a fortified rectangular shape rounded off with guns defining a second town some six hundred years ago. Many upper storeys of the houses there date from the 19th century but most are more modern and have been adapted for commercial purposes. During the period that filming took place in the area, lots of extras were milling about and one guy, said to be a student, saw a pile of parkas on the floor ready for the 'Mods' to wear and so he put one on.

Shooting commenced and as the action kicked off, he continued running after the scene was cut taking the coat with him and allegedly wasn't even an extra! The former bookshop next to the Wimpy bar where the Mods fight outside of is now called Pine Secrets. Chalky spots one of the Rockers that ran him off the road whilst on the way down to Brighton and it is his action that causes the violence to begin. He and hundreds of other Mods run across King's Road and in to the café where six or seven Rockers are set upon.

East Street Snack bar Today, the structure is entirely unrecognizable and is the kind of place that if you did not already know that it was used in Quadrophenia you would have absolutely no idea at all. Management at the Queens hotel, which has swallowed up the snack bar, has seen ownership change hands many times since 1978 and therefore no one could clarify when its newer, post-Quadrophenia extension work was completed. What is known is the fact that a small shop did once occupy a nearby space that might well be the one that became a café. The filmmakers made canny use of locations mixing them up, as they do here, to create a semblance that is not as it seems on screen. "You can't see the join." As Eric Morecambe used to say. Character's restaurant fits in to a totally remodelled corner entrance that mark it out as sharing hardly any similarities with its celluloid past. Peculiarly enough, the snack bar seen in the film, where the Rockers are attacked by a throng of chanting youngsters baying *"Mods! Mods! Mods!"* has its window shattered during the sequence yet there is another premises claiming to be the location used by the production crew. After being referred to the owners of a corner shop Fish & Chips takeaway on nearby Ship Street [a little further along Kings road], I was informed that this was indeed the location where the window was smashed. Looking at the exterior, it very much has a similar appearance to the 'Quadrophenia' one but how can it be the one seen in the finished film when clearly, shattered glass falls out onto the road outside, we can see that it is East Street! [metal railings opposite have remained halfway up on the exterior façade of the New Heart and Hand [Prodigal pub].

To the right of its corner-positioned entrance a sign reading "East Street" can be deciphered above a Lyons Maid ice cream logo on top of which a canopy with a no entry sign, which is still enforced, can be found. In addition, visible to the right of the screen is the signage of the Queen's hotel present in the film but since removed. How can I be certain of this information? Initially I assumed that the corner entrance of the New Heart and Hand public house was the location of the snack bar but the one shown in the film has three windows running alongside it as it leads on to East Street from the promenade, whilst the Hand [now the

chasing the wind BRIGHTON

[Below] : the cafe manager at the East street snack bar.

Prodigal] has only two.

Only half of East Street is seen on screen, up to Bartholemews, where the old Town Hall stands. With some very crisp cutting the filmmakers created the impression that it is a bigger space than it really is. An example being when Sting is arrested and the police van zooms off down Brill's Lane, a tiny space between the ABC Cinema and the Prodigal pub. However, the street continues on revealing a little piazza in an area regarded as the Bond Street equivalent of town, with designer clothing stores flowing out on to the town's busy North street. Whilst closer to the seafront end, it has long had a grubby image with many a derelict shop back in the Seventies. Signage seen in the film such as the Hudson Brothers vertical shaped sign observed high above the street level near to Pool Valley is no longer here. As well as John King's photographic suppliers shop, with its Kodak logo outside seen during the fighting on East Street, which is now occupied by a chic vegetarian restaurant called Terre a Terre. Sting smashes a large shop front window opposite the Pickwick pub, next to the wooden window framed exterior of premises now called Metal Guru. Its

86

black framed frontage is shown as the Mods run past, today, it is painted white. The premises are not recognizable in the film. See also: Extras, pubs, Quadrophenia alley, snack bars.

Florida Rooms "Adjoining the Aquarium."
[Press advertisement from the early-Sixties]
Found to the left of the Aquarium, it was here that The Who played on nine occasions in 1964 as well as gigging under The High Numbers banner. This popular local venue was often advertised as 'Adjoining the Aquarium' or even the 'Aquarium Florida Rooms' due to it being a part of the overall Aquarium building. In Quadrophenia it is not acknowledged other than the entrance to the Aquarium being retitled 'ballroom' which is incorrect because the entrance was to the left of the main entrance into the Aquarium. The Who dedicated their Quadrophenia album partly to the fans that came to hear and see them play here in the summer of 1965. Little surprise that their management team, Lambert and Stamp, termed the group as the purveyors of the "Brighton sound." Known previously as The Winter Garden and Prince's Hall it opened in August 1873, became known as the Florida Rooms by 1961 with dancing, and live bands playing there for a 1/6 entrance fee. Daily events were added constantly with others organised to cater for the younger clientele, in June of that year there was an "All-Night Rave" for a 10/- entrance fee as well as a 'Big Beat Record Show', 'Top Live Bands direct from London' [Fridays] and bingo on a Sunday afternoon and 'Jiving' nights
azz and the occasional RnB night also featured.

The Grand Hotel [Background picture]. December 1862 saw Brighton's most luxurious hotel open its doors for business, situated on the King's Road, next to the Metropole Hotel on its right, and the Brighton Centre to its left. Its elegant facade polished off by gilded bronzed balconies in a Mediterranean style with its Union Jack flying above.

chasing the wind BRIGHTON

The Grand plays its part in the one of the final scenes in Quadrophenia when Jimmy spots the beautiful chrome Vespa owned by the Ace Face parked up at the far end of the building's frontage. The railings seen behind the scooter glimpsed as the camera pans around it have remained and beneath them is the Midnight Blues bar [not shown in the film]. Four concrete bollards now block the space where the scooter once stood, in an attempt to prevent vehicles parking there. Bell Boy mentions that one of its windows was smashed by marauding Mods in 1963, including Jimmy and the Ace Face, and it is also name checked on the 1973 album in a

BRIGHTON   A QUADROPHENIA ANTHOLOGY

news report mentioning Mods chasing 'leather-clad' Rockers into the hotel. The Grand has changed a lot structurally due to the October 1984 terrorist attack upon the Tory cabinet members in attendance for their party conference. Four people were killed by the impact termed "Horror at the Grand," in the local press. Originally, the centrally located hotel had an open-plan front with a terrace subsequently constructed in 1934 before its fully enclosed appearance of the present. The location of photographs taken by Ethan A. Russell which accompany the original Who album can be matched-up by walking in to the foyer; however, its black marble columns therein [shown in the pictures, one with the bellboy standing outside and the other with Jimmy seeing him scurrying after a guest carrying suitcases] are not as they seem. The columns are mainly hollow structures, a result of the bombing. Much of the entrance was destroyed by falling debris but it is still a striking vision and if anything, Russell's photos fail to frame the vastness of the building. If you fancy staying in one of the 260 rooms set out on nine stories, a single costs £155 and a double is £220. See also: Midnight Blues club, Union Jack .

Hippodrome Tucked away on Middle Street, near the old North Laines, is where you will find this former theatre now in use as a bingo club. It was here that the High Numbers AKA The Who, The Beatles and The Rolling Stones all played in 1964. Formerly a part of the Moss Empire circuit, it closed as a theatre that same year after more than six decades as a variety venue. Gigs continued with The Who appearing there on Sunday 24 April 1966 a day after the Small Faces.

Jimmy and Brighton Mixed emotions are experienced by the little Mod when he returns alone, wearing his own "badge of loneliness" just as Pinkie, the lost soul in Graham Greene's Brighton-set novel Brighton Rock does. When Jimmy returns once more, he utters few words, only swearing in the alleyway, and repeating his despair of *"Bell Boy!"* and *"ME! "* on the cliff top at Beachy Head.

Live gigs and such - 1961 to 1963
'The Florida Room - Adjourning Aquarium.' [Local press listing].

Jazz, jazz, jazz and occasionally R&B were popping-up at venues all over Brighton, including 'The Florida Room at the Aquarium.' Virtually every night a specific theme would be presented for local youngsters such as The Big Beat, Dancing For Joy, Record Nite & Teen Beat at an admission of 1/6 and 3/-
1962 An increase to five shillings admission for visitors to the popular records nights at the Aquarium. 'Top live bands direct from London' performed every Friday in the year that Keith Moon's favoured fashion fellow; Cecil Gee [still there] opened a branch on East Street. April saw the British Lambretta Owners' run to Brighton continuing the events that had been going since the late-Fifties.
1963 The Aquarium's Florida Room presenting 'Top Twenty' new records and bands nights at the venue marked by the 6,000th girl member being admitted at the Brighton Chinese Jazz Club [held at the Aquarium every Friday evening]. Coffee bars were more popular than the emerging clubs though The Starlight Rooms on Montpelier Road was also another savoured mod haunt in Brighton; often more than the Florida Room.
1964 From March 1964 through to November 1965 The Who played Brighton a dozen times. Words that have now become common such as rave and discothèque had their origins back in the early Sixties and were used to promote the latest type of music/ dance event in the town. The short-lived Cinerama film fad arrived in Brighton and picture houses across the country. March found the increase in popularity of music-based events ['discotheque', 'R&B - Blue Beat', 'Record Session - TOTP'] at the Florida Rooms seeing April gigs by The Animals, Georgie Fame, The Pretty Things and The Byrds. Rolling Stones played to 850 at Hove Town Hall gig 22 May.
Whitsun bank holiday weekend - 16 / 17th May. By the Monday, with the temperature down to 56 degrees from the Seventies over the weekend, many trippers watched what scuffles there were between youngsters and the police as the media grabbed the chance for a great story and enlarged the little violence that took place turning it into a panic of mass proportion. Those remaining, just as many girls as boys, were steered through the streets of the town up to the train station by the police who lined the route from the seafront along Church Street and Queen's Road [validating the significance of the events in the eyes

of many youngsters and expending the worries of adults]. "There a cordon of 50 policemen stood guard." Reported an Argus hack. " Until the last of the long-haired rabble-rousers had boarded trains." Between 2000-3000 were caught up in the seafront scrapping depending upon which source quoted (the Argus said 3000). Photos of the period feature youngsters lying face down on the ground along the seafront. Extra officers were brought in from East and West Sussex, Hampshire and Brighton and many were on duty for more than 16 hours. Police horses and dogs were used to restore order. Kim, a twelve-year-old white police horse was put in to action for the first time [other than as a mascot] to break up the crowds with charge hand PC Ken Thomas. Commemorated with the Henry V histrionics seen in the film by a horseback police officer. The police succeeded in breaking up the large crowds in to smaller, more manageable pockets of a hundred or so. At some time in the recent past, 30-35,000 visitors came to Brighton on Whit Sunday but in 1964 it was down to 24,000. By Thursday, the Brighton League of Friends met to discuss the recent events at their annual meeting surmising that if young people had a worthwhile job then they would probably not be a Mod or indeed a Rocker. Arthur Peacock, then a Middlesex County Council youth officer countered, "Stop telling them that youth was never like this in your day. They don't want to hear about the past. You must find a way of training them for the future." Following the Clacton altercations, almost all national press printed similar stories; except The Times on that Monday. The now-defunct Daily Sketch [18 May] exclaimed, "Wildest Ones Yet" with additional sub-heads of "Stabbing, stoning, deckchair battles as riots hit new peak" and "Holidaymakers cower on the beach." The Who played the Florida

Doorway where Ace assaults the police officers.

chasing the wind   BRIGHTON

Rooms on the 12 and 19 July, both Sundays. **August bank holiday weekend - 16 / 17th** The Showcase album by Buddy Holly was in the Top 10 as the Rolling Stones claimed the top two spots on the album and singles charts. "It wasn't so much violence as hordes of young people running around and looking for the excitement that others were committing. We were like a huge mobile audience though in fact we were the main act." Explained a teen-aged John Alban in Beat Merchants. It was a quiet, contained weekend in Brighton with little signs of the trouble seen at Whit sun. Visitor numbers were down on the preceding year. The beach opposite the pier [in front of the Beach Café] was overflowing with a teenager presence precluding any sign of family holidaymakers there. A heavily visible platoon of police nearby resulted in keeping holidaymakers off the pier too. There were some skirmishes but mainly consisting of threatening behaviour, obstructing the police and one of a lad carrying an offensive weapon [a stone]. On the Sunday a crowd did build up next to the Aquarium but those that did not move on when ordered to do so, were arrested under the new Police Act (1964). Literally just becoming law, the legislation meant that police had the power to inflict a £20 fine for unruly behaviour raised from a maximum of £5. No scooter invasion occurred with the whispered rumour that something was going to kick-off at Hastings and Great Yarmouth. Despite this, around the town traders were making hefty profits. The promenade was like a battlefield only on this occasion it was full of litter rather than fighting youths. Fourteen young people and one adult appeared in court on the Monday following the weekend. A vintage photo from the period shows that Rockers *did* wear those awful black leather caps just like the one worn by an older follower beaten up by Dave on the beach or by the Village People [only minus the handlebar moustache]. Gig-wise, The High Numbers played the Florida Rooms on the second and returned to another Brighton venue, the Hippodrome, on the 9th and 23rd as a support act for a collection of Sunday concert bookings. Gerry and The Pacemakers headlined in two shows at 6 & 8:30 p.m. Whilst the second gig found the band supporting the 'Fabulous' Dusty Springfield with tickets for the 6pm & 8.30 p.m. shows priced from 10/6 to 5 shillings a piece. **November** The Florida Rooms advertised, "From London's Marquee – Faces Night with The Who" with an admission of 4/-

92

[or 3/' before 8pm] for a Wednesday night gig on 25 November. The first of five consecutive Wednesday night gigs there.

1965 "We were playing at the Brighton Aquarium [17 April] and I saw about two thousand Mod kids and there were three Rockers up against a wall." Recalled Pete Townshend in an interview with the NME of 3 Nov 1973. "They would obviously just come in thinking that they were going to a party and they were scared as hell, and the Mods were just throwing bottles at them. I mean, there's no sort of hero in my eyes in something like that. There's no nostalgia..." The Who played a further gig in November at an unrecorded venue.

1966 The Who played the now-forgotten New Barn Club on Saturday 12 December although Irish Jack Lyons' lists it as Sunday 12 December in The Who Concert File book.

1967 The Brighton Arts Festival on 21 April of that year found The Who along with Cream and The Merseys playing at the Dome theatre in the town.

Location filming - 26 September 1978 According to Toyah Willcox, Leslie Ash and Phil Daniels stayed in a posher hotel than others in cast. Location filming started on 26 September 1978. To recreate the original 'High summer of the Mods,' The Who Film company auditioned for 'Mods' and 'Rockers' extras needed for the crowd sequences. A publicist for The Who felt that they were not that many Mods still haunting the sea towns any longer so therefore, youngsters turning up at the job centre were given one of two cards dependent upon how they looked. "Mods used to rule the roost," remembered original modster Mike Housden in the Evening Argus, "we would come down sixty or seventy at a time." Two police officers were provided to support the filming for the production by controlling traffic flow on the sea front, a long way away from the mass of officers involved in the authentic '64 battles.

Madeira Drive Known as Madeira Road until the late Thirties, it leads on to Madeira Walk, a now quiet but once popular promenade. Lettering reading 'THFC' can be seen sprayed on to the wall along Madeira Drive as the camera pans along the throng of parked-up scooters in front of a row of shops in an area now known as Madeira Colonnade. The initials presumably belong to Tottenham Hotspur Football Club and probably sprayed by one of the visiting Londoners.

However, back in 1964 I doubt that aerosol cans were prevalent amongst graffiti artists, wasn't a brush and paint the more likely culprit? Maintaining the football theme, a scruffy looking Mod can be seen wearing a red, white and black scarf during the sequence in East Street when Jimmy and the others mingle amongst the crowd and passing band. The drive is popular amongst bike and transport enthusiasts and it is the finishing point for the annual London-Brighton car run which dates back to 1896. The event, held each November was popularized in the Fifties movie Genevieve. See also: Peter Pan's and the 2 photos below, as the area looks nowadays. Its exterior is pictured below.

Midnight Blues Club It was here in 1997 that the post-film screening party for the reissued Quadrophenia took place. Located between the Grand hotel and the Brighton Centre, the metal railings to this basement club can be seen in Quadrophenia towards the end of the story, where Jimmy discovers the Ace Face's scooter [the club is directly behind it]. At the party, cast members enjoyed fish and chips with champagne! See also: The Grand Hotel.

The New Hand and Heart pub Coated in a heavy pale blue in the filmed scenes around East Street, this pub is now called the Prodigal, and has been so for nine or ten years now. Its reputation was on the distinctly rough side.

Newspapers - [1] **Evening Argus**, [2] **Brighton and Hove Gazette** & [3] **The Brighton and Hove Herald.** Regional newspapers for Brighton and the surrounding areas reported on the Whit sun and August Bank holiday youth invasion of the town. "Rioting Rockers Plan Raid on Brighton Soon" Evening Argus, 13 May. A correlation with the news report heard on Jimmy's transistor radio on the morning of his departure down to Brighton spoke of the concern by

Madeira Drive: as it is today; the pillars are still there

shopkeepers and the like about the possible visits to Brighton and other seaside towns of youngsters looking for trouble. The Argus again reported on Monday 18 May with the banner article, "BATTLE OF BRIGHTON - Mods let fly at the Rockers in fierce seafront clashes." Monday had felt chilly along the south coast but by Thursday the temperature had risen to 62 degrees. It did not last. Trouble flared soon after 9am with a squadron of Mods searching for Rockers along the seafront. A stone thrown from the beach smashed a police squad car window whilst a large group of youngsters made their way down the promenade from the West Pier to the Palace Pier knocking over anyone unfortunate enough to be in their path. A two hundred-strong throng chased a thirteen year-old boy across the beach exemplifying the randomness to come. Police reinforcements brought up the total to about 150 coming in from East and West Sussex and Hastings to combat trouble. At their peak the crowds numbered 2000–3000. Police eventually rounded-up youngsters ushering them away from the pier and along Madeira Drive but some broke away and attacked Rockers on the Aquarium Sun Terrace.

This scene was re-enacted by Pete and the other London Mods in the film when they force some boys over the edge of the terrace. Outnumbered on the day by a ratio of 10:1 the unfortunate victims were forced to jump down 20ft drop to safety. A 20-year-old Brighton lad involved in throwing deckchairs was found to have been carrying a starting pistol loaded with blanks, ownership of which he denied. Subsequently, he was jailed for five months and fined £2. Further sporadic outbursts occurred with the police condemning the public for hampering their task by the holidaymakers scrambling to watch. "The whole lot should be locked up." Cried a middle-aged woman during the scuffles. "No sooner had she expressed her views than a slight howl went up from the beach below – and I watched that woman," recounted Mr Maurice Sayers in a letter published in the Herald, "fighting with elbows going six to the dozen, to get a

front-line view at the railing."
'Court applause for the police. Brighton: Eight Sent For Detention'
Evening Argus, 19 May 1964.
In specially convened juvenile and magistrates sittings on the Monday and Tuesday following the bank holiday consisting mainly of visiting Londoners up on offences including insulting behaviour, carrying an offensive weapon [a stone/ milk bottle/ 3ft steel pipe/ chains/ sharpened knife etc], wilful damage, using threatening behaviour and obstruction. The Argus reported that the public benches applauded the comments made by the chairman that acknowledged the role of the police over the holiday weekend. It took the juvenile court more than four hours to dish out fines amongst the teenaged defendants and nine were sent to detention centres. Out of the twenty-six, two further at Margate and fifty four at Bournemouth], only one was female. The father of one boy arrested for being in possession of an offensive weapon [a belt] was flabbergasted, "I never knew it was an offensive weapon," he told the court, "I always thought it was for holding up your trousers." The following Saturday saw a front-page photo of fighting youngsters accompanied by the headline 'Bank Holiday Hooliganism in Brighton – The day that the Mods came.' Reporting about questions being asked in Parliament about the events of the week before following "A situation that was perhaps without parallel in English history. For Mod violence is a phenomena of the Sixties."
[2] The Gazette gave considerable coverage following the weekend with photos illustrating the sheer volume of crowds on the beach [Friday 22].
Photographs of deckchair abusing youngsters were presented and incidentally, Gazette snapper Alfred Mead captured that famous shot of deckchair tossing youths reigning down upon leather-clad opponents. "What Makes Them Tick?" Not being a town known for its sense of moderation, the response to the skirmishes was outrageously over the top, a local restaurateur blurted in the Gazette; "These young Mods and Rockers are just a lot of yellow bellies. They are cowards. I saw hundreds of them come swarming across the road..." And his response as to what could be done to combat further aggravation was an acerbic one, "issue 1,000 boys with armbands and put them under police

control, and these thugs [I believe he is referring to the teenagers here] won't dare come near the town."

[3] "The Problems MPs Face" Brighton and Hove Herald, Saturday 23 May, 1964. Photographs appertaining to the fighting youths around the promenade areas were heavily illustrated with a supporting text asking what MP's should be doing about such violence. "...about the uproar, the chaos, the damage caused by rampaging teenagers..."

In June 1964, the local press reported a Brighton chemist being arrested for selling "special aspirins" over the counter. It was revealed that he had illegally sold 13,000 Dexedrine pep pills over a two-year period. Reported was another drugs-related story, with a sixteen-year-old boy being fined £15 after the revelation that he had been floging Purple Hearts at local coffee bars.

Odeon Cinema The premiere for a freshly re-issued print of Quadrophenia took place on 29 January 1997 at the West Street Odeon with a post-screening party at the Midnight Blues nightclub located beneath the Grand hotel [below the spot where Jimmy sees the Ace's scooter parked outside]. "I'm delighted the movie is being put out again. A whole new generation can now enjoy it." Commented Phil Daniels to the Argus [30 January]. "It's a nostalgic night for all of us and I've come to enjoy and celebrate a good part of my life." Mark Wingett, said to live locally, added, "When we were making it we had no idea that it would have such an impact." Other cast members in attendance included Gary Shail, Garry Cooper, John Altman and Franc Roddam. See also: John Altman.

Palace Pier Opened to the public in May 1899 concluding eight years of construction work, the 521m structure upholds the best traditions of tacky seaside sense. A photo of The Who decked out in their Pop Art clothes with 'Brighton Greets You' in the background was used in the long-forgotten magazine Fabulous. The sign was positioned above the theatre which once stood at the back of the pier but should you go looking for the spot today you will be disappointed; it was flattened in the Eighties. When Jimmy walks from the beach following his solitary return, we see the gaudy capital letters of the Palace Pier name with a Union Jack above it in the distance, exactly as it was a decade earlier. Apparently, the structure was to have been removed and stored off site with the proviso of returning after additional space for rides had been allocated but astoundingly, its shell was somehow lost! Scenes shot on Brighton seafront were based upon actual photographs from the period showing boys dressed in fur-lined and battered plain hooded parkas. Some 30,000 visitors stepped on to the Palace Pier over the Whit sun holiday weekend in 1964. See also: Arches.

Peter Pan's amusements, Madeira Drive To hazard a guess, I believe that this is the location where the Brighton Ace Face and his posse of scootered Mods drive around in the early hours following the ballroom events. See the full scene chronology at the back of the book for fuller details.

Pickwick pub: see under pubs.

Quadrophenia Alley Film fans seeking to make a connection with Jimmy can often be found skulking down the narrow 'twitten' [alley] snapping away on their cameras or scribbling on the wall outside the infamous doorway. Found in the alleyway that leads to Little East Street [look for the Long Tall Sally store and the jewellers W G Bishop at number 11, and you are here]. A small blue sign directs the visitor "to Little East Street" where not much has changed in the intervening years since location filming in an area so narrow only one person can squeeze threw it at a time. The former Celtic Crafts shop seen momentarily when Jimmy and Steph rush back out on to East Street directly opposite the entrance is now an American diner after many years as a Chinese restaurant with varying names. The door that Jimmy opens the old metal handle of and sneaks behind with Steph, has remained, only its painted red rather than the white seen in the movie. All graffiti is painted over but some years back it was plastered with the stuff from visitors' worldwide. Today, it mainly seems to consist of snippets of dialogue such as Jimmy's "That's why I'm a mod" eulogy. Choy's, the owners of the Chinese restaurant that allowed the space to be used so memorably in the film, does not encourage visitors and more often than not offer a curt rebuke to anyone that asks about it. The area is simply a fire escape at the rear of their premises. The Choy's sign, to the left of the exterior of the door glimpsed briefly on screen, is now a rusted shell whilst a battered notice informs us that the area is covered by security camera [which it is not]. If you do visit, which you must, hang around and you might just see behind the door where the minuscule love making spot will surprise. A camera being positioned on the metal fire escape stairwell that rises to some considerable height captured the scene. In the alley itself and to the left of the doorway, the bulbous stone wall against which Jimmy laments his moment with Steph, remains but has recently been rendered flat. Continuing around the pathway brings you out on to Little East Street itself. Above the famous doorway a row of rusted, curved, sharp edged railings remains.

Queens hotel Situated on the top end of East Street and primarily along Kings road, on the seafront, the Queens played its own part in Quadrophenia. It was used as the site of a small snack bar where the Mods charge at some

[above]
Quadrophenia alleyway as it is today and behind that famous door.

chasing the wind   BRIGHTON

rockers whom Chalky believes were responsible for having run him off the road whilst travelling down to Brighton. Debate has raged as to whether or not it was indeed the location used or that clever use of editing made it appear to be in East Street. However, visual evidence points to its authenticity rather than that of another premises on Ship Street. A Street sign proclaiming 'East Street' can be observed just above the centred-entrance as what looks like hundreds of youngsters charge across Grand Junction away from the police and in pursuit of some violence.
See also: Snack bars, East Street.
Volks seafront railway Long established site on the Brighton seafront with its track running from the top of Madeira Drive right down to wards the Marina. Its step-on point is briefly glimpsed behind the Mods as they march along the promenade to the chant of *"We are the Mods, we are the Mods, we are...etc"*
Western Road Pete Townshend opened a tiny discotheque up on Western Road above a Wimpy bar, and called it The Box. You can see a Wimpy in East Street where scuffles ensue as people continue eating inside.
See also: The Box.
Wimpy burger bar Amazingly, this bastion of 1970s fast food has remained on East Street some twenty years after the location filming. Its exterior [complete with diners tucking in to their burgers inside] is seen in Quadrophenia whilst fighting Mods rucking with police officers right in front of its glass-paned frontage. References consulted for the compilation of this section include the following titles, all of which are highly recommended as a guide to the town. Brighton Rock by Greene Graham [Penguin], The Brighton Story by John Huddlestone, [Thanet Books, 1999], Brighton Sketchbook by John Montgomery, [Perspective Press, 1979] and 'Around Historic Sussex' an Evening Argus, 2 May 1975. See also: Mod.

> 'Brighton was very kind to us as a location."
> Quadrophenia director Franc Roddam

Ray Brooks *"I was waiting, she was in the wrong place..."* So floated his velvet hued tones over a French New Wave-style footage accompanied by an Onedin Line sounding soundtrack. However, it is the young woman seen in the commercial that catches the attention of Jimmy from within the projection box within which he is ensconced. It is the voice of Brooks we hear as Jimmy plays cards with Harry and Des [Timothy Spall and Patrick Murray]. An actor born in Brighton back in 1939 his career as a voice-over artiste has been nothing less than prolific. He has, in addition, appeared in seminal sixties films The Knack and How to Get It (1965) and Cathy Come Home (1966). Ray voiced Rupert Bear in a children's animated series shown in the 1970s and coincidentally, a Pop Special Festival guide from a late-Sixties Evening Standard found Pete Townshend leap frogging over a superimposed Rupert is reproduced in Annie Nightingale's Chase the Fade: Music Memories and Memorabilia. Small screen success came calling in the Eighties series Big Deal and most recently a role in EastEnders. See also: Bibliography, Annie Nightingale. CONTACT: Marmont Management, Langham House, 308 Regent St, London.

James Brown The self-proclaimed Godfather of Soul and prolific music maker amassing a huge selection of album and single releases spanning a magnificent career. His single, Night Train, also covered by Duane Eddy and Georgie Fame, can be heard on the jukebox at Alfredo's café in Quadrophenia. The album of the same name never charted here. The Who did a cover of one of his hits on their debut album My Generation, released in 1965, after performing Brown's Just You and Me, Darling back as far as 1961. Best recalled for Papa's Got A Brand New Bag and a tempestuous private life, Mr Brown had singles put out on the Fontana label next to artists such as The Pretty Things and The High Numbers [whom, better known as The Who recorded Brown's Shout and Shimmy]. See him strutting his

101

funky stuff next to John Lee Hooker in The Blues Brothers (1978). Also check out The Commitments movie for a very witty name check!

Cars and Vehicles The only transport that plays a major part in Quadrophenia is that of the two-wheeled variety but others are glimpsed during the film. The most memorable being the two Triumph cars [I think one of them might be the 2000 mk.II model produced in 1969] caught up in the overflow of Mods dashing, en masse, across the promenade towards East Street. Observe the soft-top model as it almost strikes one of the marauding throng whilst heading west on the road towards the pier. You will also see a smart Jaguar and Rover parked up outside of the Grand Hotel when Jimmy returns to Brighton towards the end of the film. The Who name-check Jaguar in the track of the same name on their 1967 concept album The Who Sell Out whilst in the film Jimmy, Chalky and Dave smash up the Jag belonging to drug dealer Harry North. A Citroen was adapted by the filmmakers to shoot some of the close-up moments with Phil Daniels during the Beachy Head scenes at the end of the film. In some shots Jimmy is seen riding his scooter along the cliff top in a culmination of cuts were filmed with Daniels perched on the rear of the car all the while aping the steering of the scooter. Watch the video and all is revealed after the final credits have passed. Police vehicles such as cars, old black Mariah vans and a bus feature in the rioting sequences. Over the course of the Whit sun bank holiday weekend of 1964 the Sunday found some 2000 vehicles flowing through the town according to AA reports. One or two Ford Cortinas can also be glimpsed during the scenes we see of Jimmy riding his scooter around London. See also: G.P.O van, goofs, video release.

Jack Carter Recognised as the Construction Manager on Quadrophenia, Jack worked with Stephen Frears on Gumshoe (1971) and The Hit (1981) as well as additional film projects The Mission (1986), Privates on Parade (1982), Nuns on the Run (1990) and most notably, Tommy (1975). See also: Simon Holland, Bill Rowe, Andrew Sanders, Derek Suter, Terry Wells, Christian Wrangler.

The Cascades Forever committed to memory for their single Rhythm Of The Rain, this five-piece, California-founded band came together in the late Fifties but had disbanded by 1969. Steph and Pete dance closely to the soft vocal, it's that kind of song, at the house party, only to be interrupted by a jealous Jimmy changing the disc for the more robust echo of My Generation. Interchangeable versions have come from Maurice Chevalier and Sarah Brightman.

Celtic Crafts Glimpsed directly opposite the alleyway which Jimmy and Steph dash down during the East Street scenes filmed in Brighton. If investigating its location today, you will not find it because its frontage has been redeveloped and now houses a smart Chinese restaurant called Sun Bo Seng.

Charges Of those youngsters arrested by police at many of the seaside resorts the charges incurred included: the use of threatening behaviour or threatening words, carrying an offensive weapon and obstructing the police primarily. Fines dished out by Magistrates ranged from £10 - £75 to six months custodial sentences at Detention Centres. See also: Curts, New Society magazine, Police

Chasing the Wind For who can know what is good for a man in this life, this brief span of empty existence through which he passes like a shadow? Ecclesiastics 6:12. A loose translation of the Japanese rendition of their poster of Quadrophenia, titled The Pain of Living reads as follows: Fuck Off heartbreak!/ I am the wind/ I just wanna take drugs/ Ride on my scooter/ Listen to Rock & Roll / And fly with my wings. See also: Existentialism, Sartre.

The Chiffons A four-piece girl group created in 1961 with all its original members growing up in the Bronx, New York, when they hit the charts worldwide by selling more than a million copies in America alone of He's So Fine [heard on the jukebox at Alfredo's in Quadrophenia] in April 1963. One Fine Day and Sweet Talkin' Guy followed on from that success. They demo," remembers Chords member Billy in a letter to the author, who felt that the band were a little too Who-like and not an atypical R&B band that the filmmakers wanted, "we got the usual nice letter saying the usual. I think we were a bit raw then." Interest in the band has returned in the late Nineties acknowledged by compilation album This Is What They Want. Various websites are dedicated to them so take a look at www.beakz.net/thechords/discography/
See also: The Jam, Mod.

Jeremy Child Born in 1944, he plays a part in a bitingly

chasing the wind A TO Z ANTHOLOGY

funny moment with Benjamin Whitrow [Pictured opposite, Jeremy on the right] and Phil Daniels in another lavatorial scene only this time at the ad agency rather than at a pub. The two older executives are discussing the pros and cons of the *"For people like you..."* campaign launch, *"It's the Cs & Ds I'm worried about."* Grimaces the careworn Fulford [Whitrow] to the younger Michael [Child]. They continue chatting, whilst shaving, until along comes Jimmy, all coughing and spluttering as he walks up to use the washbasin between them. Neither acknowledges the other and Daniels plays the scene beautifully: totally deadpan. Akin to Ben Whitrow, Jeremy was predictably cast in the spruce former public school boy mode next to Gary Shail in Paul McCartney's film-with-music tale Give My Regards to Broad Street (1984) On television, Child was part of the cast of The Happy Apple (1983), which coincidentally starred Leslie Ash. Other work incls: A Fish Called Wanda (1988).
See also: Patsy Pollock, Benjamin Whitrow. CONTACT: PFD, Drury House, 34 - 43 Russell Street, London.

The Chords Part of the brief mod revival of 1979 – 1980. The band submitted a demo for the chance of playing the "Mod" band seen gigging at the Goldhawk in an early scene, after reading about the film in the NME. "We submitted a demo," remembers Chords member Billy in a letter to the author, who felt that the band were a little too Who-like and not an atypical R&B band that the filmmakers wanted, "we got the usual nice letter saying the usual. I think we were a bit raw then." As we all know, the role went to Cross Section. However, interest in the band has returned in the late Nineties acknowledged by compilation album This Is What They Want and various websites exist detailing the band's history. See the website at www.beakz.net/thechords/discography/
See also: The Jam, Mod.

Cigarettes *"...There's something about Private Blend. For people like you."*
Advertising campaign slogan accompanied by a grainy black and white film devised by the agency where Jimmy works as a clerk. Somewhat cliched, with a happy ending to boot, the concept finds a youngish man and woman (an un-

named Czech starlet according to Phil Daniels) meeting in a park to the accompaniment of an heavy stringed soundtrack. Curiously, the same snatch of music can be heard in the awful British sex comedy The Adventures of A Private Detective (1977). Priced at 4/6d for twenty, Private Blend is quite expensive when a pack of Park Drive retailed at 3/1d for tipped or 3/8d plain. It certainly is not a brand favoured by any of the young Mods in Quadrophenia; Jimmy is seen holding a pack of Senior Service cigarettes whilst the lads attempt to get in to the house party in Kitchener Road, as indeed is Steph at Alfredo's during the last time we see the main cliché together. Notice how large the broad packaging looks in her hands. Senior Service had various ad lines throughout the Sixties, two in 1965 read; 'Above all Senior Service satisfy. Britain's outstanding cigarette.' While a third was 'The perfection of cigarette luxury.' They are still available today at around £4.40 a packet. At the supermarket where Steph works we see a poster advertising Player's cigarettes and our introduction to Dave at the Goldhawk finds him smoking as does Kevin when he meets up again with Jimmy in an early scene at a cafe. Most of the others smoke too, the Ace Face has a snazzy case to house his stock and Jimmy's father is a smoker also. He can be found puffing away one morning whilst setting off on his way to work unaware that Jimmy has been sleeping rough in the nearby garden shed.

Clacton "'Wild Ones' Invade Seaside – 97 Arrests" Daily Mirror, 30 March 1964, front page headline with "Scooter gangs 'beat up' Clacton." A small holiday resort on the east coast of England with little in the way of amenities [just like the nearby Great Yarmouth, another trouble spot in the Sixties]. Significantly, following the confrontations between visiting Mods and local Rockers, the media labelled both as violent creatures. Moreover, what this did was to build up the anticipation in other youngsters looking for a scrap and curious holidaymakers as well as the greedy press for more trouble to flare up.

Alan Clarke An exemplary director whose work arouses furious debate; Scum (1979), Made in England (1983) and Rita, Sue and Bob Too (1986) perfect

105

examples. "My performance in Scum is Clarkey's performance, not mine." Conceded a modest Ray Winstone in an interview recorded for a biography of the director's work. The original 1977 TV version of that film, a tale about life in a harsh young offender's institution, was deemed to strong to be screened by the BBC. Busybody Mary Whitehouse attempts to keep it that way succeeded until in 1979 it was re-shot and released in cinemas instead. With much the same cast, including Ray Winstone, Phil Daniels, P H Moriarty and Patrick Murray whilst incurring some slight changes the theatrical version is generally considered a lesser film than the original. Nonetheless, seek either version out for the legendary *"I'm the daddy now!"* proclamation from Winstone after clobbering poor old Phil Daniels.

It is Daniels and Ferdy, alias Trevor Laird that both pop up in the Clarke-directed Billy the Kid and The Green Baize Vampire (1985), a musical comedy that Channel 4 sometimes screens and about which a review in Sight and Sound regarded as "...weird and not to say downright perverse." Phil takes on the part of Billy Kidd, a cocky young pretender seeking to take the crown from the local snooker hall king. Trevor is seen as Floyd. Subsequently, Phil Davis [Chalky in Quadrophenia] would be heavily influenced by his role in The Firm (1988), a made-for-TV film regaling the middle class, mobile phone organised football hooliganism of the mid-Eighties. Davis would write and direct I.D (1995) a story of an undercover police officer submerged and ultimately consumed by the calculated underworld of pre-arranged violence. Gary Oldman, the lead in The Firm, went on to direct Ray Winstone in Nil By Mouth (1997) and coincidentally, Tim Roth, so outstanding as the skinhead in Clarke's Made In Britain, also directed Winstone in The War Zone (1999). Both fledgling directors had acted together in the Mike Leigh feature Meantime (1983) which gave a role to one Phil Daniels. To read interviews with many of the above actors discussing their working relationships with Clarke see Alan Clarke, ed. by Richard Kelly (Faber and Faber, 1998). The book contains many photographs of the Quadrophenia actors in their Clarke acting guises. See also: Phil Daniels, Phil Davis, Patsy Pollock, Ray Winstone.

Bryan Coates Formerly co-Location Manager for Quadrophenia, Bryan was tragically killed in a plane crash whilst returning from Morocco after scouting for locations for the Michael Douglas/ Kathleen Turner comedy The Jewel of the Nile. He was sixty-three. Other work incls: Raiders of the Lost Ark (1981), Clash of the Titans (1966)

Stanley Cohen A Sociologist at Essex University, in 1972 his seminal text on the Mod versus Rocker youth cult, Folk Devils and Moral Panic, was published. The title refers to a group in society that is seen as being different from the perceived norm, viewed as an ill-conceived threat i.e. the Mod and/ or the Rocker in Sixties Britain. A little dry in its academic study it is worth a read if you want to determine an understanding of the period.

Coca-Cola "Coke after Coke after Coke…" The Who Sell Out album.

Its logo is seen at the café where Jimmy goes for pie and mash at the beginning of Quadrophenia whilst Pepsi is seen at Alfredo's and Brighton. Mods tended to favour Pepsi, recognised by them as having a discernably modern branding rather than the tradition of Coke. The Who recorded two mock radio jingles for the brand in their The Who Sell Out album. The album was released as a double-album along with A Quick One (Happy Jack in America) in the early 1970s and its cover can be seen above the record player during the Kitchener Road house party in Quadrophenia.

Coffee bars: See snack bars.

Frank Conor The unit photographer responsible for shooting the Quadrophenia film and of whose work is included in a special photomontage segment at the end of the 4Front video release. A stunning collection of images not just of scenes from the film or photos that are well known, but also a large selection of informal shots taken during filming and in-between. Conor captures the delight on birthday boy Phil Daniels' face when he is presented with a special scooter-designed cake to commemorate his nineteenth birthday. There are also some beautiful pictures of Phil Daniels with Leslie Ash and a curious one of Ms Ash posing rigidly as a fashion model dummy on Brighton's East Street. Pete Townshend is captured with Daniels eating pie & liquor on location, and Sting standing in front of a poster advertising a gig by The Yardbirds/ Pretty Things and Zoot Money at the High Holland Club. The segway edited by John Pledot

chasing the wind A TO Z ANTHOLOGY

and Danny Perkins features four songs from The Who heard in the film. However, most noteworthy of all has to be the cast photo of the actors dressed as they were before filming commenced in 1978 and don't they look different!

Garry Cooper *"That flash cunt!"*

Dave's acerbic opinion of Pete as told to fellow mod, Jimmy.

Of all the Mods in Quadrophenia surely Peter 'Pete' Fenton is the most dislikeable? He may dress well but he is also racist, distant and surly. Pete is not alone in spouting off his narrow mindedness as both Kevin and Chalky come out with some nasty stuff too. On the corrugated iron fence outside of the scrap yard owned by Fenton's uncle, Jimmy rides his scooter in to the entrance past a none-too-subtle piece of graffiti mirroring that of Pete's own prejudiced viewpoint. It looks as if it reads 'NF is opium', the initials relating to the National Front racist movement of the late-sixties and seventies. A prime example of Jimmy's shifting ostracism from the mod ethic of working for a living to sustain the life and look bamboozles the older mod, *"you don't work you don't get money,"* pontificates Cooper to Daniels, *"and I like money."*

Initially cast to play the Ace Face, Hull-born Garry looks to be just a little bit maturer than most of the other actors but his behaviour is spot on; watch how he starts up his scooter and allows Steph to get on first before taking his place and driving off after the party at Kitchener Road. It reeks of Mod etiquette whether or not it was, is not the point the action feels and looks right. In amongst the herd of Vespas and Lambrettas parked outside the house his is pallid and quite nondescript oddly enough, it is Jimmy's that is most noticeable even though the scene takes place at night. Watch it and see if you agree. Wearing what could be deemed as his 'Sunday best', a fabulous three-quarter-length leather coat [hardly conducive for scootering!] Pete does not belong to the main mod group in the film and he and Steph duely arrive at Madeira Drive in Brighton seafront, a little after Jimmy and the others have. Hugely excited by the army of scooters lined up, Jimmy briefly gets to talk with her before she is whisked away by Pete. *"Where'd the bird go?"* gasps a puzzled James. By now the two have become an item and perhaps with Fenton pairing off with an American girl at the Aquarium ballroom, to the envious distaste of Chalky and Dave, this explains the disintegration of their own relationship.Either that or it's indicative of its brevity. Following Pete's abandonment, Steph eventually gets it together with Jimmy until casually abandoning him for Dave. Unfortunately enough, it will be Jimmy that suffers as a consequence of Pete, Dave and Steph's behaviour. The last occasion we see Garry is on the day of the battles on Brighton promenade; he blocks the escape route of a rocker and gives him a severe kicking that has a frightening air of authenticity. Away from Quadrophenia Garry has been cast in a diverse range of films, the most curious being Beautiful Thing (1996) preceded in 1986 with Caravaggio. Demonstrating the Mod connection, he acted in an episode of Boon alongside Mr Cooper Senior, Michael Elphick. A part in My Beautiful Launderette (1986) was directed by Stephen Frears, himself the main force behind Bloody Kids, an important film for seeing the launch of one of the Rockers that attack Spider, in the form of Gary Holton. More recent work has come via television roles. See also: Stephen Frears. CONTACT: Stephen Hatton Management, 1a Shepperton House, 83 Shepperton Road, London N1.

The Cooper House The home of Jimmy, his mum and dad and sister Yvonne. For the hallway confrontation between Jimmy and his mother, a soon–to-be demolished terraced house in south London was used or according to another source, it was in Wells Home road, Acton. The hallway, carpeted sparingly only in the middle of the stairs, is drab and offers the impression of a quite poor family residency. The functional kitchen is glimpsed briefly because of Jimmy's delayed return home from work one evening, with his tea on the hob.

i. Living room / lounge - Its drab palm tree print wallpaper offers little comfort to the eye when seen during the time when Jimmy watches Ready Steady Go! They do have some ornaments; a vase and sideboard cabinet but little else.

ii. Jimmy's bedroom - lots of photos and Mod violence-related newspaper cuttings over the walls, a full-length mirror for maintaining appearance and horrid stripped flannelette sheets with leopard skin bedspread round of the eclectic feel. Yvonne's bedroom, in keeping with her brother's, is again drab only enhanced by photos of pop bands like The Beatles.

Jimmy Michael Cooper Alternatively, to give him his full name, James Michael Cooper, the main protagonist in the Quadrophenia film definitively played by Phil Daniels. Incidentally, the lad used for The Who's Quadrophenia album photos was Terry Kennett.

Ray Corbett Supporting the main direction of Quadrophenia by Franc Roddam, Ray was the first Assistant Director. The Mod sauce was added to an already tasty anthology of films stretching over some forty years; Mona Lisa (1984) with its closing scenes shot on Brighton Pier and the celluloid adaptation of the Colin Macinnes novel Absolute Beginners (1986) both seeing Ray as First A.D. Babylon (1980) was another recognisably British themed picture where he was employed as the Production Manager on a film written by Quadrophenia co-scriptwriter Martin Stellman. In addition, in the role of Beefy was Trevor Laird. Other work incls: Monty Python's The Meaning of Life (1983).

Courts Hearings dealing with youngsters arrested over the bank holiday periods often had their primary stages arranged when the courts would not normally sit i.e. bank holidays, Sundays etc. See also: Brighton, Margate.

Crash helmets It was held as a common characteristic of a 1960s Rocker to wear a helmet but in the film some are seen to do so whilst others do not. An example being the crew on their way down to Brighton whilst those that harass Jimmy on his way down to the Goldhawk club at the start of the film are all helmet-wearers. Legislation made it compulsory to do so with the introduction of the Road Traffic Act of 1972.

Crawdaddy club Famous R&B club, which alongside the Flamingo, Marquee and Scene, was popular amongst Mod audiences. We see a poster promoting a gig by The Yardbirds on the stairwell to the Goldhawk during the moment when

Jimmy and the others come dashing outside to find that Spider and his girlfriend have been roughed up. Both the Yardbirds and the Rolling Stones were resident house bands there at one time or another. See also: Jesse Birdsall, Gary Holton.
Davy Crockett *"Thinks he's Davy Crockett!"* One of the bikers to Chalky prior to forcing him off the road whilst riding down to Brighton for the holiday weekend. Crockett was an American frontiersman and politician born in 1786 whose life was popularised on the U.S television show of the same name in the mid-Fifties. His motto was "Be sure you're right, then go ahead." He died back in 1836. 
Visit the website at www.geocities.com/TelevisionCity/Set/1486.
Cross Section The young group seen and heard performing Hi Heel Sneakers and Dimples at the Goldhawk club as Jimmy and we, the audience, first meet up with the other Mods. Oddly, apart from these two songs being featured on the film soundtrack, Cross Section *[lead singer Phil Kitto is pictured opposite]* never had a single or album entry on the UK charts despite beating a number of groups to appear in the film via an ad in a music paper in March '78. All teen-aged at the time, the band spent a couple of days shooting their involvement in the film.
Seen dressed casually in horizontal patterned sweaters and striped shirts. See also: The Chords, John Lee Hooker.
The Crystals Da Doo Ron Ron was a hit in June 1963 making number five and charting again in 1974 climbing to fifteen. This American girl group is also remembered for their Then He Kissed Me single. Da Doo is heard being played by the disc jockey at the Goldhawk, before and after the news of Spider and his girlfriend's assault. Subsequent interpretations of the song came from artists such as Bette Midler and The Searchers. 
Bill Curbishley In association with Roy Baird the two worked together as producers on the Quadrophenia film and almost all of the subsequent Who-related projects [solo or group] thereafter, including The Kids Are Alright (1978)

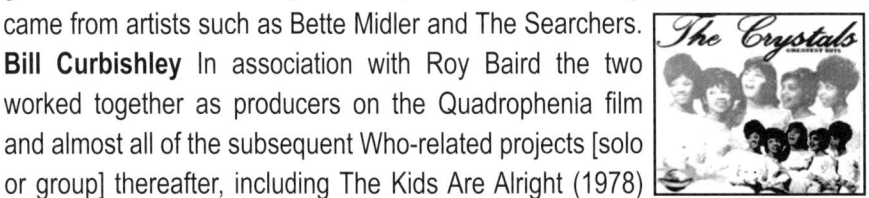

documentary, The Who Rocks America (1982), McVicar and Buddy's Song. Furnishing either the Producer or Executive Producer duties on all the above, Bill produced or executively produced many classic Who albums and a trio of Pete Townshend solo efforts. For Buddy's Song, a pet project for former Ted Roger Daltrey, Bill and Roy stamped the film with their Curbishley-Baird Enterprises mark. Known for his candid and forthright nature, Curbishley joined the Track Records/ New Action team back in 1970 before succeeding John Wolff and Pete Rudge in The Who management chair in the summer of 1974. Another grammar school associate of Chris Stamp and Mike Shaw, Bill co-managed a group in the mid-Seventies with former High Numbers maestro Pete Meaden. See also: Roger Daltrey, Pete Meaden and The Who Concert File book.

Cut My Hair A news report included on the song and narrated by John Curle, speaks of the confrontation between factions of youths and the police in Brighton. The track, taken from the Who's original Quadrophenia album, is featured in an early scene set in Jimmy's bedroom. Zoot Suit, an early Mod favourite item, is referenced in the lyrics. Also, Pete Townshend repeats the remark of why he should care, as he does in Cut My Hair, at the beginning of 5:15. See also: The Grand Hotel, Zoot Suit

Roger Daltrey Water.
The author realised that he had become a Daltrey fan after noticing a commercial for his single After the Fire on TV in the mid-Eighties. This Pete Townshend composition never dented the charts. Puzzling in that it is such a good tune. From 1973 to 1985 Roger released eight singles in Britain with deteriorating success; from the respectable number five of his debut Giving it all Away through to the watery number fifty of After the Fire in 1985. Album wise, four were put out over the same ten-year period, the most commercially successful being Ride a Rock Horse [peaking at fourteen]. One solo recording that included the Townshend-penned Fire was Under a Raging Moon, a direct reference to former drummer Keith. The explosive stream of intensity that

is Love Reign O'er Me is, for me, with 5:15, the defining sound reverberating from the Quadrophenia film. "They [The Who] weren't pretty but had style," commented rock writer Nik Cohn. It was from an invitation to join the Detours made by Roger, never actually trained as a singer, to John and Pete that set the foundations for the genesis of "the greatest band in the world." NME scribe Alan Shacklock freely admitted to being intimidated when meeting Daltrey, "There's a sort of vicious strangeness about these four beatsters...and they admit it." He remarked in a 1965 interview with the band. Roger is listed as Musical Director and Executive Producer for the Quadrophenia movie and can be seen enjoying the sunshine with Phil Daniels in a break from location filming in the on-set photographs shot by Frank Conor. At Alfredo's Espresso bar, George Innes [is his character the man in question?] has photos of Elvis Presley on his wall complimented by a poster featuring Buddy Holly inside the cafe itself. Roger is a big fan of Holly, as was Keith Moon who acted in a film derived from a title of a Buddy hit, and it was Daltrey who developed a TV and film drama called Buddy's Song in 1990. The production duo of Roy Baird and Bill Curbishley worked with him on the project for which The Who singer was involved with the music and acting side of the productions. Michael Elphick, Jimmy's dad in Quadrophenia, played Des. Having experienced what could only be called an eclectic career incorporating advertising campaigns for American Express and Kickers boots, trout farming, singing and acting, Daltrey maintains a physique to belie his years. Over the same period as collaborating with Ken Russell on Tommy (1975) Roger was again directed by him in Listzomania, with the mod association preceded with Peter Brayham [Quadrophenia's stunt arranger] employed in a supporting role and utilizing his skills as a fencing master. Subsequent Quad crew members Bill Rowe and Roy Baird colluded with Tommy actors Paul Nicholas and the late Ollie Reed in a hectic production year. Mr Daltrey contributed musically to the film by writing some lyrics and singing too.

McVicar presented a major role for Roger and is a film for which more than a half-dozen Quadrophenia crew members worked on. He would attain success on the American Billboard charts with a single put out from off the soundtrack and The Who [with replacement drummer Kenney Jones] were to receive a

chasing the wind A TO Z ANTHOLOGY

Music Consultancy credit. Years later, Roger was to make a surprise guest star appearance in The Bill, after acting with one of its cast, Billy Murray, in the above film. A 1984 part in Pop Pirates, a children's adventure story, was memorable for its score being co-written by none other than Gary Shail, the 'monkey-brained' Spider. An anthology of his solo recordings came out in 2000 and joins the 1997 package Martyrs and Madmen – The Best of Roger Daltrey. A live version of After the Fire can be heard on the live Who CD released over the internet, The Blues to the Bush. Further information about 'The Duchess' as he is known in Who circles, can be found at rogerdaltrey.netl.
See also: Leslie Ash, Frank Conor, Buddy Holly, Levi's, Keith Moon, Toyah, The Who. CONTACT: Conway Van Gelder Ltd, 3rd floor, 18/21 Jermyn St., London SW1Y 6HP.
Dancing "You stop dancing..." Roger Daltrey lyric heard at end of film as the Ace's scooter stolen by Jimmy back in Brighton goes flying over the cliff top.
Its line is used to great dramatic effect as the bike smashes down on to the rocks and the end credits come up on screen. Choreographed by Gillian Gregory, the cast members were taught all the relevant dances over a three week period at a Soho studio prior to filming. Phil Daniels, as Jimmy, dances like a boxer psyching himself up for a fight or a woodpecker with his chicken-head movements cluck-cluck-clucking away. In Quadrophenia we see both Monkey and Jimmy dancing individually, a common sight amongst Mod circles whose etiquette allowed solo dancing, with a boy or a girl or in a group. Just like much else to do with being a Mod, it was important to get the movements spot on. Sixties pop show Ready Steady Go! had ones called the Hitchhike, Shake and The Dog whilst other mod ones developed with two basic steps, the block and bang, both hard to do!
Phil Daniels Like a man that's lost his shadow.
John Paul Sartre.
Pictured above, with Toyah in Quadrophenia, Mr Daniels ably carryies the film as manic mod Jimmy Cooper and remembering that he was still only twenty-one when the film

(Above) Jimmy (Phil Daniels) and Monkey (Toyah) at the houseparty.

was released, Phil's performance is all the more remarkable. As the onset photographer, Frank Conor's pictures show a genial Daniels minus his furrowed brow that would formulate itself as his dramatic angst took root. Get a hold of the 4Front video release for a special montage of the images wrapped up with a soundtrack of Who songs. Born on 25 October 1958 and growing up in London's King's Cross, Phil had already acted in a half-dozen films before Quadrophenia. Of relevant interest is The Class of Miss MacMichael (1978) which had Oliver Reed and Patrick Murray in its cast. Murray and Daniels had worked together on the small-screen in Alan Clarke's Scum (1977) and they would again repeat their parts in the 1979 feature film version. A graduate of the Anna Scher Children's Theatre, as was friend Trevor Ferdy Laird, success continued for Phil after Quadrophenia with his portrayal of Danny, the wide boy manager in Breaking Glass (1980). Dave, aka Mark Wingett, co-starred as band member Tony in the fictitious group managed by Daniels. Glass followed on from Phil's celebrated roles in Quadrophenia and Scum, both showing in cinemas in 1979. Gary Holton and Patrick Murray were also in the film and Caroline Hagen as Production Assistant, reconvened her same duties from the Quadrophenia shoot. Billy the Kid and The Green Baize Vampire saw Phil being directed by Les Blair, in a working relationship that continued with Bad Behaviour in 1993, a novel little comedy that gave Daniels fans a two-for-the-price-of-one special due to his appearances as twins! Still Crazy (1998) finds Phil again in the shape of a band manager only this time Timothy Spall appears as drummer Beano. A cameo from Phil Davis as a limo driver is wasted in that he has nothing remotely to do. Neither of the three Quad actors are seen on screen together alas. Closing the musical avenue in 1994 Phil played trombone, horn and narrator on the Blur single Parklife as well as stealing the spotlight in the accompanying video clip. Writing in the definitive Blur 3862 days - The Official History [Virgin, 1999] Stuart Maconie defined Daniels' contribution as giving "the narrator just the right tone of voluble idiocy and wit and a modern classic was born." Blur had, with the likes of Pulp and Oasis been pigeonholed under the Brit Pop banner of the mid-nineties and the boys were already big Daniels fans before working with him, "We were all really amazed when he turned up;" recalls one of the band, "'cos we were expecting this sharp cool mod from Quadrophenia and he had this long hair and straggly beard." Never one to stagnate, Phil had been playing a tramp in a theatrical presentation of the musical Carousel at that time. Career diversification has involved acting in a Shakespeare TV adaptation and a stage role in A Clockwork Orange back in the eighties. Returning to Blur, a boisterous partnership culminated in Phil's presence rounding off their 1995 concerts to perform Parklife, including their mammoth London gig at Mile End. With The Who reviving Quadrophenia for The Prince's Trust concert in the mid-eighties and the subsequent American tour of 1986, Phil did the vocal narration heard at the shows. A photo of him with 'Irish' Jack Lyons, a character cited as one of Townshend's influences for creating Jimmy, taken at a Madison Square Garden Who gig in 1996 features on Lyons' link from the official Who website [found at www.thewho.net]. Daniels has acted with Quad co-star Ray Winstone in both versions of Scum and in Number One (1984). P.H Moriarty, who played a barman in Quadrophenia, Winstone as Timmy and Phil as Terry the Boxer acted in a movie that was alternatively known as Streetwise.

Embracing his London tones as Jimmy, a particular favourite of mine being his intonation in retelling Steph and Dave as to why he quit his job at the ad agency, Phil has flexed his vocal muscles in many an advertisement, "Blitz those zits with Oxy" one that I recall. Summer 2000 marked the release of Chicken Run, the first feature-length animated film from the makers of Wallace and Gromit, with Phil playing a fellow rat with Timothy Spall!

A TO Z ANTHOLOGY   A QUADROPHENIA ANTHOLOGY

Benjamin Whitrow, the exacerbated Fulford from Quadrophenia, also voiced a character. A little known bit of trivia being that Phil and Benjamin do on occasion enjoy a round of golf together. Franc Roddam in The Bride (1985) again directed Phil, although in a wholly different standing, next to the old gang of Sting, Timothy Spall and Gary Shail. He has won more substantial acting parts in recent years on television rather than film. Holding On and Sex, Chips & Rock n Roll have been specific favourites for the character actor. A 1990 episode of Boon, the Michael Elphick drama series saw Mr Cooper Senior and junior all to briefly reunited. Whilst Nasty Neighbours (2000) and Goodbye Charlie Bright (2001) are amongst his more recent cinematic performances. That's not forgetting his role in Freebird (2)))?) as a greasy biker, the antithesis of Jimmy Cooper from all those years ago. 'I thought it would be good fun to turn the tide a bit.' Commented Phil regarding his role in that film.

But for me, and I am sure for you, he will always be the bug-eyed, chicken-dancing mod of whom a way of life is only found through great cost. Phil followed his Quadrophenia co-stars Michael Elphick & Mark Wingett upon joining EastEnders for a stint in 2006. See also: Trevor Laird, Toyah, Benjamin Whitrow, Youth. CONTACT: ICM, Oxford House, 76 Oxford St., London W1.

Phil Davis Dizzy in the head.

As Chalky his inauguration in to the mod milieu comes in a pub toilet where Dave, Spider and Jimmy and the rest of the cognoscenti are gathered. All laughing and joking whilst checking their looks in the mirror, it is a great establishing scene that is laced with atypical young male humour. Although at twenty-five, Phil was a little older than most of the other cast members. However, he is easily able to relay to the audience, as does Phil Daniels, that sense of awkwardness of no longer being a child but existing in the space between that and adulthood. A piercingly sharp dresser, Chalky looks resplendent in a dark blue suit, lime shirt and cuff links

117

prominently displayed; so much so that he offers an appearance definable as androgynous. Not quite leaning towards effeminate his hair is just that little bit longer than most others is and can be seen in parallel with Gary Shail as Spider: both opaque in their Modliness. What do we learn of his background? At most that he is also from Shepherd's Bush and like many youngsters of the period, he still lives at home. Can you imagine how much harder it must have been to maintain a mod look if you had to pay rent rather than spend all your spare cash on clothes and records? Remaining in the gents, Dave declares that if his father had padlocked his scooter [as had Chalky's old man] preventing him from getting involved in any bank holiday violence then he would sort him out physically.

This bravado will be demonstrated at Brighton where both prove themselves able scrappers [despite Phil's diminutive stature]. Interestingly enough, following the attack upon Spider and his girlfriend, it is Chalky who is keenest to seek retribution. And again, when he is run off the road by some bikers whilst on the way down to the coast, his actions are conveniently validated. It is his speculative spotting of one of the former that presses the detonator to the elongated violence on the sea front area. Chalky *'the ponce'* may have been the first to gain revenge for Spider but it had already been observed at Alfredo's Cafe that he was keen to *"knock off"* some greasers/ rockers prior to this. That same scene had clearly shown that Spider's uninvited mingling amongst the Jimmy/Dave/Chalky clique caused a barely suppressed sigh most prominently expressed by the attitude adopted by Dave. After agreeing that a large quantity of pills will be a necessary sustenance for the bank holiday weekend the guys go in search of Ferdy and it is here that Chalky's uncomfortable ness in being found in an unfamiliar domain presents itself badly. *"It's like bloody Calcutta..."* he bemoans anxiously. *"Calcutta's in India."* offers Dave as they wait outside a house. *"Yeah. West India."* concludes Chalky. Wingett laughs as does the audience but it is a moment that could easily have been offensive if it was not delivered in such a resolute manner. Contrast this with the distinctly bitter after taste left by Pete's racist remark about Ferdy [when Jimmy goes to ask him for a drugs contact].The detachment of the childish ignorance of the former, does not bode well with the latter and it is little wonder that virtually nobody cares for Fenton. Chalky is oblivious in his attitude towards women; it is only after Dave has declared his lust for Steph to him in Brighton that sex appears to occur to him at all. As a Mod, his scooter is an extension or rather continuation of his identity and personality: accessorized and sprayed with tribal colouring. In a later moment, the witless Chalky [what is his actual name?] riding ahead of the other Mods, is forced off his scooter in spectacular fashion by a troupe of bikers and ends up sprawled out next to a pile of rubbish containing discarded mattresses. *"It looked good from back there."* giggles a soon arriving Jimmy with Dave. Momentarily checking that he is okay the others ride off leaving him to make his own way towards Madeira Drive on theBrighton seafront, the rendezvous for everyone. Chalky eventually arrives, with his battered scooter disfigured by broken mirrors and dented side fins.

Later in Brighton, following Jimmy's self-inflicted ostracism from his friends, Chalky and Dave spend a lot of time together whilst things had been different following their earlier failed attempt to buy drugs from Harry North [John Bindon]. Exemplified in their Three Stooges ineptitude during a night-time raid on the chemist shop where Monkey works. The contradictions blur an overtly adult behaviour combined with a childlike attitude comes together in our perception of Chalky here. His concerns for being identified by his footprints is a logic that only a child could have derived contrasted with an adeptness at opening a packet of condoms adopted in a most idiosyncratic manner [to avoid finger prints!] Giggling constantly throughout the burglary Chalky even goes back to take a bottle of talcum powder home for his mother. Disappointingly Davis has little more to do after the Brighton moments of the film but he is included in the final group scene at Alfredo's where Jimmy reacts to Dave's snide goading and lashes out at his former friend. Chalky says nothing at this time but assists Ferdy ans Spider to keep the two former pals apart.

Philip, or Phil as he is sometimes known, as well as having acting experience has written and directed films. In 1995 he directed I.D, a Brit thriller with football hooliganism at its core. He also provided the voice-over for its subsequent video release. A role in a similarly themed TV film The Firm (1988) left a last impression, "You look at The Firm and it really sums up the Eighties." remarked the actor in a book about director Alan Clarke. Hold Back the Night (1999) was another feature helmed by, but not starring Davis. It received limited cinematic exposure in London and is available on video. His beautifully understated playing of Cyril, pictured opposite, in High Hopes (1988) ably supports Mike Leigh's proclamation that Phil was one of his favoured actors. Hidden beneath a woolly Marx-inspired beard and wretched-looking glasses, he offers a characterisation a world away from the dandyism of Chalky. Trevor Laird and Timothy Spall can each be seen in Leigh's award-winning Secrets and Lies (1996) as may Phil in a tiny cameo. Speaking of which he can be glimpsed in an entirely superfluous part as a limo driver in Still Crazy, a decent British comedy written by Dick Clement and Ian Le Frenais, the duo behind Franc Roddam's Auf Wiedersehen, Pet [again with Tim Spall and an intermittent host of Quadrophenia actors, as mentioned previously]. Face (1997) another Brit-flick; saw Phil lining up with the rocker that he beat up almost two decades earlier, Ray Winstone. Each had been cast in the early-eighties telly adaptation of Robin Hood and in 1999 they came together once more in mini-series Births, Marriages & Deaths. His career goes from strength to strangth. See also: Brighton, Alan Clarke, Phil Daniels, Mike Leigh, racism, scooters, Mark Wingett. CONTACT: William Morris Agency (UK) Ltd, 1 Stratton St., London W1X 6HB.

Deckchairs Like sweet pink rock, buckets and spades or candyfloss, the deckchair has long been a staple of the seaside and it has remained so in Brighton. In the film we see a middle-aged attendant methodically placing some along the seafront whilst the London Mods make their way along the coast road on their scooters. There was some 15,000 stripy ones in the Brighton of 1964, with twenty-three casualties recovered from the sea following the Whit sun holiday. A further figure, estimated at 2000, was said to be the total deckchairs scattered over the beach. On average, the council would expect to lose fifty or so but that year 260 lost their lives many seeing a distinctly unorthodox usage on the sun terrace at the Aquarium. See also: Brighton, The Jam.

Desert Boots Jimmy and many authentic mods would wear them for their comfort when riding on their scooters. You can see Jim's when he sits with Dave inside the Goldhawk club during the scene where the former is also moodily cloaked in wraparound sunglasses. As well as when the crew make their way towards Brighton, Chalky, Dave and Jimmy all wear them whilst riding their scooters. Manufactured by companies such as Clarks, the two-holed eyelets date back to 1950. Hush Puppies also resembled the same product. See also: Clarks shoes, Pete Meaden

Dexy's Midnight Runners Formed in 1978, the band sought to evoke the Mod sound that was popular in the decade before with a soul influence. They of course took their name from a popular drug used by youngsters in the Sixties called Dexedrine. See also: Drugs.

Dimples "I love the way you walk…I got my eyes on you…" John Lee Hooker. "Now you're losing all your dimples…" I've Had Enough, The Who.

Pretty apt for its adaptation as Jimmy's lustometer for the alluring Steph. His attraction towards her is clear when we spot him watching her at the Goldhawk club. Written by American blues man John Lee Hooker, it is the second of two guitar-driven tracks performed by Cross Section in an early scene set there. Along with the similar sounding Boom Boom, Dimples has been covered by many beat groups in the Sixties [such as The Animals] and guitarist Duane Eddy. The track was a hit in Britain for John in August 1956. Never one to let a good riff go, Dimples was reworked in the guises of I Like To See You Walkin' and I Got My Eyes On You for subsequent recordings. Evoking the nuances of Green Onions and Hooker's own Boom Boom, if Dimples gets you moving just as much as it seems to do to Jimmy and Dave, check out The Best of John Lee Hooker on the Music Club label (1991). See also: The Chords, John Lee Hooker.

Doctor Jimmy Includes John's theme, Is it Me? Heard over the closing credits of Quadrophenia, a minute of atmospheric sound from its introduction was erased by John Entwistle for his 1979 remastering of the Who album of 1973. Written expressly for inclusion in the film, Dr Jimmy plays over the closing credits of the film. See also: gin, Levi's.

Kevin O'Driscoll Production Manager on Quadrophenia.

Drowned Piano accompaniment played by Chris Stainton (in the time before Pete Townshend could play) he also features on 5:15. The song tells of Jimmy's paralysis and his overwhelming desire for love. Let Pete Townshend, quoted here from Quadrophenia.net, explain further, "It's a love song, God's love being the ocean and our 'selves' being the drops of water that make it up." Has an echo of 5:15 within it if you listen closely, a trait running through many of the tracks on the Who album.

Drugs - Mod multivitamins. "Once the pills start to take effect you can't stand still for a minute...when you feel that confident it's like an unstoppable energy." Relays Irish Jacks Lyons, an authentic Goldhawk Mod of the Sixties, on his site contained within the official Who site. References to drug use swarm through the Quadrophenia album and theme in such tracks as The Punk and The Godfather, I'm One, Dr Jimmy, Cut My Hair, 5:15 and I've Had Enough. In 1964, the Drugs [Prevention of Mis-use] Act made it illegal to possess or distribute amphetamines without a licence although its implementation simply pushed up the street price from 6d to 9d. In Brighton that year, a survey conducted amongst 14-21 year-olds at cafes, dancehalls and on the street, found that 62% of Mod youngsters and 42% of local Rockers had said they had tried drugs.

Amphetamine is an entirely synthetic drug that is a stimulant to the central nervous system. Purchased in London coffee bars and jazz clubs, Mods took them mainly in pill forms but they can also be inhaled or injected. 'Speed' was the most common type amongst Mod users. Amphetamine/ speed in its commonest form of blues pills or powder wrapped in cigarette paper aka 'bombers', was sold at a shilling a piece. This came after its introduction into Britain in the guise of the Benzedrine inhaler in 1932. During the Twenties its medical potential was first explored following the synthetic manufacture of amphetamine in Germany back in the late-1800s. By the Twenties the effects of inhalers given to asthma sufferers showed that they perked the user up and stifled the appetite. Amphetamine misuse in Japan and Scandinavia was documented as being at an epidemic proportion. Given to troops in WW2, following this period the potency of the drug was realised by governments and consequently, was only available on prescription. During the war years they were used by U.S. service personnel to give them an energy boost and increase aggression before engaging in, or sustaining combat. At the beginning of the Sixties adolescent children discovered the potency of the drugs and began stealing them from their mother's or burgled chemists. LSD and marijuana replaced amphetamines as the decade progressed.

Black Bombers High-level stimulant AKA Durophet used for treating obesity. A small dark blue capsule, triangular containing dexamphetamine [a stimulant] and amlobarbitone [a hypnotic]. Chalky asks Jimmy for some of his supply during the scene set in the gent's toilet at a London pub. Said to be extremely potent with three-dimensional after-effects experienced once they start wearing off. And all for about two shillings each.

Dexies - Dexedrine / Dexamphetamine: yellow in colour and a shilling a time.

French Blues Purchased at places like the Goldhawk for sixpence a time. Light blue in appearance with a line down its centre, 'Blues' were known to be twice as strong as Purple Hearts, so it was important to chew gum when using.

Purple Hearts Its name was taken from the U.S Army medal awarded to those wounded in action [Drinamyl, a stimulant made from a mixture of amphetamine and barbiturates.] A Purple-blue appearance with a curved triangular shape, they were found at mod haunts like the Goldhawk, although originally prescribed for the treatment of neuroses. With a retail value of sixteen shillings for a hundred, on the black market they could be bought for a shilling or 7/6- each. After their demise, French blues, Dexedrine and Durophet slipped down the mod throat. As a part of the brief Mod revivalists groups of the late Seventies, The Purple Hearts took their name from the drug and utilised the Lambretta typeface for their own logo.

Side effects: paranoia, anxiety, aggression, reduction of libido and depression.

Plus points: increase in mental agility, energy and sense of euphoria. Mods took them so they could stay awake for the weekenders events involving dancing etc.

Come down: exhaustion; downers could be taken to limit the body's awareness of the unpleasant effects or more speed. Said not to be addictive, speed clearly is. Addiction worked in that you had to take more to have a sustained effect the more tolerant the system becomes. The media of the early-Sixties honed in upon the drug scene amongst mods and a front page Sunday Mirror headline made their opinion clear: "Exposing the Drug Menace." This May 1964 article informed parents of the misuse by their children, with the exposition that heroin and cocaine, "two drugs that almost always lead to death before the age of thirty-five," was a natural follow-on from amphetamine abuse.
See also: bibliography, Brighton, slang.

Eastman Colour American Cinematography pioneer George Eastman invented the film stock Quadrophenia was shot on.

Ecclesiastics And I saw that everything was emptiness and chasing the wind, of no profit under the sun. Ecclesiastics 2:11. Biblical text often related to Jimmy's spiritual/ existential plight in Quadrophenia. However, it seems more pertinent to Pinkie, Graham Greene's anti-hero of Brighton Rock. In the former, Jimmy is initially seen to be awakening in to the light with everything else a rewind of his life up until this point whereas Pinkie kills himself by leaping from a cliff edge in to the sea. See also: Chasing the Wind entry.

Michael Elphick *"... You're no son of mine. You just wait until your father comes home!"* [Kate Williams aka Jimmy's mother in Quadrophenia].
Formerly an Electrician, Chichester-born Michael has played innumerable parts with a visibly rough sheen; typical examples being as a heartless exploiter in The Elephant Man (1980), Jake in Withnail & I (1987) and as the brutish Magowan in Auf Wiedersehen, Pet. In an elongated career, latter years have provided a succession of lighter roles specifically in TV series like Three Up, Two Down, Harry and in his most popular part as Ken Boon in eight series. Ex-Fire-fighter Boon rode a 650cc BSA motorcycle the like of which screen son Jimmy would never have been seen on: not that he could have even started it if the back yard scene with Ray Winstone was any indication. Boon warrants further mention due to the string of roles that it offered former Quad actors:

chiefly Timothy Spall, Hugh Lloyd [Mr Cale in the ad agency post room], Daniel Peacock, Garry Cooper and Ray Winstone. In the bulky form of the white vested George, Mr Cooper Senior, Elphick's character appears only able to express his concern for Jimmy through physical means i.e. clumsily knocking him down the stairs after his son returns home late one evening. Clock how Jimmy has his fist clenched in anticipation of a further attack a moment later. Fortunately his dad actually proceeds to articulate his confoundment by questioning the pack mentality of his son and friends, *"...got to be a mod or this or that, haven't you got a mind of your own?"* All the while his mother persistently harps on about her son's odd behaviour not being *"normal".* It is revealed that Michael's character is just as afraid of his son as Jimmy is of his father. This is symptomatic of his generation, one that never had been availed the extraordinary freedom, the new code of living, presented to Jimmy. For the younger generation, the first to be termed teenagers, they had no real memory of the Second World War and thus had nothing to fear or feel guilty about. Commenting in 1965, a then twenty-year-old Pete Townshend enhances upon the point, "The big social revolution that has taken place in the last 5 years, is that youth, not age, has become important." This point is further confounded by the No Man's Land that the teenager growing up in the sixties were lost in, young people," elucidates Polly Powell and Lucy Feel in their book Fifties and Sixties Style, "could no longer be classed as either children or immature adult they had a completely different set of values and requirements..." In each of their scenes together, all situated at the basic family home, Elphick and Daniels sparkle and the similarities between screen father and son are plentiful. It is self-evident that Jimmy could fall in to an analogous adult life similar to that of his father, what with both employed in dreary manual jobs. Elphick rides a pushbike to work uniformed in a black donkey jacket [also worn by Dave for his job working for the council street cleaning department] heading a family well defined as working class and plainly intoned by the scriptwriters. Glancing at the exterior of the Cooper family home its three windows-and-a-door drabness marks it as a plain and almost naturalistic presence diametrically opposed to Jimmy's inclinations. Michael Elphick puts in an affable performance as a man who does very little after working all day other than drink himself in to oblivion using bottles of Guinness as his carriage. Meanwhile Kate Williams as Mrs Cooper [we never get to know her first name] stares intently at the television. Their introduction to the story shows little harmony as Jimmy hears their voices off-screen as he returns home late one evening. But for all that he does notice his son and even recognises Jimmy's state of mind however, no professional help appears to be suggested in the film version of the Quadrophenia story [the original Townshend album being different in this respect]. George and Jimmy Cooper share a sense of humour demonstrated by their interaction whereby Jimmy is teased by his father when Ready, Steady, Go! comes on the telly and draws the complete attention of the mod son. A Who performance of Anyway, Anyhow, Anywhere prompts the elder Cooper to mock *"I can sing better than that little ape,"* grins Elphick looking at Roger Daltrey, *"sounds like a dead dog."* As George, he does not commit the cardinal sin of dampening his son's enthusiasm even if he cannot condone it. Take for example his baffled response to Jimmy telling him that to wear new Levi jeans you have to first shrink them to fit the contours of your body. Great humour. After being kicked out by his mother Jimmy returns home one last time in a plea for help but painfully [yet understandably so in a way] none is forthcoming. Perhaps kicking the front door and calling your father an *"old spunker"* is not the most fitting means of communication. Watching this very short scene unfold the empathy felt for Jimmy is considerable even as his father makes a half-hearted grab at him from the safety of his scooter. The observer almost wants him to catch hold of his son [think Renton in Trainspotting] not literally but metaphorically. Alas, he is not the person to help Jimmy. A major part in the Roger Daltrey pet project Buddy's Song, a film both starring and produced by Daltrey, was released by the Quadrophenia production team Curbishley-Baird Enterprises in 1990. Memorable too, as has already been mentioned, was Elphick's interpretation of Magowan in Auf Wiedersehen, Pet; a series which in turn featured Timothy

Spall and Gary Holton in leading roles. Ray Winstone also acted in an episode. The Comic Strip's big-screen comedy The Supergrass (1985) finds Michael as Collins, with Daniel Peacock as Jim in a further acting engagement for the two actors [Peacock would act with Elphick once more in an episode of Boon and in the spoof horror flick I Married a Vampire Motorcycle]. The early months of 2001 saw Michael join the cast of the BBC drama series East Enders. Other work incls: The Knowledge (1981), Privates on Parade (1982). See also: John Altman, bibliography, Franc Roddam.

Ben Elton With a CV listing TV's The Young Ones, The Thin Blue Line, half-a-dozen novels and plays, and a career as a stand-up comedian, the accomplished Mr Elton is said to be glimpsed in Quadrophenia during the Kitchener Road house party. I think that he is the drunken youngster bundled out of the way by Pete as he and Steph leave the party and then again by Jimmy as he comes out looking for her. Or is Elton one of the guests seen drinking a pint as Jimmy struts into the living room where everyone is dancing and chatting?

Employment Jimmy, Steph, Monkey and Dave all have manual jobs such as a mail clerk, check-out assistant, chemist shop assistant and council refuse worker respectively but what of the other characters? The most shocking discovery is made by Jimmy upon discovering that the Brighton Ace Face is employed as a humble bell boy at the Grand Hotel but what do Ferdy, young Chalky and Spider do to sustain their modly lifestyles?

Brian Eno "I thought, 'Oh-oh, rock music is going to do something.'"
Commented Eno after hearing My Generation.
A successful producer and artist, he has worked with U2, Bowie, Talking Heads, Ultravox and on the Dune soundtrack, a film starring the Ace Face, Sting. Interestingly enough, Eno was an art school protégé and was taught by Roy Ascott, the same tutor as would guide the young Pete Townshend in the period before he left college to play with the Who on a professional basis. He was the founder of Seventies sensations Roxy Music. See also: My Generation.

John Entwistle. Air. "I ain't quiet, everybody else is too loud..."
[The Quiet One from The Who album Face Dances.]
Interviewed for Rock Docs: Second House - The Who and shown on BBC2 in

1993 [actually recorded in 1974] a good humoured Townshend elucidates on the character of Jimmy consisting of 4 archetypal personalities; 1) Roger - tough and assertive, 2) Keith - a 'devil-may-care' type, 3) Pete - the mystic, frustrated seeker in a state of spiritual despair and, 4) John - the secret romantic, dream-laden with a perfect ideal of life and love. Born to musical parents in Chiswick in 1944 John is credited as Musical Director/ Executive Producer on the film. Accompanying Pete, in 1959 he joined trad jazz band The Confederates after switching instruments from trumpet to bass guitar [and Pete from banjo to rhythm guitar] in the year before. Eventually rounded off with the arrival of Roger Daltrey and Keith Moon on drums in 1964, the band became The Who. On stage John remains motionless, a Bill Wyman of The Who if you will, as the cartoon histrionics from Pete, Roger and Keith splashed their Technicolor all about him. But how could anyone compete with such vivacity anyhow?

Nicknamed The Ox, John has appeared in many Who-related film and concert work and he surfaces as a guitar-wielding associate welcoming new arrivals at the Marilyn Monroe iconoclastic church in the film version of Tommy. Dwelling in Tommyland, John contributed two songs, Fiddle About and Cousin Kevin, as well as writing the most irritating Who song, Boris the Spider. His musical activities outside of The Who culminated with the recent Left of Live album under the John Entwistle band label. Previous albums had been recorded before this one reaching a pinnacle in 1996 with The Ox (Track 1970). Thunderfingers: The Best of John Entwistle [others include: Smash Your Head Against The Wall, Whistle Rhymes, Rigor Mortis Sets In, Mad Dog & Too Late The Hero]. Low key gigs featuring Who songs not written by himself have gained good feedback from fans and in the throes of their penultimate American Who tour his guitar solo on 5:15 was regarded as one of the focal points. Back in 1988 he auctioned off a selection of his guitar collection, which had totalled more than two hundred. Up until his early death John lived on a family farm supplemented by 13 dogs.

Martin Evans Electrical Supervisor for Polytel Films [the Production Company that along with The Who, released Quadrophenia]. Martin was responsible for all location lighting and was guided by Director of Photography Brian Tufano. He has seen employment as a Best Boy, Gaffer, Mini-Effects cameraman and

A TO Z ANTHOLOGY   A QUADROPHENIA ANTHOLOGY

electrician on Return of the Jedi, Carrington (1995), Pink Floyd - The Wall (1982) and the Spielberg-directed Raiders of the Lost Ark (1981).
Evening Argus: see Brighton newspapers.
Extras "We told all the kids that this was only acting and we would be using rubber bricks and rubber sticks [I forgot about the latecomers]." Remembers professional extra Harry Fielder at www.harryfielder.co.uk. Harry, an extra for some 32 years, was brought down to the south coast along with 30 or so others employed as policeofficers seen in the film. "After two days filming we all had a few bruises but w weere well paid for our trouble. "I can look back and laugh now at being kicked up in the air by a group of latecomers because I was dressed as Old Bill." Although the director was not too pleased with these pro extras.
Remaining in Brighton, the woman in the yellow coat that gets knocked over by marauding mods, whilst sitting in a deck chair on the beach, was said to be a stuntwoman. One extra punched a police officer counterpart during the Brighton sequences but as it turned out he was actually a genuine one! No charges were made. Allegedly, a member of a scooter club broke his leg during the filming Brighton extras were paid £10 a day or £15 if you owned and brought along your own motorbike. Also, an ambulance was said to have accidentally knocked down one of the extras. There are some 600+ extras featured in the film. One local extra, Dougie Macdonald, was hospitalised after being bitten by an Alsatian dog whilst shooting on East Street in Brighton. The scene can be seen in the film when Sting pulls a police officer down from his horse in amidst the riot on East Street. The injured extra was presented with a £14 sweetener as compensation for his injury and ripped jacket. His account of events appeared in the Brighton and Hove Gazette of 19 October 1979. Film production was delayed for two months after a pile-up between scooters and motorbikes saw many of them damaged and unusable for the additional scenes that they were needed for. The rocker whose escape on the promenade is prevented by Pete, and then severely beaten prior to being thrown over the walkway below was in actual fact a stuntman. Real mods from scooter clubs around the country turned up for the open casting sessions in Brighton. Curiously enough, during the curtailment of the East Street rioting, director Franc Roddam filmed the actors and extras standing around without their knowledge. Only Trevor Laird was aware of the

camera being on and watch how he offers a shrug all the while another young mod extra stares into the camera before sheepishly realising!

Fashion *"Dressing up like a freak."*
According to the Daily Mail of 1964 "Today's Mod buys", [see how many items you can spot in Quadrophenia]: mohair suits, hipster trousers with 15" bottoms silk-lined, chukka boots, slip-on moccasins, all Italian shoes, corduroy hipsters, pastel colour shirts, button-down collars, specific ties, waistcoats, jackets..."
John Stephen, an early Carnaby Street fashion entrepreneur and owner of eighteen shops across the country, six on that street alone, summed up the intensity of being a mod, "They need to be able to afford a new fashion, often." See also: Carnaby Street, hair, mod, suits.

5:15 "...write another song that Jimmy heard the day he caught the train..."
Ocean Colour Scene, The Day We Caught the Train.
Composed by Pete Townshend whilst he was in between appointments around Oxford Street and Carnaby Street, recorded in June 1973 and released as single that September with a two-year-old unreleased track Water as its b-side [it made number twenty and stayed on the charts for six weeks]. Unusually, no demo of the song was made by Townshend prior to the track being recorded. The piano accompaniment heard on the track was played by Chris Stainton whilst the many remaining components such as Keith Moon's tumbling drumming and Roger Daltrey's howling vocals allow the song to synchronise beautifully with the train scene where Jimmy is on his way back to Brighton. Beginning as it does with a refrain from Cut My Hair, Pete's vocal is overrun by Roger's in a tale involving references to drugs, cross-dressing, isolation, harmony and love.
Listen out for the "m-m-m-my generation" stammer. Reissued and remixed with I'm One on its b-side it oddly failed to chart in Britain in 1979. The song appears on a number of compilation albums as well as on the Quadrophenia soundtrack including on My Generation: The Very Best of The Who, The Who Collection, Hooligans, The Blues to the Bush and on the Thirty Years of Maximum R&B video. The 2001 covers album Substitute – The Songs of The Who has a version of the song performed by American thrash metal band Phish. See also: Brighton,

Ocean Colour Scene, Sea and Sand.

Film Certification Upon its theatrical release Quadrophenia was awarded an 'X' certificate which meant that you had to be eighteen or over to see it. This proved problematic for Mark Wingett, aka Dave, who couldn't legally see his own performance in the film back in 1979! As well as the broad church 'U' certificate, there was then an 'A' category which allowed both children and adults, then the 'AA', which was a film that could only be viewed by fourteen year olds and above. Common in the late-seventies was for a main film to be supported by a lesser feature and in the case of the Mod tale, King Kenny ('A') was that secondary picture. The film was launched in Brighton on Thursday 18 October 1979. Back then, the latest films came out on a Thursday rather than the traditional Friday of today. For its 1997 re-release, Quadrophenia was '15'.

Flags What looks like a Danish flag is seen on the back of one of the scooters belonging to a member of the Brighton Ace Face's posse when we first see him come along Madeira Drive shortly after Jimmy's arrival. It is again seen flying opposite the Grand hotel where of course, the Ace Face works as a Bellboy. Resembling the red and white Dane flag, the Danneborg, or the very similar but differently coloured, Swedish one. In actuality, the flag represents the number four in the international code of signals, the maritime equivalent of Morse code. The Union Jack is prevalent on scooter designs in Quadrophenia, as well as being sported in various guises by male and female Mods in Brighton. Some have it on the back of parkas, and one even has a shirt made out of the pattern! The Who used it a lot at gigs, with Pete Townshend and John Entwistle both seen wearing a jacket made up of the flag [they also had others made to support appearances in Wales, Scotland and Ireland]. The Rockers in the film favour instead the Confederate flag of the American South more commonly recalled for

131

its place atop the Dukes of Hazzard's racing car in the Eighties tea-time show. See also: Union Jack.

Alan Fletcher Story Consultant on Quadrophenia next to Chris Stamp and Pete Townshend. Alan wrote the Corgi-published novelisation [with Pete Townshend receiving a special credit of thanks]. Now sadly out of print, one version of the paperback has an lurid air brushed scooter upon its cover. The paperback is illuminating in that it puts some flesh onto the bones of the sparse screenplay. An entertaining example is the mutual antagonistic relationship between the Cooper siblings, Jimmy and Yvonne. This is only glimpsed in a single scene at the beginning of the film when Jimmy asks to borrow a pair of scissors from her. Transposing details and chronology the novel is somewhat variable with the running of its scenes often different to the filmed ones. Alan has published three additional books symptomatic of the Mod psyche; Brummel's Last Riff, The Learning Curve and The Blue Millionaire. The first, a tale of a trio of sixties Mods and the second, with a modish inflection. You contact him c/o Chainline Publishing, 149 Hilton Road, Mapperley, Nottingham. Or pay a visit to the following site: modernist.com/modcrop/learning.html

Florida Rooms See: Brighton.

Michael Flynn Recruited to the Quadrophenia crew as Second Assistant Director. Michael has worked extensively with Stephen Frears on films including Gumshoe (1971), The Hit (1984), The Grifters (1990) and High Fidelity (2000). See also: George Innes, Andrew Sanders, Derek Suter, Christian Wrangler.

Folk Devils: see Stanley Cohn.

Food Mark Wingett [Dave] is memorable for his moment at the Beach Café in Brighton where he sets about devouring an oozing egg sarnie. Jimmy fairs less well in a scene at a London café where his enjoyment of pie and mash is spoilt first by the arrival of leather-clad Kevin [Ray Winstone] and then by the former's Mod acquaintances. The Quadrophenia album also has an appetising photo of a greasy meal in amongst its photos that accompanied its release [you can also see Jimmy in a window seat at a traditional Brighton seafood café].

A QUADROPHENIA ANTHOLOGY

Four Faces Along with Joker James and Get Out and Stay Out, this was the third new song added to the 1979 film reissuing of Quadrophenia. Significant in that the trio of songs were the first recorded with former Faces drummer Kenney Jones playing with Entwistle, Daltrey and Townshend after Keith Moon's death.

Stephen Frears An especially commendable British director born in Leicester in 1941. Stephen helmed Bloody Kids [made in 1979 but released in cinemas in 1980], which included early roles for the Quadrophenia faces Gary Holton, P.H Moriarty and Jesse Birdsall. Set in Southend, its story had a "head on energy leaving most contemporary offerings on the sate-of-the-nation looking distinctly lame." [Chris Peachment,Time Out]. Screenplays by Hanief Kureishi, Roddy Doyle and Stephen Poliakoff have each been given visual resonance from a creative persona whose career stretches back to the early-Seventies.

See also: George Innes, Andrew Sanders, Derek Suter, Christian Wrangler.

Fred Perry "Worn with feeling." [company advertising slogan, 2000]. Jimmy wears a white coloured short-sleeved sports shirt endorsed by the former British tennis player when going to the villain's pub to buy drugs for the planned Brighton beano. With its distinctive laurel wreath logo proving a constant favourite amongst Mods Jimmy can again be seen dressed in the same shirt at Alfredo's coffee bar and on his ill-advised visit to see Pete. Dave probably has one too although it is not entirely certain but when he has his red v-neck jumper on in Brighton the heavy collar to his buttoned-down top looks like it is a 'Fred'. Fellow Mod John is wearing a white one during the courtroom scene set in Brighton. When the Mod look died out, it continued to be a favourite amongst the skinhead [derived from hard Mods] of the late Sixties and even today. "Shirt by Fred, 'nuff said." As the skins used to spout. A 1990 BBC2 documentary Design Classics: the Fred Perry Shirt, two Who songs can be heard and there is some excellent footage of scooters and Mods.

Marvin Gaye A firm favourite amongst the British R&B groups of the early-Sixties, his soulful sound on tracks such as Let's Get it On, Sexual Healing and I Heard It through the Grapevine has meant that his records are still played nearly two decades since his death. Gaye played the Brighton Centre in 1980 as well as appearing on the Mod favourites', Ready, Steady, Go! in 1964 and 1965. Marvin's take of Baby Don't You Do It, a hit on the American chart in September 1964, can be heard on the jukebox at Alfredo's during the final group scene with Jimmy and the other Mods.The song, which The Who, Stevie Wonder and the Isley Brothers have all covered, is part of the Marvin Gaye 'Super Hits' album released in 1970. For a comprehensive account of his life read Trouble Man - The Life and Death of Marvin Gaye by Steve Turner [Penguin, 1999] otherwise visit www.sedgsoftware.com/marvin.

Gin "He only comes out when I drink my gin…" Jimmy's use of the beverage is mentioned on the Who track Dr Jimmy and we see him swigging it back with some amphetamines on the train platform at Waterloo station whilst waiting to make his return to Brighton. In the Quadrophenia album notes Gilbeys gin is name checked by Jimmy. See also: The Punk and The Godfather.

Girls There is a broadly held view that girls were secondary to boys in the Mod pecking order, and it has to be said that there is a lot of truth in this in particular in its early development. "The true Mod was," explains Jonathon Green, "above all [an] incestuously, narcissistically male environment." However, the primary difference between a Mod girl and a female Rocker presented itself in the beach scuffles of the early-Sixties; where the former waded in whilst the latter did not. Girls associated with the Rockers were less well-favoured, "Their girls looked like men in drag." Offers George Melly, " The Rockers were noisy too. There was nothing hip or cool about them." Girls liked The Who for their fashion ideas and it's probable that someone like Spider's girlfriend; with her closely cropped hair just flopping over the top of her ear, red leather jacket and pixiesque look would have too. Monkey sometimes looks awful, in a brown skirt and blouse, all dreary Fifties but the true mod girl looked clean, crisp and neat, somewhat boyish in appearance. Toyah's character has the right hairstyle but look at the ugly, v-striped and distinctly unflattering grey dress worn by her at the Brighton ballroom more Fifties than anything else. Mod fashion may have succeeded in blurring the line between male and female, you only have to look at the make-up that Jimmy and his friends regularly wear in the film, Steph on the other hand, may not dress absolutely Mod but she has the contemporary attitude alright, turning the tables on an emasculated Jimmy in her casualness about their relationship. She has a sexual confidence that represents itself through choice.

Girlfriends Joker James mentions some girls in Jimmy's life as does The Real Me and Sea and Sand.

Bobcat Goldthwaite An American comedy actor who adopted a screeching voice for his character seen in Police Academy II - IV. Is he one of the bikers, seen to Chalky's right, which causes him to crash his scooter whilst travelling down to Brighton? See also: John Hannah.

Goldhawk Social Club A popular Mod haunt along with the Flamingo, the Scene and Marquee [all in the West End area of London], the Station Hotel [Richmond] and the Norick in Tottenham, east London. Now called the Shepherd's Bush Club, 205 Goldhawk Road / Stamford Brook. Its reputation as a rough venue to play is confirmed by anyone that attended a gig there. The Who returned to play a one-off gig after the success of debut album My Generation, which saw an angered Pete Townshend destroy one of his guitars. It was an occurrence witnessed by Italian film director Antonioni who used its imagery in his film Blow Up. The original Quadrophenia album of 1973 was partly dedicated to 'The Kids of Goldhawk Road.' See also: Irish Jack Lyons.

Goofs It has to be pointed out that the following production errors are included purely as a part of this project for no other reason than objectivity. Still, there are quite a lot of them to be found if you look but few spoil the enjoyment of the film. However, they are broken down in to three sections, 1 Brighton, 2 Beachy Head and 3 London.

Brighton: 1.*"Look at that! That is Brighton, my son!"* Jimmy informs the mod posse that the coast below is Brighton, it is not: the scene belongs to Eastbourne. 2.A Motorhead t-shirt exhibited by one of the extras is said to have been visible during the seafront clashes between the Mods / Rockers / police. A mistake in that the metal group, led by Lemmy, was not formed until the 1970s and Quadrophenia is set in 1964. Still, Lemmy played guitar for The Rockin' Vicars in 1965 who released a Pete Townshend song titled It's Alright [later reworked into The Who's The Kids are Alright]. 3.Watch the scene where Jimmy, Steph and Dave come together with the mass of young Mods in on the Brighton seafront. A press photographer steps in front of them causing Gary Shail [Spider] to start the *'We are the Mods!'* chant and keep your eye on Mark Wingett on the left of the screen, as he walks along next to Daniels and Ash only to stumble and disappear from the sequence. You can hear him say 'Ow!' and the very next moment he has vanished off the edge of the promenade pavement and off camera! 4.See Dave [Mark Wingett] during the fighting scenes on the beach and observe the disappearance of his beloved pork pie hat whilst he's scraping only for it to return again in the next sequence. 5.The exterior display boards of the ABC cinema in East Street are seen when a girl cuts across the road and in front of the camera as the Mods march down towards the beach. Look closely and you will see Heaven Can Wait and Grease are both being presented at the cinema odd in that both films were released in 1978 not 1964. 6. Is there a mistake in continuity when Mark Wingett wears a red jumper on the Brighton promenade then disappear? 7. Evidently one of the parka-wearing Mods seen on the beach during the tumultuous moments of violence can be spotted with The Jam logo pasted on to his back. Regrettable in that this particular band was not formed until 1976. 8. Police officers viewed trying to control the youngsters on the beach and around Brighton's East Street, the pier and Aquarium areas are seen to be topped off with both black and white helmets, surely an error? Well no, dating back to the Thirties, Brighton officers would adopt white coloured helmets for the summer months. 9. A motley looking crew of parading air cadets [or are they sea cadets?] are seen to be sporadically clad in service-issue jumpers, a specifically Seventies adaptation as in the Sixties they would have been given battledress tunics to wear. 10. A very obscure one now, see how Steph's white heeled [stilleto] slip-on shoes change to heavier black/brown lace ups when she and Jimmy break away following Sting's smashing of a shop window on East Street. But by the time the two move towards the alleyway, her white shoes have returned.

Beachy Head: 11. Observer the windshield of the Ace Face's stolen Vespa as it vanishes and then re-appears as Jimmy makes himself ready for the cliff top denunciation towards the climax of the sequence. Pay particular attention as he heads towards the cliffedge. 12. Also at Beachy Head, the shadow of the helicopter, used so effectively in capturing the moment when Jimmy rides the scooter off the cliff edge, has its shadow revealed moments earlier. It can be glimpsed for a very distinctive split second after the scooter's exhaust is seen heavily smoking as it makes its way along the green carpeted cliffs. 13. Watch carefully during a long shot of Jimmy riding on the grass where two figures are clearly outlined in the distance. The camera cuts the angle to hide their positioning as the scene is cut with Jimmy zooming past what appears to be a white wooden marker point positioned close to the cliff edge. 14. Another question, after watching the film a few times doesn't it become obvious that it is not Phil Daniels riding the scooter along parts of the cliff top? See for example in the cut before the close-up of a bobbling head Daniels [filmed on the back of an adapted Citroen car rather than a scooter] where the chap riding the scooter clearly is not the actor we all know. 15. Finally, again during the final climactic sequence, why should there be track marks in front of Jimmy as he chugs along the cliff top if he had not been there before? Obviously from earlier takes in what is quite an extended scene with both long shots, over-head and close-ups for one extensive setting. Roddam has lamented the restricted budget resulted in the tracks not being artificially removed prior to the film being released.

London: 16. A red Mini with its V or W registration plate is glimpsed driving away from the camera just before Steph comes out of the supermarket to discover Jimmy sitting on his scooter waiting for her. 17. And again, glancing at the traffic as they drive along the busy road a number of vehicles can be observed, many of them newer models than circa 1964. 18. My Generation : The anthemic Who single was put out as a single in 1965 and not 1964; which is when Quadrophenia is set. However, its appropriateness outweighs any debate to its exclusion. 19. A Quick One/ The Who Sell Out compilation album of two separate Who long-players from 1966 and 1968 respectively, is none-too-subtly positioned on top of a record player at the house party. Watch how initially its cover is seen standing on its side but when Jimmy moves to put on My Generation it magically realigns itself in to an upright position and thus clearly readable. In real-time, it was not released until May 1974. 20. Whilst riding as a convoy on the coastal road towards Brighton, Jimmy brings his scooter to a halt and proclaims that the coast line below is Brighton but take a look at the stripped-down scooter behind him; would such a style be relevant for 1964 when the film is set? 21. During the scene where Chalky brings news that Spider and his girlfriend have been attacked by a mob of Rockers, one of the Mods, played by John Altman, is seen to dash off on a scooter only for the next scene to reveal him dancing along with the others inside the Goldhawk when we have just seen him leave. Thanks to John for pointing this one out to me. 22. Whilst in the projection box at the ad agency Jimmy clearly addresses Timothy Spall as 'Des' on three separate occasions however, when he motions to leave to catch up with his work errands, Jimmy calls him Harry! But isn't Patrick Murray's character called Harry? 23. In an early morning scene set in Jimmy's bedroom, the black and white portrait photograph of Pete Townshend re-appears upon the wall above his bed after vanishing from earlier scenes. 24. A train with Seventies rolling stock is seen passing over a bridge during the time Jimmy spends readying himself in his room on the morning of the Brighton weekender. 25. Observe Spider's tie as he and the other Mods screech at the young host in the doorway at the house party. Watch as Gary Shail's tie is undone an inch or so then miraculously moves back up again. Interestingly, both Jimmy and the Ace Face can be observed with their ties loosened just a touch in alternate scenes. 26. Whilst engrossed in Ready Steady Go! on the television The Who perform their single Anyway Anyhow Anywhere a 1965 release whilst the Manfred Mann record 5-4-3-2-1 playing over the opening titles was a hit in February '64.

G.P.O. Van *"All you fucking Mr Postman...Fuck Off!"*
Jimmy involved in an accident with a post van that destroys his scooter in a scene following his exhaustive confrontation with Steph. In fact, in Quadrophenia, most alternatives to scooter transportation prove to be hostile to the Mods i.e. the Triumph car that hits one of them as they dash across King's Road along the Brighton promenade; the Rockers use their bikes to force Chalky off the road and others that attack Spider following his scooter breaking down whilst on the way to the Goldhawk.

Grease The late 1970s phenomenon that made stars of John Travolta and Olivia Newton John is advertised as one of the four films presented at the ABC cinema in Brighton in scenes that are supposed to be in 1964. Watch as the camera passes along the East Street side [the cinema also had a seafront entrance] revealing the large spotlight lettering.

Greasers: see Rockers.

Gillian Gregory Wholly successful as the Choreographer on the film [just think of Jimmy chicken dancing during the Brighton ballroom scene] as well as for Tommy (1975). The cast was put through three weeks of dance class prior to filming. Gillian also worked on Privates on Parade in 1982, a movie with Mr Cooper Senior, Michael Elphick amongst its cast. See also: John Altman. Other work incls: Return of the Jedi (1983), Mahler (1974).

Greenwich Village The bohemian area of New York from which the longhaired American girl tries to tell Pete that she hails from when they get chatting at the ballroom. Come the end of the evening, she and Pete leave thus concluding the relationship between him and Steph.

Grooming *"Leave me hair alone will you Dave!"*
Mods were not at all averse to preening themselves in any available mirror and in Quadrophenia this trait is demonstrated by Jimmy and his mates in the pub toilet where Chalky is introduced to the story. Jimmy also has his own full-length mirror in his bedroom.

Guinness In the early 1960s some five million units were sold each day in the UK. Jimmy's dad enjoys a bottle or two of the dark stuff whilst the younger Cooper favours a Newcastle Brown Ale at the house party. Interesting in that as with the connotations of drinking either Pepsi or Coke each brand is perceived differently. The advertising of the product here has seen an attempt to appeal to all social classes over the years but clearly its working class association is evident. For an account of the psychology of the Guinness branding read The Guinness Book of Advertising by Brian Sibley [Guinness books, 1985]. See also: Coke, Newcastle Brown Ale, Pepsi.

Freddie Haayen A former m.d at Polydor Records responsible for signing The Who to the label. Now retired, Mr Haayen, a Dutch native, is name-dropped on the closing film credits as Freddie Haaven.

GUINNESS IS GOOD FOR YOU

Caroline Hagen One of the two Production Assistants for Quadrophenia; the other being Ken Tuohy. See also: Mark Wingett.

Hair *"Poofs wear lacquer, don't they!"* Jimmy's to his barber [filmed in Islington, London] on the day before the Brighton trip. *"I have lacquer!"* responds a deadpan Dan unaware of the irony. Many hairdressers advertised their ability to offer the latest Mod cuts demonstrated in 1964 by hairdresser Julian Maurice who told the Hairdressers' Journal, "All Mod styles have a common factor," they are round [high on top] and low [neckline an inch or so from the collar]." Looking at vintage Sixties photographs of The Who is a good way to source the various Mod cuts adopted by Keith Moon and Pete Townshend during their Mod dalliance. Pete was seen to have a straight fringe with hair covering half his ears, as was Moonie. In the film, Steph wears her hair heavy over the forehead and down to her shoulders whilst being very plainly made-up. Spider's un-named girlfriend has a fine Sixties look, all pixiesque and boyishly feminine. It is left to Monkey and her bottled blonde feather cut to uphold the Mod accuracy. Ray Winstone has since shuddred at his embarrassement of his 'Liberace' quiff seen in the film as Rocker Kevin.

Slim Harpo Born in Louisiana in 1924 as James Moore, he died in 1970 just as the popularity of this drawling vocalist with his trademark harmonica breaks was beginning to brighten once more. Known in his early career as Harmonica Slim, Harpo was a big star on the R&B stage. Check out The Best of Slim Harpo [1997] available on the Hip-O label. See also: The High Numbers, I'm The Face.

Hastings Jimmy has a copy of the newspaper article reporting the non-events at Hastings over the August bank holiday of 1964 titled 'On The Run.' No violence occurred, just lots of youngsters dashing back and forth chased by anxious police

140

officers. "The Mods and Rockers invade...but this time it's an 'itchy feet' invasion...The time, YESTERDAY. The place, HASTINGS. The tempo, QUICK, very QUICK." See also: Newspapers, Toyah.

Hats Playing an integral part in the features that make up Dave and Ferdy in Quadrophenia, they are the only youngsters to be seen wearing them in amongst the Mod group. However, such accessories were popular, as the following ads show, "Hats for Mods" – Fabulous for style, quality, comfort and value at 69/6." Advertisements in Sixties music papers offered the choice of mid blue, slate grey or donkey brown fashioned hats detailed as having "high crown and high ribbon". 'The Fab' was another style available for both sexes to wear at eighteen shillings or so. By the time of the Mod revival of the late Seventies, 'pork pie' hats were being sold in amongst the pages of the NME for £8.50. See also: Fashion, Trevor Laird, Mod, Suits, Mark Wingett.

Heaven Can Wait This 1978 remake starring Warren Beatty, a big star back then, can clearly be seen advertised outside the Brighton ABC cinema at the top end of East street during the Mods scuffles with police. Noteworthy only because Quadrophenia is, of course, supposed to be set in 1964/ 5! Not that it matters.

Helpless Dancer Roger's theme. A track included on the original Who album but not on the soundtrack release to the film in 1979.

High Heel Sneakers Covered by John Lee Hooker in a set that also featured Dimples and Boom Boom. This infectious little number was performed by Cross Section during an early scene in Quadrophenia set at the Goldhawk club. Alternate versions have been crooned by Bill Haley, Elvis, Adam Faith, Paul Weller/ Noel Gallagher and Waylon Jennings.

The High Numbers A reference to the t-shirts worn by many Mods that had numbers on them as a fashion. Before making their name as The Who, the High Numbers were rejected by EMI records but not before having recorded four tracks; I'm The Face / Zoot Suit / Leaving Here / Here 'Tis. Bootleg copies of other songs are available including a version of Green Onions, a true classic instrumental track recorded by Booker T and The MGs and heard in Quadrophenia at the Brighton ballroom. As the Numbers they played the local music scene highlighted with a Tuesday night show at the R&B Club, the Railway Hotel at Harrow and Wealdstone. The cost of admission was a princely 3/6. The High Numbers changed their name back to The Who by November 1964. I'm The Face / Zoot Suit was re-released in 1980 leading Who completists to push it to number 49 on the charts. Originally selling 500 copies, half being purchased by Mod maestro Pete Meaden and two by John Entwistle's grandmother. See also: Booker T and the MGs, I'm the Face, Pete Meaden, Zoot Suit.

Hire Purchase AKA "HP" Came in to its own in the early-sixties and made it simple for young Mods to obtain the latest scooters by way of a deposit and one to one-and-a half years monthly repayments. A new Vespa 90 cost a little over £114 in 1964 and could be attained by leaving a 25% deposit.

Holidaymakers At many seaside resorts involved in skirmishes between factioned youths and the police, both the latter and the media have reported on the phenomenon of people watching the confrontations with much relish. The Times commented of the Whit sun 1964 troubles at Margate, "Thousands more stayed on, hanging over the promenade railings, to watch pitched battles in which Mods were the undoubted aggressors."

Simon Holland Production Manager on Quadrophenia. He continued his workmanship on Scandal (1989), as did former Quad Location Manager Redmond Morris. Simon worked with Roger Daltrey on the TV film Magical Legend of the Leprechauns aired in 1999. Other work incls: The Emerald Forest (1985), Nuns on the Run (1990)

Buddy Holly Born in Texas in 1936 Buddy was a competent piano and guitar player when still a child. His influence on musicians was strong, being cemented by hits like Rave On, That'll Be the Day and Peggy Sue. Roger Daltrey would star in a film and telly series called Buddy's Song and Keith Moon acted in the 1970s film That'll Be The Day. A poster featuring the bespectacled singer can be spotted at Alfredo's cafe which Jimmy and his mates frequent. Holly had a hit album in the British charts in 1964 and his records continue to sell to this day. In

1978, a film biog titled The Buddy Holly Story was premiered. 
Gary Holton *"Which one are you?"* asks rocker Holton to Spider before doing him over outside the Bramley Arms pub, *"'Cos it's hard to tell with you lot..."*
A minute later he and Jesse Birdsall within a gang of a half-dozen others goad a reaction that ends violently. After flooring the lonesome mod and his helpless girlfriend, watch how Gary struggles with the sheer weight of his motorbike before finally speeding away. The wafer-thin actor and musician looks much the same in Quadrophenia as he does in the Franc Roddam devised Auf Wiedersehen, Pet telly series of the early-eighties.

Before finding fame in Pet, Holton was one of the lead cast members in Bloody Kids, "a manic study of urban anarchy [a low budget, British Warriors in other words]" according to the Guinness Book of Classic British TV. Both he, Ray Winstone and Kate Williams appeared in the same episode of eighties comedy drama classic Minder. Gary portrayed a punk guitarist in Breaking Glass that also cast Jimmy and Dave, Phil Daniels and Mark Wingett in major roles. In addition, he toured in stage musicals including one with Kiki Dee. As the libidinous Wayne in Auf Wiedersehen, Pet he appeared in two series along with Timothy Spall and Michael Elphick, memorable as the psychotic Magowan. Gary died during filming aged thirty-three in October 1985. See also: Bibliography, Jesse Birdsall, Chris Menges, PH Moriarty, Steven Poliakoff, Christian Wrangler.

John Lee Hooker His tracks Boom Boom and Dimples were each a considerable influence on the bands playing R&B in the early 1960s in amongst which was The High Numbers / The Who. The latter song, with its "bombs in the base and knives in the treble," as described by Charles Shaar Murray in his comprehensive biography Boogie Man – The Adventures of John Lee Hooker in the American Twentieth Century [Penguin, 1999] was a hit in 1956. John worked directly with Pete Townshend and the remaining members of The Who for the short-lived musical adaptation of The Iron Man in the mid-1980s. Hooker followed The Who and The Kinks by being inducted in to the Rock and Roll Hall of Fame. Album success continued in to the Nineties with Mr Lucky and Boom Boom charting in the UK. He passed away in June 2001.

See the website www.virginrecords.com/jlhooker.

See also: Dimples, Ready Steady Go!

Dave Humphries As one of three contributors to the Quad script Dave had previously completed the screenplay to a 1976 supernatural tale starring Mia Farrow called The Haunting of Julia. He also scripted the 1978 hit The Stud. Furthermore he was a member of the sound department on the following films; Sunday Pursuit (1990, Sound Mixer), A Casual Affair (1994, Subbing Mixer), Bright Hair (1997, DM) and Sound Recordist on Beautiful People, a 1999 film including Garry 'Pete' Cooper. Credited as David Humphries on some films.

Dewi Humphries Camera Op on the 1978 shoot of Quadrophenia.

I Am The Sea Known as the four themes representative of the members of The Who; Is It Me?, Bell Boy, Love Reign O'er Me and The Real Me. The rush of the sea and the moan of the instruments are swept away as the track plays at the start of the film where we find Jimmy on the cliff top at Beachy Head.

See also: The Real Me.

I'm One "And I can see that this is me..."

Pete Townshend's gentle, nasal voice feels very apt coming as is does after the house party scene, expressing Jimmy's developing sense of frustration. Heard when he sits on his scooter feeling blue besides the canal. Its sentiments express his strength of feeling that he upholds his Mod allegiance in spite of the uncertainties of everything else in his life. See also: Levi's, Mods.

I'm The Face "On their first outing, 4 hip young men from London say..."

Early High Numbers/ Who promoter Pete Meaden proclaimed the snappy track that's over in a little more than two minutes and twenty seconds as the first 'authentic' Mod single. Loosely based upon a debut solo recording by early R&B man Slim Harpo called I Got Love If You Want It of which he freely acknowledged, Fontana pressed a thousand copies of the single releasing it on 3 July 1964. Love was a favourite song to be covered by up-and-coming bands like

The Kinks and The Yardbirds who both recorded versions. I'm The King Bee, another Harpo song, was covered by the Rolling Stones on their first album released in 1964. An original red labelled seven inch single-sided acetate cut from the demo tape in 1964 when The Who were using the High Numbers name is valued at £150/ 160. Face appears as track nine on the 1974 Who compilation album Odds and Sods and is included as a part of the Who's Thirty Years of Maximum R&B box set. It never made the charts despite receiving valuable airtime to support its release. Townshend repeats some of its lyrics at the end of Sea and Sand on the original Who Quadrophenia album. See also: Slim Harpo, Pete Meaden, Zoot Suit.

Tom Ingram Played one of the Rockers contained within the policevan that Jimmy get's put into following the Brighton rioting. I think he is the John Hannah lookalike.

George Innes 'A charming bloke.' Franc Roddam. Portraying the nameless and slightly greasy moustachioed proprietor of Alfredo's Italian Espresso Cafe, George has been acting since the Sixties. Alfredo's is given a stamp of mod approval by way of the mass of scooters parked up outside. He tolerates the rowdy youngsters [Jimmy especially] because he takes a lot of cash from their custom mainly it would appear from the sale of bottles of Pepsi Cola at *"one and tuppence"* for two. His Buckaroo pinball machine is also a success with Jimmy and the others to. With tea towel over his shoulder and wearing a chequered shirt and severe period side parting, observe his glee in tallying up the day's takings in the seconds before Jimmy gives Dave a thrashing. Lamely banging on the window from within he does not choose to get involved in the scuffle erupting outside. At the beginning of this scene seeing Jimmy returning alone after being arrested in Brighton, Innes says to him, *"...you lose a shilling and find a sixpence?!"* A common saying prior to decimalization and clarified upon knowing that a shilling was the equivalent of five pence and a sixpence to 2.5 pence. Around the plainly attired cafe photos of Elvis can be seen behind the counter and a poster using Buddy Holly to advertise something or other is seen behind Steph and Jimmy. Holly was in the top ten of the album charts throughout the summer of 1964, the year in which the Quadrophenia film is set [although The 1973 Who album mentions 1963 in Bell Boy]. There was an actual Alfredo's Cafe on Essex road, Islington and a plaque above its main entrance states that it was established in 1920; it is now open again as the Sausage & Mash cafe. Meanwhile, away from playing the nameless cafe owner [could he be Alfredo's son?], George has acted with Oliver Pierre [the harassed tailor having to deal with the finicky Dan aka Daniel Peacock] and on Gumshoe (1971). Innes and Michael Elphick were jointly cast in The Odd Job (1978) and Ordeal By Innocence (1984). Born in 1938, he also appeared in Last Orders (2001, with Ray Winstone). CONTACT: c/o Spotlight.

Introduction to characters in the film :
1. Jimmy on the cliff tops at Beachy Head, 2. Ferdy outside Goldhawk, 3. Spider, Monkey, Dave and John at the Goldhawk along with Steph, Dan and Pete.4. Mr and Mrs Cooper and Jimmy's sister Yvonne at the family home. 5. Kevin at the public bathhouse, 6. Chalky and Dan in the toilets of a pub just prior to the Kitchener Road house party, 7. Fulford and fellow executive, Michael in the gents at the advertising agency where Jimmy works as a clerk. 8. Des and Harry in the projection booth at the ad agency, 9. The Brighton Ace Face, at Madeira Drive along the seafront. 10. Harry North at the unspecified villain's pub.

John Ireland Sound Engineer on Quadrophenia. With an extensive CV incorporating the James Bond thriller Tomorrow Never Dies (1997) and the Brit horror adventures of Pinhead in Hellraiser I & II, John has been in the film industry for almost thirty years. Other work incls: G.I Jane (1997).

Is it in My Head An old Who track, The Kids Are Alright, features at its start. Its opening and closing lyric of "I see a man without a problem" is adapted as the last line before the closing titles of the film, sung by Roger Daltrey after Jimmy's scooter flies over the cliff tops at Beachy Head. It is also heard when we see Jimmy riding in the back of a police van with the Brighton Ace Face.

I've Had Enough This six-minute Who song with its sound effects conclusion plays a major part in the story of Jimmy. Observe the front cover of the Who album and what do you see? Why a parka-wrapped Jimmy on his scooter with his back to the world. In fact, this is the song that finds him questioning the whole Mod edict, played so effectively during the climax of his struggle. On the 1973 album it does not have the line added to the version that appears on the 1979 soundtrack closing the film with Roger screeching,"You stop dancing." With its piano introduction pre-empting the incoming storm echoed by rumbling, crashing cymbals taking its energy to a crescendo of emotion only finding momentary relief in the gentleness of Daltrey's quest for love to reign forth. Interposing Roger and Pete, it comes across as two or three separate songs with detailed information relayed appertaining to Jim's mod lifestyle. In the film, Pete sings about the type of jacket and scooter worn by the young mod is delivered only once but in the song on the album, it is repeated twice. Released as a single in 1978 with Who Are You, in Italy and France, a 1980 issuing also appeared.

See also: Prokofiev.

The Jam Formed in Woking in early 1973 the band was a leader in the new wave Mod revival of the late-Seventies / early-Eighties. Often categorised under the punk or New Wave [think The Police or The Pretenders] banners of the mid-Seventies the Jam were more the latter whilst engaging in the punk ethos. A 1976 gig at 100 Club in London found the band's sound heavily influenced by Townshend's songs even to the extent of the press terming them "the new Who". On to 1977 and their album In The City shared its title with the Who song and The Jam reproduced a number of Who / Mod references throughout their career and continue to do so with its former lead singer, the "Mod father", Paul Weller. For example, the new band posed in front of Big Ben ALA My Generation wearing suits made from the Union Jack insignia whilst another photo places The Jam in the middle of Carnaby Street with the same collective uniformity of dress. Wearing their jackets next to the Houses of Parliament for a magazine cover shot in 1977, the one worn by drummer Rick Buckler recently came up for auction at Christies with an estimated sale price of £462. Their album All Mod Cons presents the results of a photo shoot at which Paul took to sticking two arrows [made from tape] emblazoned on to his jumper aping Roger Daltrey from two decades earlier. Drummer Buckler wore a Union Jack badge on his chest also. For In the City they took to adopting a totally Mod look in a black and white promo poster reading 'Most R&R Maximum RnB' in 1976. The band covered the So Sad About Us and Disguises from The Who back catalogue and their 1977 debut album has similar chord structures to early-Who stuff. The middle-eight of In The City is not dissimilar to the second half of Anyway Anyhow Anywhere. Melody wise, it is reminiscent to the second half of I'm A Boy. City also shares its title with a track that was co-written by Keith Moon and John Entwistle found on The Who's Direct Hits '68 album. Maintaining the Moon connection, the back cover of their single Down in the Tube Station at Midnight, has a photo of Keith Moon, with its b-side being So Sad About. Paul Weller had first discovered The Who back in 1974 after hearing My Generation on the soundtrack of Stardust, a film in which Keith Moon acts. With a highly-held reputation as a powerful live band The Jam set included version of So Sad About Us and Heatwave, the latter a favourite Who cover that is located on their A Quick One album and on Pete Townshend's demo collection Scoop. Similarly, the short and sweet Batman TV theme was a big favourite at Jam gigs as an encore number, and can be found on the album. That particular theme was also recorded by The Who and can be heard on their Ready Steady Who! EP. In their heyday, The Jam had the opportunity of supporting The Who on tour but turned it down. As a renewed interest in all things Mod, it was often through listening to The Jam that youngsters were turned on to The Who because Paul Weller mentioned the band. The Jam were more vociferous than many of their punk counterparts of the mid-Seventies and although the safety pin followers did not like the suit-wearing trio, the band attained massive commercial success well in to the early-Eighties when singer/ lyricist and eternal Mod, Weller split the band up. Scoring more than a dozen Top 40 hits, three in 1979 alone, Beat Surrender, their last group single, hit the top of the charts in December 1982 at which time they played final gig at the Brighton Centre [a pillar of which can be glimpsed by a departing Jimmy after nicking Sting's Vespa from outside the neighbouring Grand hotel].

Living up to the Modernist maxim, the songwriter then formed The Style Council with keyboardist Mick Talbot, himself a former member of Mod revivalists Merton Parkas enjoying fresh success. There exists an eerie photograph of a fresh, sleeked-back hair Weller walking past a group of young, be-suited Jam fans still sporting parkas. Disguises was the flip-side to their Funeral Pyre single and is included on The Jam's Extras album and on The Who covers tribute Substitute: The Songs of The Who. It has since come to light that the band was offered a spot in Quadrophenia but declined fue to not wanting to be typecast with the mod resurgence of the time. See also: Direction, Reaction, Creation (1997) box set, The Jam - Our Story, Bruce Foxton and Rick Buckler with Alex Ogg (Castle, 1993), Kit Lambert, Pete Townshend, Paul Weller.

Jewellery Jimmy can be seen throughout the film wearing a ring on the second finger of his right hand.

Glyn Johns Credited as the engineer and associate producer with The Who on Love Reign O'er Me and Is It In My Head? on the Quadrophenia album.

Jukebox As an American invention of the Twenties many were first imported in to Britain in 1955 and by 1957 around eight thousand were familiar features in coffee bars across the country. In Quadrophenia, Alfredo's has one that plays Baby Don't You Do It, Sweet Talkin' Guy and Night Train. An American record is only heard in the film when it is played on a juke box or at a café/ house party. Only The Who features as an enhancement to the theme of the film.

Kevin *"That's why I joined the army – to be different."*
Better known as 'Kev,' actor Ray Winstone puts in a decent performance as the straight-talking but not always logical motorbike enthusiast and old school friend of Jimmy Cooper. Appearing in only a few scenes the last time we see him is outside of Shepherd's Bush market before he takes a hammering from an unbeknownst Jimmy and his mates. See also: Aden, racism, Ray Winstone.

Kingsmen Louie Louie, their only UK hit in January 1964, is played during the ballroom sequences at Brighton. At one stage in their career, their one hour live set consisted entirely of variations upon this track. Of suspect content with a covert sexual nature, the Kinks and Motorhead have also covered it. Written by Richard Berry back in 1956, a U.S. governor called it 'pornographic' due to its debatable sexual connotation. A version by The Kingsmen, the one heard in the film, was released as a single on the Pye International label in 1963 as was Hi-Heel Sneakers by Tommy Tucker in 1964. Go to www.eskimo.com/~craigb/kingsmen.html.

The Kinks 'Everybody's acting a part.' Ray Davies, 1965.
Songwriters Ray Davies and Pete Townshend both attended art school prior to finding success with their own respective bands, The Kinks and The Who. Both have since been inducted into the prestigious Rock 'n' Roll Hall of Fame. The Kinks, like The Who, made their own concept album in the mid-Sixties, called Arthur, it sadly flopped. They would both, with differing success, share the skills of Who producer Shel Talmy, who had engineered the very first Kinks recording session in 1964. Beginning their career as the Ravens, the Kinks played with The Who when they were called the High Numbers. Gig-wise both were on the same 1964 show bill in Blackpool, when the former were top of the charts with You Really Got Me, coming after a memorable performance by the band on Ready Steady Go! It became a part of The Who's live repertoire shortly after. As with Anyway Anyhow Anywhere, Me was chosen to be the sound heard opening the show as had been awarded to Manfred Mann. Set in 1965, Jimmy sings to the song twice in the film, firstly in competing with Kevin at the public baths and secondly, in the mailroom at the advertising agency. The track was re-released in the Eighties in a special target picture disc. The Who's early single I Can't Explain was directly inspired by the Kinks hit which in turn it can be said has echoes of Louie Louie. Again, Me and My Generation have kind of matching guitar riffs. Their first single, a cover of Long Tall Sally, is coincidentally the name of a clothing store in East Street, next to the alleyway that leads to where Jimmy and Steph consummate their relationship. In his autobiography, Kink, guitarist Dave Davies remembers them as a serious bunch of fellas all that is, apart from Mr Moon.

Notably, The Kinks feature in the excellent collection of groovy shots collected by snapper Jan Olofsson in his book My Sixties. Kinks member Pete Quaife can be met sitting on his ornamented Lambretta scooter bedecked in a parka, roll neck sweater and baseball boots in an evocative collection of images. See also: Bibliography, Ready Steady Go!, You Really Got Me.

Kitchener Road The location for the house party visited by Jimmy and his mates early on in the film. More than a half-dozen locations sharing the same name are recorded in the London A – Z guide. However, an actual house in Clarendon road near Lee International studios, Wembley was used for filming. All the night interiors were shot there, causing a number of lighting problems but it looks good on screen.

Trevor Laird *"How much do you want?!"*
Cast as Ferdy, a man who keeps all that he values under his hat, Trevor was twenty at the time of casting. Fashion-wise, he is impeccable in his dark suits and customary pork pie hat and upon occasions is seen to wear black, wrap-around shades. This trait is echoed by Jimmy in that they each use them for reasons other than practical; Ferdy during the evening arrival at the house party whilst Jim sports his at Alfredo's and at a local dance club. To be found wherever the young Mods are, be it dance clubs, cafes or down in Brighton, any degree of character progression is not forthcoming. Aside from his dealings with Jimmy his role is functional in keeping everyone going by providing the necessary special vitamins. The film premise of Quadrophenia is set in 1964 but the look adopted by Ferdy is akin with the Jamaican Rude Boy [or 'Ruddies']: sharp and cool. This look came back in to fashion in the late-Seventies popularised by The Specials and The Selecter, bands that were a part of the Two-Tone/ Ska beat of that period. A second of three known examples of racism rears its ugly head in the idiocy of Chalky in the course of their visit to Ferdy's neighbourhood, the third elsewhere in the nastier tones of Pete. Writing in Sight and Sound [Feb 1997] Jon

Savage raises a strong discourse, "As the true retardation of Jimmy's friends is slowly revealed, with their casual sexism, homophobia and racism, you're so in the seventies that you think, well why doesn't somebody challenge them? And then you remember that Oh, we're supposed to be in the mid-Sixties - before all these pesky-isms had invaded youth-cult discourse." Ferdy features in many of the group sequences and can be spotted as the camera lingers over the exhausted and deflated mod faces on Brighton's East Street. A scene set up by the director somewhat covertly attempted to catch the actors/ extras unawares but Laird realised the camera was on and watch his method-like, 'fuck you' shrug. The last time that he is seen follows the tumultuous dénouement reigned over Jimmy's mates by a maniacal Phil Daniels both inside and out of Alfredo's coffee bar.

As an actor Trevor has performed elsewhere with some of the Quadrophenia co-stars in Secrets and Lies (1996, with Timothy Spall and Phil Davis), Billy the Kid and The Green Baize Vampire (1985, with Phil Daniels), The Long Good Friday (1979, with PH Moriarty and Oliver Pierre) and Love, Honour & Obey (2000, with did Ray Winstone). Babylon (1980) written by Quad scripter Martin Stellman numbered crew members Ken Wheatley and Ray Corbett behind the scenes. Laird played in a 1986 episode of Doctor Who and guessed on Mark Wingett's This is Your Life in April 2000. Billed as Trevor Laird in Quadrophenia he is now goes by the name Trevor H.Laird. Trivia fans might like to know that he and Phil Daniels are best-mates off-screen and share a love for Chelsea F.C.

See also: Alan Clarke, Phil Daniels, drugs, fashion, Lee Lighting Ltd., racism.
CONTACT: Hamper-Neafsey Associates Ltd, 4 Great Queen St., London

Christopher 'Kit' Lambert The Who: Maximum R&B.
After stumbling across the band whilst under their brief High Numbers banner, Lambert devised the above declaration splashed across posters promoting Who gigs. Accompanied with a striking black and white image of a guitar strumming Townshend the image was devised by Brian Pike with creative input from Pete Townshend and others. The impact of the logo [still used by the band] with its thrusting arrowhead above its

lowercase 'o' accompanied by the first two letters linking with the second 'h', its initial visual impact around the centre of London and surrounding locations was immediate. Kit had already been intrigued by the throng of scooters parked outside that 1964 gig at a club venue within the Railway Hotel, Harrow, and he was suitably impressed by what he saw both on stage coupled with the reaction of the energised audience. That gig accommodated an audience numbering seven hundred in a venue that had an official capacity of 180! Born in May 1935 Kit met his future Who managerial partner Chris Stamp whilst both men worked at the BBC in advance of freelancing on various projects. With the support of Mike Shaw, a school friend of Stamp's, and future musical co-ordinator on the Quadrophenia film, their alliance with the Who was initiated with Lambert and Stamp taking over the management of the former High Numbers. It was Lambert who shot the b/w film of Mods and scooters used for the Who video clip for their single I Can't Explain. Perceived as an unusual partnership, the skinny, desert boot wearing Stamp standing much taller than the heavy foreheaded Lambert [think Bob Newhart mixed with Stephen Fry and you'll be about right] worked hard to bring success. Kit would have a profound effect upon the iridescent Townshend, being looked upon as a mentor to the eager teenager, always enthusing and encouraging. Provocative media sound bytes advocating the vitality of the ephemeral Pop Art movement, to which the Who were drawn, would all be incited by Lambert through Townshend. "It's representing something the public is familiar with, in a different form." Pete explained in a 1965 Melody Maker interview with Nick Jones. Success for the band blossomed, sealed by an unprecedented Tuesday night stint at the Marquee club in London [with admission at 5 shillings]. Meanwhile Kit concentrated on attempting to crack the European market whilst Stamp's focus was on breaking the band in America, a wholly more elusive task. Lambert and Stamp originated their own record label, Tracks, releasing thirteen Who singles over a six-year period from April 1967 [with Pictures of Lily] to October 1973 with the stunning 5:15 from Quadrophenia. Not only engaged in a managerial capacity, Lambert also produced some of the Who records before creative differences fuelled by his lack of technical proficiency, led to Pete Townshend controlling most of the duties thereon in. All professional associations between the band and Kit Lambert was dissolved in 1973, however, the day-to-day management of the Who had long since passed to others within the fold. For a salacious insight in to the decadent life of Lambert read You Don't Have to Say You Love Me [Ebury Press, 1999], the autobiography of former Yardbirds manager Simon Napier-Bell. First published in 1982, and reprinted in 1999, Napier-Bell recounts the endurance that life on the road with the Who demanded. Simon was the-then manager of a support band and the title of his book relates to his co-writing of the Dusty Springfield of the same name. Alternatively, see The Lamberts: George, Constant and Kit by Andrew Motion [Chatto and Windus, 1986]. A photograph of Kit with Keith Moon is included in Tony Fletcher's excellent Dear Boy biography of the latter. Elsewhere, A Decade of The Who also contains a picture or two of Mr Lambert. Kit passed away in 1981. See also: Bibliography, Bill Curbishley, Keith Moon, Pete Townshend.

'Cy' Langton In a film such as Quadrophenia, where music plays an integral part, he was the remixing engineer. His working relationship with the Who is substantial; combining with Roger Daltrey on McVicar and on Roger's Martyrs and Madmen compilation album in 1997. In addition, independently of the group, Cy engineered and played guitar on the John Entwistle Anthology album released in 1996. As well as which he was the Sound Editor on The Kids Are Alright (1978) documentary. Cy formulated his association with the band when becoming their first full-time roadie back in their formative years followed by producing and engineering a 1982 flexi disc version of My Generation for Richard Barnes' Maximum R&B Who book.

Leather Jackets A favoured item by many a biker and seen in Quadrophenia to a great extent. It's interesting that the leather jacket, like blue jeans, has been used as a symbol of rebellion in popular culture for some time. Wrapped around the punks during the 1970s, seen in left field film Easy Rider, Brando in The Wild One, box office sensation Grease and even on sanitised American TV show Happy Days, the cult has also journeyed to the celluloid future of Terminator and the Mad Max pictures too. Kev [Ray Winstone] shocks his old friend Jimmy by his reappearance in leathers. Equally a favoured item by the more Modly characters; Steph and the Brighton Ace Face both wear three-quarter length leather coats, as does Pete. Check out The Leather Boys (1963) for an interesting account of the early 'ton-up' boys and their love for speed, leather and coffee at the famous Ace Café in London. See also: Hamlyn 20th Century Style - The Leather Jacket [Hamlyn Publishing, 1997] or The Black Leather Jacket by Mick Farren [Abbeville Press, 1985].

Lee International Studios Co-owned by The Who these Wembley-based film studios were used to shoot many interior shots for Quadrophenia. It was also utilised for Tommy in the early Seventies.

Lee Lighting Limited A company with extensive experience in the film and TV industry furnished the Quad shoot with grip and lighting equipment. LLL also worked on Babylon, a film with major mod connections as has been detailed. See also: Trevor Laird

Mike Leigh British filmmaker given to heavy improvisation workshops prior to a completed script being developed with actors cast in his projects. Phil Daniels, Gary Oldman and Tim Roth acted together in the Leigh film Meantime (1983). Oldman and Roth have both since directed their own features each having Ray Winstone in a leading role. Fellow Quadrophenia actors directed by Mike Leigh include Trevor Laird and Timothy Spall. The excellent but terribly underused Phil 'Chalky' Davis acts in his High Hopes (1988) and has a cameo in Secrets and Lies and in Vera Drake. Peter Brayham, the Stunt Arranger on Q, was called upon for Life is Sweet (1990); a story featuring David Thewliss, an actor whom played in an episode of Only Fools and Horses alongside Daniel Peacock. Fools as it turned out, gave Patrick Murray a stock character part as Mickey. See also: Patrick Murray, Daniel Peacock, Timothy Spall.

Levi and [Blue] Jeans *"They're Levi's you gotta shrink 'em on you."*
Jimmy's explanation to his father about his new 501's jeans.
Name checked within the lyrics of I'm One, Dr Jimmy and The Punk And The Godfather Who tracks they were given a special credit at the end of Quadrophenia as 'jeans by Levi'. Adroit advertising tactics has made them known as the original and definitive jeans. Dave [Mark Wingett] wears them as does Jimmy and many of the rucking youngsters during the rioting scenes in

Brighton. Jimmy also takes the piss out of his work colleague played by Timothy Spall about the uncertainty of larger sizes being available. Patented in 1873 by Levi Strauss, a Bavarian immigrant, with material originally intended to be used for tents and baggage during the California gold rush. However, it was suggested to Strauss that what was really needed by the workers was clothing and hence he adapted the use of the material into work wear. In the late-Fifties and in to the next decade, finding Levi jeans was a hard task and once located, they were expensive: around 42/6d. Worn with a one-inch turn-up so that the inner seam just showed through they were later adopted by hard Mods and then Skinheads of the late-Sixties. Seen as symbol of rebellion in American movies think James Dean in Rebel Without a Cause or Brando in The Wild One or Thelma and Louise etc. Jimmy name checks them in the Who album notes. By 1979 more than thirty brands of designer label jeans were all available in the UK. Versace, Calvin Klein, Chanel, and Vivienne Westwood all vying for a stake for some of the 55m jeans sold pa [by the Nineties]. A dynamic, stage-set photo of a guitar-wielding Pete Townshend was used to promote the brand in an American ad campaign in the Eighties supported by a copy line of 'Quality never goes out of fashion.' Dressed in black DMs and blue denim, the ad covered an entire side of a skyscraper. Many of the youngsters in the film both Mods and Rockers, can be seen wearing jeans. Handy to wear whilst riding your scooter I'm not so sure that Mods would choose to wear them today - far too mainstream. Elsewhere, the Rolling Stones album cover of Sticky Fingers (1971) by Andy Warhol shows a close-up of a male crotch, and the brand was heavily utilised by Bruce Springsteen, see his Born in the USA album cover as an example. Website address: www.eu.levi.com. See also: Vintage Denim by David Little, photographs by Larry Bond [Gibby Smith, 1996], Hamlyn 20th Century Style - Blue Jeans [Hamlyn Publishing, 1999] or Blue Jeans, [Channel 4,1995].

Hugh Lloyd The veteran small screen comedy actor, pictured opposite, is Mr Cale, Jimmy's immediate boss at the ad agency. Cale may have risen to office manager status but the sensitivity shining through his eyes betrays the fact that he was once like Jimmy, only a long, long time ago. He gazes forlornly in remembrance of the sheer enjoyment of being young and having money in your pocket whilst giving Jimmy and a co-worker their weekly pay packets. Cale attempts to conciliate the antagonism between Fulford the agency manager [played by Benjamin Whitrow] and Jimmy by warning the younger on his nonchalance to his daily duties. This is a poignant role for Hugh especially upon seeing him watching the youngsters disappear off for their weekend adventures all the while leaving him with his lament for the past burning forth through his hollow eyes. Part of a troupe of character actors in the Tony Hancock comedy shows of the late Fifties and early Sixties [others included Sid James and Kenneth Williams], Lloyd is most readily remembered for his part in The Blood Donor episode. He signs-off his screen time by pocketing the laconic Hancock's wine gums during the lad's pompous pontification. Hugh Lloyd can be spotted in an episode of the Michael Elphick series Boon and likewise, in the Leslie Ash telly drama CATS Eyes. Fellow Quadrophenia actor Timothy Spall can be seen in conjunction with Hugh in The Clandestine Marriage. The author contacted him in relation to Quadrophenia but such was his elongated career that the actor had no recollection of the project! Try to find a copy of his autobiography, if you can (no real mention of Quad though but still an entertaining read).)Mr Lloyd was awarded an M.B.E in the New Year Honour's list 2005 and died in recent years.

Locations [in no particular order] : Bramley Arms,[found by getting off the tube at Ladbroke Grove [the Hammersmith & City line], London; Southgate, London [night club]; Lewes Magistrate's for the Brighton court scene; Wells Home road, Acton for Cooper house, public baths in Portchester, west London, barbershop in Islington, chemist on King's road, Hammersmith; Shepherd's Bush, Alfredo's Cafe, Essex Road, Islington; Brighton, Eastbourne [for the Brighton Coast shot], Barnet night-club used for the Brighton ballroom [although the Royalty ballroom in Southgate, north London has also been muted; Lee International in Wembley, London, used for interior shooting.

London Goldhawk Building Society "Cultivates your Interest" [Advertising slogan]. Glimpsed on the railway bridge under which Jimmy and Steph pass

157

whilst the former takes the latter home, is a sign advertising this particular organisation. That scene was shot in the Shepherd's Bush area of London. Research would point to the society no exists as such today.

Love Reign O'er Me. Pete's Theme.

The more times that you watch Quadrophenia the more fitting the music seems; this is a song that really cannot be anywhere else than with Jimmy on the cliffs at Beachy Head. It is a scene that succeeds perfectly well without its inclusion in fact; some feel that the moment where the scooter shoots over the cliff edge and crashes on the jagged rocks below is spoilt by the volume of the track.

Similar in meaning to Drowned on the Quadrophenia album, its theme addresses Mehebar Baba's idea that rain and thunder are blessings from god. So as to immerse one's self in god.

Its striking chorus is included on I've Had Enough sealed with Daltrey's perfect vocalisation. Laid down in June 1973, this pleading, vulnerable and energised track was one of the four songs played by The Who at the Live Aid concert in 1984. Just listen to how Moon's drum rolling technique stretches on until the guitar pulls it back in. With Water as its b-side it made number seventy-six in America(MCA/ Track) in 1973. In Thailand, Love was released as a single accompanied with a trio of other artists. Included on Who's Greatest Hits [see Union Jack] Released as an edited single for America, with Water as its b-side. A 45-rpm for the Belgian and Dutch markets exists with its b-side consisting of Is It In My Head? Check out Scoop, a collection of Townshend demos to find another version of the song.

L.S Lowry A print of one of his 'matchstick' people paintings is seen in the lounge of the house party on the wall above where we see Monkey snogging Jimmy. Lowry's work focused on the industrialised North of England, littered with images of smoking chimneys, ant-like people and factories. Art purveyors contest the merits of his importance as an artist but he most certainly made a valid contribution as social commentary. One of the appealing aspects of his work is simply that there is a great deal to discover and re-discover in the detailing i.e. whilst people are captured dashing from here to there some faces can be seen looking out of the painting.

Derek Lyons Remembered for a recurring character role in The Bill and many other uncredited film and television appearances, Derek can be seen in Quad as one of the Mods.

"Irish" Jack Lyons Known as an original Goldhawk Mod and part of Townshend's inspiration for Jimmy Cooper, Lyons has published his own reminiscence of his Who connections used in the excellent The Who Concert Files, co-written with Joe McMichael [Omnibus Press, 1999]. Visit his website at thewho.net/irishjack/ to view pictures of Jack at the Who's 1996 Hyde Park concert and with his semi-fictional counterpart Phil Daniels at their July 1996 Madison Square Garden gig and to read one of his many stories. His 'Irish' prefix was given to him by Who manager Kit Lambert.

Lyons Maid Logo seen for this popular brand of ice cream seen at the East street café attacked by the Mods.

Manfred Mann Their catchy 5-4-3-2-1 single was selected to be the theme to seminal Sixties Mod pop show Ready Steady Go! It's opening bars are heard by Jimmy on the television in the lounge whilst he chat's with his dad in the kitchen. It peaked at number five in the hit parade of January 1964. As a live band the Manfred's were backed by a group called the Detours at one point. Pretty Flamingo and the Bob Dylan-penned Mighty Quinn were put out as singles, three of which hit the top spot and a further trio all got in to the Top Ten. See also: Anyway Anyhow Anywhere, goofs, The Kinks, Ready Steady Go!

Margate "...the dregs of these vermin who infested the town..."
A Margate Magistrate commenting on the second day of court hearings to deal with the aftermath of the skirmishes between youths and the police. Chalky talks about Margate in a scene set in a pub. Along with Bournemouth and Brighton, the resort saw trouble between Mods and Rockers during Whit sun 1964 following on from Clacton. Coming as it did with thirty-six arrests, the resort made the front page of the Daily Express with the infamous diatribe from local Magistrate Dr G Simpson. John Phillips gives pretty much all of the speech during the Brighton courtroom scene in Quadrophenia with Jimmy and the Ace Face [actually filmed at nearby Lewes Magistrate's courts]. It was at Margate that an impudent teenager called James Brunton asked if he could pay by his

fine by way of cheque even though he had no bank account! Again, as with the Simpson soliloquy, Brunton's quip was realigned, in this case, to the Ace Face (played perfectly by Sting).

Marquee Club In origin, it was a ballroom that turned to playing traditional jazz and later the blues. Chris Stamp persuaded club boss and trad jazz musician, Chris Barber, to let The Who perform there with a Tuesday evening having proven to be a quiet time for business. Their first performance was not well attended but still the elongated booking was maintained. The band were resident from November 1964 for some sixteen weeks, playing every Tuesday night and eventually becoming more of a hit than previous big-time performers Manfred Mann and The Yardbirds. By 1965 the Marquee was the leading venue for live music in London virtually seven nights a week with occasional Saturday afternoon sounds too. The Who would be seen wearing different outfits each week for their twice-nightly gigs. The Marquee, like many music venues of the period, was not licensed to sell alcohol. Their Live at Leeds album from Track (1970) had two versions of artwork, one featuring a back cover shot of the cub and the other of Leeds. The Who used the studio facilities of the Marquee whilst laying down the elements that would morph in to My Generation. An album titled Live at the Marquee features The Who. See also: David Bowie, Brighton, Goldhawk club.

Mascara Amongst the Mod mates it is Jimmy and Spider whom seem to be the most prevalent in adopting a little. Jimmy also uses eyeliner, at the house party for example, most significantly seen when a female passenger opens the unlocked door to the toilet where he is revealed in the midst of applying some on the train back down to Brighton.

Masturbation Jimmy pleasures himself using the photos of the model which he was meant to deliver elsewhere in the ad agency. Also, The Who single Pictures of Lily was about such a subject with the idea for the song arriving from the swapping of saucy postcards between schoolboys Entwistle and Townshend.

Peter McNamara Television-based actor usually in an aggressive and/ or hostile role. Peter can be glimpsed squirming away in a tight collar and tie at the house party. Watch how he swears at someone off screen whilst standing stiffly in the packed lounge.

Pete McCarthy [Pictured opposite]. Pete was a well-known travel presenter/ writer and Brighton resident who can be seen goading the police at the front of the crowd on the beach. Dressed in a blue suit, at the time of filming he was going to be cast as a Rocker extra but was told to shave his beard off and play one of the Mods instead. It was to be during the tempestuous sea front moments that Pete accidentally knocked Leslie Ash over and was heavily chastised by Franc Roddam for doing so! Sadly no longer with us.

Pete Meaden "He actually made us very conscious of the audience, and aware of the idea of reflecting their feelings." Pete Townshend.

Such an acknowledgement is apt and its significance is noted due to the role Meaden played in the early chapters of the High Numbers, the band that went on to become The Who. As a freelance publicist Pete had worked for the Rolling Stones, Chuck Berry and Bob Dylan prior to being engaged to do the same for the Numbers by their first manager Helmut Gorden.

He was a Shepherd's Bush businessman who was persuaded by Meaden to change the band's name to the High Numbers, "Four hip young men from London, who say I'm The Face and wear Zoot Suits." as the publicity blurb read. Not surprisingly, it was written by Meaden with the single being promoted as the first authentic mod record. An interview given towards the end of his life included in The Sharpest Word - A Mod Anthology paints a picture of an intriguing man. He regales the mod ethos of its formative years as being a distinctly male domain, a 'society unto itself.' By linking the band indelibly to the burgeoning Mod audience the High Numbers were used to bring his own purist mod packaging to fruition. Let Pete Townshend elaborate further from Rock Docs - Second House: The Who [BBC, 1993], "What elevates you, also elevates them [the audience] so you become like a barometer." Such was the man's belief that when Kit Lambert visited the Railway Hotel for that infamous gig, Meaden thought that the well-dressed stranger was there to book them for a future gig. Little realising the significance of his own words would lead to his control of the band being displaced. Lambert and Stamp bought off his share in the group for a little under £500 [contract had proved invalid because the boys had been under-age when signing]. However, it was Pete Meaden who gave them their first taste of a recording studio furnishing them with two tracks, I'm the Face and Zoot Suit, both derivative of earlier records by Slim Harpo and The Showmen.

As a single, it was put out on the Fontana label in July 1964 after recording had finished in June. Despite the necessary airplay being obtained it failed to trouble the charts. Ironically, it was a success as a re-issued picture disc in 1980; two years after Meaden's death in August 1978. The collectibility vale for the Fontana 45 is now set at £350, whilst a stickered demo is worth in the region of £400 or £300, without the sticker. In addition, the 1980 reissue, which made number forty-nine on the charts, is of considerable less worth, priced at £10. Fittingly, the catchy Zoot Suit was used in the Quadrophenia film over a scene in Jimmy's bedroom. It is also found on the Polydor album of the soundtrack having first seen the light of day on the compilation album Odds and Sods. A final twist of the knife embedded itself in the midst of Pete's curiosity to see his old mates play a gig at the Florida Rooms at the Brighton Aquarium. Unfortunately, due to the prospering success of The Who, he was unable to get in. Such is the brusque nature of show business.

A final affirmation echoing the Meaden philosophy comes from Paul Weller, "For me Mod will never go out of fashion, and I think there will always be people who understand that and get what they want from it." resounds the ex-Jam man in Paul Weller - In His Own Words. "To me [being a Mod] is like a religion - it's like my code. It gives something to my life. I'm still a mod, I'll always be a mod, you can bury me a mod." An immensely curious figure, Meaden rejoined the Who fold in 1975 when he formed a record label with Roger Daltrey, suitably titled Goldhawk. In addition to which, he co-managed a band with Bill Curbishley on Track Records around the same period. He disappeared thereafter amongst mental ill health and prolonged drug abuse, and was finally tracked down by journalist Steve Turner for the already mentioned Mod anthology publication. Pete Meaden passed away three weeks before Keith Moon in 1978. See also: Bibliography, Kit Lambert, Mod, Chris Stamp, Paul Weller.

Media: See Newspapers.
Chris Menges A brief mention of this cinematographer turned director, for his work with Gary Holton, P.H Moriarty, Daniel Peacock and Jesse Birdsall on Bloody Kids. Christian Wrangler and George Innes were both part of the cast/crew on Gumshoe(1971; directed by Bloody Kids helmer Stephen Frears).
Mental Illness "Is it me, for a moment?" I Am the Sea.
See also: Four Faces, schizophrenia.
The Merseybeats Their version of the Bacharach and David written Wishin' and Hopin' is overhead at a record store where Jimmy enjoys looking at the photographs of the model and hearing The Who whilst in one of the listening booths. Their take reached number thirteen on the charts in July 1964, a strong year for the group with three singles and two albums released rounded off by a gig at the Florida Rooms in Brighton that November. Originally starting life in the early Sixties as The Mavericks they were briefly managed by Beatles maestro Brian Epstein on the Fontana record label. Who man Kit Lambert took the reigns in the mid-Sixties resulting in a couple of hit singles. Most of the original group still tour today after getting back together in the Nineties. See their promotional website at http://website.lineone.net/~the_merseybeats/
See also: David Bowie, Brighton's Florida Room
Midnight Blues Club: See Grand Hotel.
Mod "An aphorism for clean living under difficult circumstances." Pete Meaden. Concerned with the individual within the context of a collective, the Mod was quite often influenced from the general neatness of their parents but where the Mod kids differed was in the extent of the details. Self-expression was made possible within a clique but equally important was the approval from others. Quadrophenia finds Pete Townshend writing one last time from the premise of a teenager, on this occasion, Jimmy the Mod. Being a Mod was all about the perception of being: *"That's something, isn't it?"* pleads Jimmy to Steph during their last muted meeting.
1. The Who connection "Wherever you looked there were Mods. Some were so well dressed it was sickening." The Who's Quadrophenia booklet given away with the album.

"Townshend was never a real Mod, but he was a middle-class voyeur close enough to the phenomenon to hide the difference." The Beat Goes On book. Never slow on the uptake, Townshend knew what made the Mods tick, saying that The Who "caters for aggression" which the young male audience related to. Pete Meaden had already attempted to use the band as a focal point for a Mod audience. The Scene club in London's West End was where the authenticity of The Who, then known as The High Numbers, was vetted amongst the hardcore Mods that frequented the place. "They weren't exactly Mods but Mods liked them." Jimmy, Quadrophenia album notes.

2. The Quadrophenia connection In the film, Jimmy wears a three-buttoned jacket with the top button left un-done in a typical Mod trait.

Definition of Mod Waves/ strands

"The Number, The Face, the Ticket, or to use the generalisation, the Mod, is a product of this day and age." Pete Meaden, publicity blurb for The High Numbers. There definitely seems to be a confusion or contradiction as to when specific waves started and ended so the following is an informed guide only: Replacing the Beatnik the first Mods were into existentialism, John Lee Hooker, Modern Jazz, Sartre, American Soul and were users of amphetamines. With a love for R&B [and later, The Kinks, The Moody Blues, The Small Faces, The Animals and Ska] c.1960 or 1958 to 1961, they were known as 'individual stylists' or 'purists' that was not picked up upon by the media of that period at all. Often affluent Jewish middle class youths with money to spend on clothes, they did so with relish. Ephemeral. Originating in London prior to spreading and transforming itself in to a collective, herd-like mode. Interested in all things Continental - French movies, haircuts, suits, frothy coffee and so on, there was a link with homosexuality. Author Kenneth Leach defined the authentic Mod as a 'homosexual phenomenon.' Not only that, the Mods, Jimmy and the others all wear make up and are shown to constantly preen themselves without fear of embarrassment. Writing in England is Mine, make a broader acknowledgement, "...combining a bisexual mixture of extreme violence and extreme sensitivity...mod, was both a reaction against adolescent [even teenage] conformity and a belief that pop could be a spiritual quest..." A resurgence came

about in the Glam Rock days of the early-Seventies.
Second wave - 1961 to 1963
"To be a Mod was a way of living – full stop." John Marsh, interviewed in All Dressed Up. You simply cannot have an elitist mass movement and therefore, by 1962 Mod such as it was, was consumed in to Modernism with all the strands coming together by 1962. This early period differed from 1964 when Mod became a broader media term for teen-aged fashion. The second wave according to author and musician George Melly was in 1963 with 1964 marking a period when the souring of Mod purity becomes known. "Inside the mind of a Mod" was a Daily Mirror article from May 1964 which had agony aunt Marjorie Proops interviewing a Mod girl in an attempt to gain a better understanding of like-minded youngsters that were very much in the news thanks to the recent happenings at Margate and Brighton. The majority of those arrested for alleged involvement in the Brighton troubles were boys with all but one being male. A fifteen-year-old girl, clad in a pillar box red cardigan and white shirt, she was arrested for her part in the scuffles following her role in throwing stones as police officers. The young lady was remanded on probation and for subsequent school reports. An additional thirty-five youths were arrested and presented at special Magistrates' courts on the Monday after the weekend disturbances.

1963 to 1966
Mainstream look including suits/ pointed shoes/ parkas/ jeans, with girl's shorthaired, deathly pale make-up and elegantly wasted [see Spider's girlfriend]. The Who and The Small Faces were deemed the top Mod groups in 1965 other leading lights were The Action and The Move. Coincidentally, Pete Townshend collaborated with ex-Small Faces member Ronnie Lane on solo album Rough Mix [1977] also, former Faces drummer Kenney Jones went on to become the new sticks man for The Who in late Seventies / early Eighties. By 1965 then, Mod was becoming something else, a lazy media terminology for youth fashion in its broadest sense. Favoured accessories, the scooter and the ex-army issue parka coat became seen as symbols of delinquency against which the public, via the media, were opposed. With skirmishes abounding at

seaside resorts, the previous Whit sun 1964, The Times categorised the Mod as "short-haired, suede booted, and jacketed, with their girls in expensive nylon anoraks." Many true enthusiasts abhorred the violence and distanced themselves from the Mod term by reverting to being known as Stylists instead. By 1966 it was all finished. In Carnaby Street, a former haunt of young Mods, as the tourists and media moved in, what Jonathon Green coined as the "Shepherd's Bush Mod", thus departed. The 'Hard Mod' of the late-Sixties was a predominantly working class youngster in jeans, work boots and denim ALA Skinhead that developed from 1966 onwards. Mod succeeded by making a generation conscious of itself. "Everybody looked the same, acted the same, and wanted to be the same." Concurs Pete Townshend in a 1968 Rolling Stone interview, "It was the first move I have ever seen in the history of youth towards unity: unity of thought, unity of drive and of motive. It was the closest to pure patriotism I've ever felt."

Into the Seventies and Eighties

A brief Mod revival in fashion and music made the cover of Time Out August 17-23 1979 spearheaded by bands like Secret Affair, The Chords, Lambrettas, Merton Parkas and The Purple Hearts. The Lambrettas put out three singles in 1980 with their biggest success being Poison Ivy, a top ten hit. The Merton Parkas with their You Need Wheels single limped in at number sixty on the chart in August 1979 [the track often turns up on Mod-themed cds such as one for which Phil Daniels did the voice-over for its telly ad. Parkas band member Mick Talbot went on to form The Style Council with perennial mod Paul Weller. Back in the late Seventies, fashion designers Roger Byrne and Jack English now with the Horse Hospital in London, created clothes that they felt were true to the mod ideal such as full-length suede coats. However, none of their work was used in the Quadrophenia movie. Instead, the producers chose Lloyd Johnson's "Johnson's Modern Outfitters" on London's King's Road to supply shirts and suits for the production. By the Eighties Mod had moved on to the casual yet expensive look of Pringle jumpers, loafers and all things branded. Whilst the Hard Mods of the late-Sixties came forth from the shadow of the skinhead of that period. 'Skins' were a continuation of many things Mod and would move on to a rather more aggressive identity of the late-Seventies and Eighties [with a minority linked to racist groups]. This time, Mod was more of a fashion than anything else. But even back in the tail end of the interest in the movement, for 1/6 a copy, the Mod's Monthly existed aimed at a predominantly female audience. Beatle drummer Ringo Starr proclaimed himself a "Mocker" when asked to express a preference in early Beatles interviews. Interesting in that Phil Daniels uses the same term in an interview with gspot.

With a resurgence in the interest of all things mod coming in the mid-Nineties with the advent of 'Brit Pop' an album featuring the last wave of enthusiasts in the late-Seventies e.g. The Purple Hearts, Secret Affair and The Chords called Mods Mayday '79, is available at record stores. See also: Brighton, Cross Section, Cut My Hair, Drugs, The Jam, Pete Meaden, My Generation, Scooters, Union Jack.

Money and metrication See the old blue £5 note that Jimmy gives to Ferdy at Alfredo's Café. Metrication came about in Britain in 1971 meaning that there was twenty shillings in a pound and twelve pennies to a shilling. 240 pence in a pound, so 120 pence made 10/- [shillings]. 6d [sixpence] = 2.5p , 1/- [shilling] = 5p, 10/- [ten shillings] = 50p
3/- = 15p and 2/2/- = £2.10

Keith Moon Fire.
The supreme melodramatist. Pete Townshend, 1978.
He was an explosion every time you met him. [Roger Daltrey, 2002].
"We'll call it The Moon Papers." Joked Moon to Annie Nightingale after suggesting that they write his life story together only a week before his death in September 1978. Annie, who got to know Keith and the band well, writes and speaks fondly of the octopus-like drummer in her book Wicked Speed, a necessary read not only for the anecdotes but additionally for the photographs of both the private and public Moon [and a couple of Who shots]. Born in Wembley, north

London in August 1946, Keith provides the mockney music hall vocal on Bell Boy; heard when a distraught Jimmy stumbles across the scooter belonging to the Brighton Ace Face [Sting] outside the aptly titled Grand Hotel in Brighton. The 'licking boots' parallel of Townshend's lyrics is apt evoking Jimmy's fetching and carrying at the ad agency and the similar duties for the grey Ace at the hotel. Upon dashing towards the main entrance in fevered anticipation the world of Jimmy Cooper finally crumbles, "I work in a hotel all gilt and flash..." *"BELL BOY! BELL BOY!"* screeches the by now devastated Jimmy. The Who played Brighton many times and notched up nine gigs there in 1964 alone. And dually, the 1973 Quadrophenia album is partly dedicated to their young fans of that period. Occasionally billed as The High Numbers they performed several times at the Florida Rooms on Brighton seafront. This was where a spot of the real bother took place during the 1964 scuffles and the location played its part in the subsequent film. The band also played twice at the Hippodrome theatre in Middle Street, now in use as a bingo club. Not too surprisingly, the High Numbers/ Who was dubbed as 'The Brighton Sound' by their management. Always happiest when playing with The Who, by 1976 Keith Moon had amassed the largest drum kit in the world and once played the drums so hard that he developed a hernia. A complex, highly-strung individual, his effect upon those around him still lingers and rumours abound about a film biography of his life is in development, with John, Roger and Pete all said to be contributing. In the interim, read Dear Boy: The Life of Keith Moon by Tony Fletcher. Published by Omnibus, it is an exhaustive and compelling account that transposes the 'Moon the Loon' character next to the many other faces of the 'patent exploding British drummer.' Alongside Dougal Butler's account of life with Keith in the guise of a personal assistant, Moon the Loon [Star, 1981], with Chris Trengrove and Peter Lawrence is worth searching for a second-hand copy.

Quadrophenia as a feature film went in to production only days after the death of Keith Moon on 7 September 1978. He was thirty-two. Fittingly, his name remained as one of the four executive producers on the finished picture. The remaining three attended the Cannes Film Festival the following year to publicise the film as well as their biography The Kids Are Alright (1979). Kids uses newsreel footage, TV clips and a mass of concert footage of The Who in a hundred minutes of vivacity. Alternatively, read an interview with the great man in the December 1972 issue of Rolling Stone magazine. See also: Bibliography, Grand Hotel, The Jam, Annie Nightingale, The Who.

Derrick Morgan The first star of Ska music, his song Burning Fire can be heard when Jimmy, Chalky and Dave go looking for Ferdy. The track can be found on Forward March, a Sixties release from Island records. The first wave of Mods was to be influenced by the music and culture of young blacks coming to Britain from the West Indies in the late-Fifties.

P.H Moriarty Paul provides a necessary physical presence as bar man at the villain's club where Jimmy goes to buy drugs from Harry North [John Bindon] following Pete's begrudging recommendation. The moustachioed Moriarty becomes all convivial once Jimmy has said the right thing and he immediately ushers the nervous young mod through a sliding door, revealing another world. An underworld where men like North thrive and people like Jimmy should not venture. Minutes before, Jimmy wearing a white Fred Perry (see the photo below) had blanked a woman who had shown an interest in him whilst they both stood at the bar. With only one thing on his mind [and Dave and Chalky]; the drugs are all that are important for him here. Once behind the door a tardis-like boxing gymnasium is revealed and it is simply a question of time before his needs are taken 'care' of but not in the manner anticipated. Filling the boots of screen characters such as Mike the Throat [in Number One], Razors [in The Long Good Friday] and Hatchet Harry [Lock, Stock And Two Smoking Barrells] the kind of roles offered are pretty clearly marked. In Streetwise aka Number One, Phil Daniels and Ray Winstone both offer performances in a film directed by Les Blair, the creative force behind Bad Behaviour also starring Daniels. Meanwhile, Moriarty also acted in the original

Moriarty with Phil Daniles

169

small screen version and later film remake of Scum in 1977 and 1979 respectively. A further Quadrophenia connection evolved with his work as a policeman in Bloody Kids a film detailed elsewhere. He continues to act. See also: Stephen Frears, Trevor Laird, Mike Taylor, Benjamin Whitrow. CONTACT: c/o Jim Thompson, 'Herricks', School Lane, Arundel, West Sussex BN18 9DR.

Redmond Morris Location Manager for Quadrophenia in partnership with Bryan Coates. Redmond has worked on many of Irish writer/ director Neil Jordan's most notable films in the role of co-producer. His production manager duties encompass the Dennis Potter adapted screenplay for Gorky Park in 1983, providing Michael Elphick, Mr Cooper Senior, with another of his innumerable yet consistently recognisable subsidiary parts.

Motorhead Formed by Ian 'Lemmy' Kilminster, a son of a vicar no less, in 1975 and best know for their hit the Ace of Spades. One of the rockers can allegedly be seen wearing a band t-shirt during the Brighton beach confrontations which were of course set in 1964!

Motorbikes *"I got a ton-five out of that."*
When Kevin pays Jimmy a visit at his shed out the back of the family house, observe the futile attempt by the young Mod as he attempts to kick start the heavier bike. Sporting flying goggles you can see them when he visits. Little wonder that they cannot agree on the definition of why they ride a bike; for Kevin it is about speed whilst for Jimmy its freedom, style and functionality placed side-by-side with being a mod. Whereas the slightly built mod would ride a Vespa or Lambretta, his counterpart preferred a Viper, Tiger, Talisman, Norton, Triumph or BSA [of which Jimmy's screen dad, Michael Elphick, used in his telly series Boon]. Enthusiasts hold the opinion that the bikes ridden by the Rockers in Quadrophenia are all wrong for the period. Being those that came in to fashion at least half a decade later than seen in the film.

Bikers back in the early-Sixties chose the Café Racer type of vehicle favoured for its rear foot rests and clip type handlebars. A sequence demonstrating the sheer weight of the motorbike is offered by Gary Holton, as one of the Rockers that beats up Spider and his girlfriend outside a pub. See how he fumbles to move his bike away following the conclusion of the attack. Interestingly, both BSA and Triumph whom, along with Norton were the makes favoured by bike enthusiasts, also brought out scooter models in the mid-Sixties. Advertisements in the Brighton press of 1964 targeted rockers with the sale of a "1964 Royal Enfield 250 Turbo Twin" which could reach 75mph and cost £200 19s 6d whilst the more powerful 250cc could reach speeds of 85 mph. Alternately, scooters were advertised with a by-line of "It's Fab! What's Fab?" the answer being the new Vespa 90. Available at £114 19s 6d [through monthly repayments] the 3-speeder could reach a maximum 45 mph. As was also common, accessories such as a spare wheel [£5 14s] and a luggage carrier [£2, 15s] could be purchased too. See also: Brighton, crash helmets, scooters.

Moustaches A number of the older characters on the periphery of the story have one of varying kinds; the café owner at Alfredo's Espresso bar has a slight, Errol Flynn-type one, Mr Fulford [Benjamin Whitrow], Jimmy's snooty boss has another. Remaining at the ad agency, the guy moaning at Jimmy for being late has a handle-bar styled one ALA Sgt. Pepper's and P.H Moriarty, the bar man at the villain's club, is also a member.

Patrick Murray Familiar to most of us as Mickey Pearce, the pork pie hat-wearing wide boy in Only Fools & Horses. Patrick appears briefly in the projection box scene at the agency. Featured as Des, he sits next to the tank top-tastic Timothy Spall, playing cards whilst the latest agency campaign is projected through to a nearby screening room.

Murray acted in Alan Clarke's cinematically released film of Scum alongside Ray Winstone and Phil Daniels. Elsewhere, on television he has acted in The Bill as well as in The Firm, which featured Philip Davis aka Chalky from the film version of Quadrophenia. Patrick was also in The Class of Miss MacMichael (1978) and Breaking Glass (1980) alongside Phil Daniels. See also: Hats, Gary Holton, Mark Wingett.

(Pictured opposite: Patrick Murray)

Music from the Original film soundtrack [released September 1979]: I'm The Face 2:31 / Zoot Suit 2:00 / I Am The Sea 2:03 / The Real Me 3:30 / I'm One 2:40/ Love Reign O'er Me 5:11 / Bell Boy 4:57 / I've Had Enough 6:12 / Helpless Dancer 0:23 / Doctor Jimmy 7:32 / Get Out & Stay Out 2:28 / Four Faces 3:21 / Joker James 3:14 / The Punk and The Godfather 5:28. All tracks written by Pete Townshend 1979 except Zoot Suit (1964, Meaden). Phonogram Polydor Records.

In addition, a further release included extra non-Who / High Numbers tracks as well as those listed above (Polydor 3577352): Hi Heel Sneakers (Higgenboatham) performed by Cross Section, Night Train (Jimmy Forrest/ Lewis C.Simkins/ Oscar Washington) from James Brown, Louie Louie (Richard Berry) by The Kingsmen, Green Onions (Steve Cropper/ Al Jackson/ Jones/ Lewis Steinberg) by Booker T And The MG's, Rhythm of the Rain (John Gummoe) from The Cascades, He's So Fine (Ronald Mack) by The Chiffons, Be My Baby (Phil Spector/ Ellis Greenwich/ Jeff Barry) by The Ronettes, Da Doo Ron Ron (Phil Spector/ Ellis Greenwich/ Jeff Barry) by The Crystals. Tracks heard over the audio soundtrack during the film but not included on the OST release are: Dimples (John Lee Hooker) performed by Cross Section. Anyway, Anyhow, Anywhere (Townshend / Daltrey) performed by The Who, Baby Love (Brian Holland/ Lamont Dozier/ Eddie Holland) performed by The Supremes, Blazin' Fire written and performed by Derrick Morgan, 5-4-3-2-1 (Paul Jones) performed by Manfred Mann, Baby Don't You Do It (Brian Holland/ Lamont Dozier/ Eddie Holland) performed by Marvin Gaye, Wah-Wahtusi (Kal Mann/ Dave Appell) by The Orlons, Quadrophenia (Instrumental) by The Who and Wishin' and Hopin' (Burt Bacharach/ Hal David) performed by The Merseybeats. The running order for tracks on the reissued 1996 Who double-album was as following: I Am The Sea (2:09) / The Real Me (3:21) / Quadrophenia (Instrumental/ 6:13) / Cut My Hair (3:44) / The Punk and The Godfather (5:11) / I'm One (2:38) / The Dirty Jobs (4:29) / Helpless Dancer (2:34) / Is It In My Head? (3:43) / I've Had Enough (6:14) / 5:15 (4:59) / Sea and Sand (5:01) / Drowned (5:27) / Bell Boy (4:55) / Doctor Jimmy (8:36) / The Rock (Instrumental/

6:37) / Love Reign O'er Me (5:58). The order of music heard in the film, including being played on jukeboxes/ record players and so forth, is as follows: I Am The Sea (THE WHO): Played over the pre-credits as we see Jimmy walking away from the cliff top and towards the camera. The Real Me (THE WHO): Heard as Jimmy heads towards the Goldhawk Club as the opening titles are presented. Hi Heel Sneakers (CROSS SECTION): Mimed to by the group inside the Goldhawk. Dimples (CROSS SECTION): The second track by the group launched immediately after Sneakers and heard as Jimmy makes his way back home on his scooter. Cut My Hair (THE WHO): Plays as Jimmy relaxes in his bedroom after seeing Steph and the others at the Goldhawk club. Be Bop A Lula (GENE VINCENT): A vocal interpretation is offered by Kevin (Ray Winstone) at the Public baths. You Really Got Me (THE KINKS): Jimmy's retort to Kevin's choice of karaoke at the baths. Zoot Suit (THE WHO): Features as Jimmy is in his bedroom preparing himself before an evening out. Baby Love (THE SUPREMES): Heard very lightly for a mere moment during the sequence where the Mods arrive outside the venue for the house party. Be My Baby (THE RONETTES): Played as Jimmy and the others eventually gain access into the house. Rhythm of the Rain (THE CASCADES): Spun on the record player in the lounge where masses of youngsters are gathered chatting and/ or dancing/ drinking. My Generation (THE WHO): Replaced on the deck by Jimmy upon seeing Steph smooching to The Cascades tune previously. I'm One (THE WHO): Featured as a backdrop to Jimmy's displacement at the end of the evening of the house party whilst he sits on his scooter by the canal side. Anyway, Anyhow, Anywhere (THE WHO): Jimmy's choice of music whilst enjoying the photographs of the model in a listening booth at a record store. Wishin' and Hopin' (THE MERSEYBEATS): Interspersed with AAA, and the selection of a young postal worker in the booth immediately behind Jimmy's. Night Train (JAMES BROWN): The featured choice playing on the jukebox at Alfredo's coffee bar, a favoured haunt of the local Mods. Da Doo Ron Ron (THE CRYSTALS): Grooved to by Monkey and a group of other girls at the Goldhawk whilst Jimmy and Dave watch from the side of the disc jockey's record deck. Quadrophenia (THE WHO): Very Tommy-like in its intonation, sections of this

173

instrumental from the '73 Who album is included throughout the film. In this instance some sounds are heard when Jimmy realises that he and his mates are bashing Kevin, his old school friend, outside Shepherd's Bush market following the attack on Spider [Gary Shail] earlier that evening. Instrumental: Not certain as to which Who track that this is taken from as Jimmy pleasures himself in his room after the heart-to-heart with his father. Burning Fire (DERRICK MORGAN): Can be detected during the evening-time visit to Ferdy's house by Dave, Jimmy and Chalky whilst in search of drugs. Instrumental (THE WHO): Plays as the lads scoot off on their bikes over one of London's bridges. You Really Got Me (THE KINKS): Jimmy again sings this catchy kinks ditty to the sound of the franking machine in the mailroom at the ad agency where he works. 5-4-3-2-1 (MANFRED MANN): Heard very quietly from the lounge whilst Jimmy chats with his father in the family kitchen moments before dashing off in to the lounge to see and hear The Who. Anyway, Anyhow, Anywhere (THE WHO): Absorbed by an enthused Jimmy whilst his bemused dad looks on, is the electrifying performance by The Who whilst featured on the teen-show Ready Steady Go! Get Out And Stay Out (THE WHO): Set in motion by Dave shouting it back at Chalky following his mate's crash whilst on the road down to Brighton. Green Onions (BOOKER T AND THE MG'S): The first of a trio of vintage tunes played inside the Brighton 'ballroom' visited by Jimmy and his mates. Louie Louie (THE KINGSMEN): Supporting the Ace Face (Sting) as he dominates the dance floor with his moves. Wah Watusi (THE ORLONS): The final song to be heard at the ballroom played as we see Steph dancing next to Ace. Quadrophenia (THE WHO): Plays during the early hours where we see the Ace leading a posse of other scootered mods in a circular formation and then zoom off. The piece continues as we see Jimmy on the beach prior to joining the others at the Beach Café. Is It In My Head (THE WHO): Heard during the aftermath of the rioting in Brighton and as we observe Jimmy in the police van with the Ace Face. Get Out And Stay Out (THE WHO): Supplements the altercation Jimmy has with his furious mother who promptly banishes him from the family home. Baby Don't You Do It (MARVIN GAYE): Used as background ambience at Alfredo's on the tumultuous return of Jimmy. Sweet Talkin' Guy (THE CHIFFONS): The second disc to spin at Alfredo's that evening. The Punk And The Godfather (THE WHO): possibly the piece used in a scene that finds Jimmy returning home one evening and harassing his parents. He is chased away by his father and the music continues as he returns to the canal side once more. 5:15 (THE WHO): Used to such good effect as a stoned Jimmy takes the train back down to Brighton. Love Reign O'er Me (THE WHO): Its elegant, pleading vocal plays as Jimmy foolishly returns there alone and forlorn. Bell Boy (THE WHO): Popped in to place at the time that Jimmy sees his former hero, the Ace Face, now working at the Grand hotel in Brighton. I've Had Enough (THE WHO): played to perfection as we see Jimmy riding his scooter along the cliff tops at Beachy Head. Doctor Jimmy (THE WHO): Kicks in as the scooter smacks onto the rocks below and the closing credits.

Musicality During the period of making Quadrophenia Phil Daniels was regularly playing gigs with his own band called Phil Daniels and The Cross [they released an album in 1980] and Toyah Willcox won a recording contract with Safari Records whilst shooting was in full-flow. Leslie Ash was also said to be in a band at some point and Spider aka Gary Shail had success as a composer of film music. Mark Wingett played one of the members of a screen band led by Hazel O'Connor in Breaking Glass (1980), a role that Toyah went up for and of course Sting, hit the big time with The Police in 1978. See also: Blur.

My Generation "People try to put us down…" We see and hear the lads at the house party as they respond to the line "Why don't you all f-f-fade away…" with something a little ruder but exactly as we all sing along to at home! Recorded on 13 October 1965 and released on Guy Fawkes Night it is regarded as The Who's coup de grace by it's composer Pete Townshend. Written in ten minutes or so, it went on to sell over 300,000 copies and heralded as one of the benchmark singles of the Sixties. Yet it was not overly promoted by record label Decca [Brunswick] who did not realise the impact that it was about to make.

Still saved as the finale to gigs today back in 1965 Who vocalist Roger Daltrey had been kicked out of the band shortly before it became a big hit but its success saw his reinstatement. Initially banned by the BBC who thought that Daltrey's vocal styling was offensive to actual vocally impaired people it will forever be renowned for its vocal stylisation. So by informing them that his interpretation of a pilled-up Mod overwhelmed by the force of the drugs was somehow more acceptable? However, the single was first laid down without such at the Marquee recording studios behind the former club in Richmond Mews, London. Coming after two failed attempts were scrapped and the fantastic John Entwistle guitar twang was expensively added [John had to buy three new electric bass guitars in the process due to stores in London not stocking replacement strings!] to the fifth version. The stuttering was on the third of the five separate recordings. "The stutter was always there," recounts Chris Stamp in the POP100 celebratory chart of Rolling Stone's December 2000 issue, "like a true piece of early Townshend brilliance." Various suppositions exist as to its origin with one being that Daltrey genuinely stumbled over the lyrics whilst a more adroit solution is that as it was about a teen-aged mod, the stammer coming as a side effect of amphetamine abuse and a part of such a lifestyle. By June 1993 it was reported that Pete Townshend remembered that the genesis for My Generation came from a roadside incident he experienced with a snooty older woman driver doubtful of his young success. It would seem that Pete's wavering memory has again proved problematic in that over the passing years, he has offered 2 other versions of the basis for writing the song. Whatever. Songs like Anyway, Anyhow, Anywhere and My Generation were demonstrative of the blossoming craftsmanship of its lyricist. "Townshend's guitar seemed to strain at the leash." offers Charlie Gillett in The Beat Goes On – The Rockfile Reader. Even more remarkable is that at the time of composing the piece the band had no rhythm guitarist so Townshend soldiered forth on lead guitar. "This song really goes," begins Tommy Smothers in his introduction to the legendary exploding Keith Moon performance on The Smothers Brothers comedy show, "and you're gonna be surprised what happens because this is excitement..." Talk about understatement. Moon, even with or despite his knowledge of chemistry, had packed too much explosives in his drum kit and consequently caused more damage [in this case, to Townshend's hair and hearing] than was ever anticipated or pre-planned. Meanwhile in the midst of playing the song at a May 1966 gig in Berkshire Pete Townshend hit Keith Moon over the head with his guitar because Moon and Entwistle had failed to turn up for the show. Keith came away with a black eye, a cut leg and three stitches! The Smothers Brothers performance can be seen in The Kids Are Alright docu-film released commercially in cinemas across Britain in 1979. My Generation Blues and a filmed studio version of the song are also included Kids, as is a part black and white [and colour] film of the band playing a cataclysmic version of the song. There is in addition a slow walkin', foot-stompin' interpretation in the documentary too. The song was recorded on the same day as Kids beginning its life as slow blues number Talkin' Generation but was changed at the behest of Kit Lambert. A rendition of Roadrunner, covered later by the Sex Pistols, flows in to My Generation and in association with Join Together, the "My Generation Blues" was to have been on the same soundtrack album but was pulled. Generation was the third chart single from The Who in 1965 following I Can't Explain and Anyway, Anyhow, Anywhere. Released three times, it made number two [1965], sixty-eight [1988] and thirty-one in 1996.

Numerous pressings of the single have been made with a b-side of Out in the Street put out by Decca in USA 1965. An alternate 12" acetate from IBC in 1965 is very sought after by collectors as are the two-hundred picture sleeves released by Brunswick but these are elusive to locate. A studio medley was recorded in August 1966 in London and was produced by Kit Lambert whilst 1968 saw My Generation / Shout and Shimmy was issued on the red Decca-American export label. Brunswick put out a French EP by the re-aligned "Les Who" with Generation the first of four tracks, another being The Kids Are Alright. My Generation, segued with Elgar's Land of Hope and Glory appears on The Who album A Quick One. Numerous versions exist and are included on the many Who compilation albums e.g. version III, a live interpretation of the song as performed in 1970 for the Live at Leeds LP whilst version iv is a part of the 1976 The Story of the Who. In addition, it can be found on My Generation: The Very Best of The Who, The Who Millennium Collection, Meaty, Beefy, Big and Bouncy and the Monterrey Pop Festival LP from the Rhino label. Generation is featured on the soundtrack of Stardust, a 1974 film that gave a role to Keith Moon and was the first point of recognition of The Who for a young Paul Weller.

A 12" promo of My Generation / I Can't Explain was released by MCA in 1984, with a second, including two other tracks was again released on the same label later that year. Not surprisingly, the song can be found on subsequent Who compilation titles Who's Better, Who's Best and The Who Collection. The band recorded a special jingle for Radio 1 using its melody, found on the BBC Sessions album as is a second live version. Its youth theme prevails in the echoing of the title in The Punk and the Godfather and 5:15, two tracks on the Quadrophenia album. The Who's debut album, also titled My Generation, was cut in an astonishing seven hours flat and saw a release on Christmas Day 1965, with the title song being found as track six [the last on side one]. In America the album was re-titled The Who Sings My Generation [featuring the first version recorded of My Generation] hitting record stores in April 1966. Its cover photography by Dave Wedgbury, house photographer for Decca Records and the man responsible for taking what has been recognised as one of the seminal band shots of the Sixties, the famed Big Ben photo. Curiously, the reality for its inspiration was more logistical, as with most things, with the record company's office situated near to the London landmark and hence the composition. The 1965 image captures a fresh-faced bunch of men packaged up and ready for consumption. A second picture made the cover of the My Generation album interesting in that it was shot from above using a technique copied much by an in-house photographer for Decca Records. The album was the first of four in a box set release by the West German Polydor label [date unknown] whilst a 1970 re-issue on the Coral budget label never saw the light of day. Covered by Alice Cooper and Oasis the sentiments of the single saw a rebuke in 1997 on Robbie Williams' Old Before I Die retort to the legendary "Hope I die before I get old" chorus with his own "I hope I'm old before I die." Both Townshend and Daltrey have admitted that it has been impossible to live up to the success of the song, "When we hit with My Generation it showed the public that we were a lot more than just another pop group." Concedes Roger in Off The Record. "The only trouble was, it was very hard to top. I don't know if we ever did." Thirty years on and My Generation was the first of four numbers performed by The Who at Live Aid in July 1985. In Townshend's entry in Who's

Who [2000] the "Hope I die before I get old" line is included. On in to a new Millennium and still it finds a place, Australian Airlines used the track for a 2000 television commercial. See also: Brian Eno, The Kinks, Union Jack, Dave Wedgbury.

Kim Neve In 1964 Beatlemania was sweeping across America and whilst a photograph of Pete Townshend was mixed with nudes and mod-related cuttings on Jimmy's bedroom walls, his sister Yvonne, played by Kim, has pictures of 'The Fab Four' upon hers. Interestingly, in the photographs taken by Ethan A. Russell featured in the 1996 re-issued Quadrophenia Who album, one shows Jimmy laying on his bed with both The Beatles and The Rolling Stones visible behind him but not The Who. Perhaps this was due to the band not having the first of their three hit singles until the following year. Disturbed by her bumbling brother coming in to her room in search of scissors, our first view of Yvonne is an eyebrow raiser. Buzzing from seeing Steph [Leslie Ash] dancing away at the Goldhawk he moves about the brightly lit room whilst she remains in the lotus position wearing only a bra and pants. With a pair of swimming goggles to protect her eyes from the artificial light Jimmy sarcastically teases her about the dangers inherent of tanning before he leaves the room.

In the novelisation of the film author Alan Fletcher adds a scene whereby brother and sister disagree about their opposing fashion ideals but warmth is felt between them through their mutual antagonism. Regrettably this interaction is not shown in the filmed version, with the scissors scene being her only time on screen. The audience never get to know what she does for a living or if she is meant to still be at school. If Jimmy is meant to be in his late-teens I think, in actuality, that Kim is a fair bit older than Yvonne is supposed to be. Quadrophenia would seem to have been the only film that Kim Neve worked on.

Newcastle Brown Ale The tipple favoured by Jimmy during the house party scene in the film. Dad is seen drinking from a trusty bottle of Guinness at home.

New Society magazine Article by Paul Barker with a headline "Brighton Battleground" written by a reporter there during May 1964. The journalist gives a perspective of what it was like to be caught up in the energy of the weekend when he travelled about with the Mods along the seafront. He begins, "Their get-up was as chic as always: the boys in razor-cuts, short-jackets and narrow trousers; the girls, mostly in nylon anoraks and stretch slacks, hair ranging from long and ragged to closer cropped than the boys'. The uniformity added to the menace." It was Barker that wrote of the media's 'shocked hypocrisy' reportage of the events of that tumultuous weekend in Brighton.

See also: Brighton

Newspapers "Wildest Ones Yet" Daily Sketch headline 19 May 1964 – Whitsun. Along with Brighton and Bournemouth, Margate saw violence between Mods and Rockers following the media pillaring events at Clacton earlier that year. Dubious in their sensationalist coverage of the skirmishes between youngsters [or more often than not, with the regional police] in the Sixties, the perceived image of the Mod or Rocker was fuelled by the re-enforcement of the latter supposedly being inarticulate and working class meanwhile; the Mod was lower middle-class and not viewed as being violent simply due to their literal neatness. "They're pin-neat, lively and clean, but a rat-pack." Categorised the Daily Mail. From Clacton onwards the labels were being placed, "The papers thus held to create the 'Mods and Rockers' myth…[it] grew, and took on a life of their own." SR Gibbons book. A good example was at Margate, where James Brunton was fined £75 but who asked to pay by cheque. It was revealed later that he did not have a bank account and that this was just a bit of bravado.

The press was barely interested in reporting this fact preferring to maintain the established perception of youngsters like Brunton held by the public. Some of the many reported events included these headlines: "Day of Terror by scooter groups." The Daily Telegraph. "Fears of another weekend of violence" – Jimmy's dad reads the Daily Mirror in the kitchen scene where Jimmy comes in wearing wet Levi jeans in preparation for the Brighton weekender. "Riot Police Fly to Seaside" Daily Mirror [3d] Aug 1964. "Battle of Brighton" Brighton Evening Argus, 18 May, 1964. "Young and foolish – with old-fashioned ideas" The Times, May 1964 "Battles between adolescents whose only point of difference appeared to be their dress." A very apt summation indeed! "Montague's and Capulets at Margate" Manchester Guardian, Tuesday 19 May 1964 [4d].

Mods let fly at the Rockers in fierce seafront clashes
BATTLE OF BRIGHTON
Fifty arrested

However, balanced reporting could be found within the paper but it bore no relation to the salacious cover headline. "In these affairs the lesson taught by the Courts – which tends to be taught arbitrarily to the least fleet-footed is probably less of a deterrent than the measures the police can take to stop the fighting." "Living for Kicks." Daily Mirror front-page headline, Tuesday 19 May 1964. "They met on the beach at Brighton yesterday – the Mod and the Rocker. And the boot went in…" Allegedly, a young girl was waiting for a bus opposite the Palace Pier when she saw a group of youngsters dressed in what she viewed as mod clothes. Accompanied by a photographer, she watched them dash across the main road where they proceeded to attack a small group of unsuspecting youths [looking like the perceived notion of Rockers] before running off. All the while the photographer snapped away. This un-named girl saw the Mirror cover many years later and realised what she had witnessed that day. Conversely, the Evening Argus [28 May, 1994] offers another interpretation, "There was no blood-smeared Rocker. The photo was staged, the story a lie. Pete Townshend, guitarist with Mod heroes The Who, even saw the fake photo shoot happen." Next a Daily Express cover headline, Tues May 19. "Sawdust Caesars." The most infamous of all the media coverage of the events at Margate and Brighton was this one. Significant in that its use of vermin terminology to categorise those involved was picked up by other newspapers and widely used. Dr George Simpson's comments made the front page in relation to the scuffles at Margate. Clacton was the next location at Easter, then Margate and Brighton weekend in May with trouble at Margate, Brighton, Southend, Great Yarmouth, Bournemouth, Clacton, Hastings and even County Durham following on. Margate, Clacton and Brighton were all popular Mod strongholds for The Who to gig at. "On the Run" Daily Mirror, Monday 3 August 1964. No actual reports of fighting or significant arrests but still heavy coverage by the media. "Youth as spectacle with a vengeance" Stanley Reynolds writing in the Guardian defined Mods as having a peculiar type of middle class, sartorial elegance whilst Rockers we seen as slovenly dressed and basically working class. In Quadrophenia, Jimmy's mum thrusts a copy of the Daily Mail with its banner of Mod/ Rocker violence splattered across its front cover whilst his dad is seen to read the Daily Mirror. Clacton "Wild Ones" Invade Seaside – 97 Arrests Mirror headline, March 1964. This was a theme continued by the Daily Sketch with their front page reporting on Brighton from 19 May 1964 – "Wildest One Yet." Whilst the Mirror had their, "On The Run" 3 Aug 1964. Jimmy has this Hastings-related cutting on his bedroom wall, "The Mods and Rockers invade…but this time it's an itchy-feet invasion." Another from that weekend, "The time, Yesterday [2 August, Sunday]. The place, HASTINGS. The tempo, QUICK. very Quick." See also: New Society, John Phillips, Rockers, Youth.

Nicknames Chalky, Spider and Monkey each have them but the origins hardly seem complimentary.

Annie Nightingale "…But most of all I loved The Who...it was like being in the front line of a war zone. There was the possibility that you might die from the sheer velocity ...that they might just decide to turn their heavy artillery fire on the audience and kill you as part of the performance." Taken from her second book, Wicked Speed, Annie. a former Brighton resident and Radio One DJ, Annie formed a personal friendship with Keith Moon and, to a lesser extent, The Who. In the early Sixties she used to write a music column in the local Brighton paper titled "Spin with Me" and I would recommended her two books, Chase the Fade and Wicked Speed, both containing extensive visual and literary references to the band. As part of a recent initiative by Brighton and Hove buses, Annie has been included amongst a succession of names with a link to the town resulting in his or hers name emblazoned across the front of a bus. See also: Brighton, Dusty Springfield, The Who

Ocean Colour Scene Their track The Day We Caught the Train name checks Jimmy and can be found on their albums Moseley Shoals and B Sides: Seasides and Free Rides. Former Jam man Paul Weller has regularly played with the band whose version of Anyway Anyhow Anywhere features on the Who covers album Substitute. See their stylish fan website at www.debrisroad.com

Gary Oldman Powerful British actor who starred in Meantime next to Phil Daniels and Tim Roth. Director Alan Clarke influenced all three actors during the fledgling period of their careers. Oldman starred as Joe Orton in Prick Up Your Ears. Watching Ears Orton and Halliwell's wall collage reminds one of Jimmy's. See also: Alan Clarke, Jimmy's bedroom.

The Orlons A mixed bag of friends and schoolmates, the Orlons, consisting of boys and girls, were based in Philadelphia up until disbanding in 1968. Their debut single Wah Watusi can be heard during the evening that the London Mods visit the Brighton 'ballroom.' See also: Brighton Aquarium

Parkas "I wear my wartime coat in the wind and sleet." [From the Who tracks Sea and Sand / Helpless Dancer / I've Had Enough]. Jimmy and Dave both wear one, as does Chalky. Oddly, in the scenes along East Street, one of the lesser known Mods, John, can be seen wrapped in one but it is the only occasion that he does so in the film, after having initially met him at the café where Jimmy and Kevin chat briefly John wears a cotton blue jacket. As a fashion item in itself the parka consistently comes back in style but if you look around Brighton today you might see a solitary Mod enthusiast cloaked in one yet with not a scooter in sight. In the film, older mod enthusiasts deemed many of those worn by the extras vastly unauthentic. This was because the originals worn by scooter-riding Mods were genuine army surplus with fishtail backs, fur hoods, double-zips, wool-blanketed lining and clip attachments. Whilst those manufactured in the late 1970s, were available through mail order as "Mod" parkas for £12.50, and even C&A, being of little comparison to the style evoked from the originals. See also: Fashion, Mods.

Daniel Peacock Viewed only on the fringes of the main Mod group Dan is similar to John [Altman] in that both fully trained actors were used to mechanically push the story forth. As one of those socially less refined in the cliché he provides the butt of much consternation when confronted by those that simply cannot deal with his Modliness. Oliver Pierre plays the unfortunate tailor that fails to meet his specific detailing requirements for a new suit and consequently gets sworn at. Again featuring Jimmy, a very witty moment occurs at a barbers where Phil Daniels' justification for refusing to use hair lacquer is by saying that 'poofs' wear it. [This from a dandy too!] *"I have lacquer!"* blurts the innocent Peacock reciprocating the Cooper point. *"Usual miracle?"* sighs the laconic, white-jacketed barber as Dan takes the seat vacated by Jimmy. Still talking away, he emits an absolute zeal for all things Mod. Peacock is a charismatic presence and comes to the fore in the beach fighting against leather and denim clad Rockers. In the bubbling froth of the Brighton tide lapping all about them both he and John Altman get stuck in. One assumes that Dan rides a scooter as he always can always be found at the Mod hangouts such as the pub, house party and down on the South Coast. Not only busy as a jobbing actor, Dan has written for film and television, embracing both duties for Party, Party (1983) a film with Jimmy's mother Kate Williams playing a role. Writing for the early Channel Four Comic Strip team he would move on to act with Father Cooper, Michael Elphick, in the Strips' The Supergrass (1985) and I Bought a Vampire Motorcycle (1990) and in an earlier episode of Boon. Toyah and Peacock co-starred in a play called Sugar and Spice. Daniel is pictured above as he is in Quadrophenia.

CONTACT: JM Associates, 77 Beak St, London W1R 3LF.

Pepsi Cola *"One and tuppence?"*
Jimmy buys a bottle for Steph and himself at Alfredo's café following the night time break-in at the chemist where Monkey

works. Spider drinks his with a red and white straw, as do the young lovers. For Mods, where details meant everything, the choice of drinking Pepsi is significant in that its perception enhances its recognition as modern unlike the more traditional brand identity of Coke. Created in 1898 by an American chemist Caleb Bradham from North Carolina, following on from the 1886 introduction of Coca Cola by Dr John Pemberton, also a pharmacist. Its circular red and blue logo is seen on a window within the café but the one seen on the bottles is an older variety, being the traditional hand-scrolled logo. Also seen at the snack bar on Brighton's East Street that is attacked by the marauding Mods and at the corner entrance point of the ABC cinema on the same street.

John Peverall Associate Producer on Quadrophenia and McVicar (1980). His filmography has seen him as Second Unit Director, Assistant Director, Producer and Production Manager.

John Phillips Aged sixty-four, John was perfect as the un-named magistrate giving the bombastic 'Sawdust Caesars' speech in a scene worth watching purely to giggle at the child-like scowl covering Jimmy's face as the camera pans across the crowded courtroom before arriving on Phillips. In actual fact that astonishing soliloquy was spoken by the aforementioned Dr.George Simpson, a Margate magistrate, whilst residing over a specially arranged holiday Monday sitting of his court. Not that this detail detracts from the gentle supposition that this judicial scene in Quadrophenia takes place in Brighton. In addition, Sting's cheeky request to pay his heavy fine by way of a cheque, is based upon fact, this again occurred at Margate and not Brighton. Returning to the actor portraying Simpson or rather given his words, John Phillips features in the solitary scene in Quadrophenia and his career was ended by his death in 1995. Telly work back in the sixties found him in Z Cars, The Forsyte Saga and Softly, Softly and next to Laurence Olivier in the 1954 film of Richard III. See also: Dr George Simpson. (John is pictured opposite).

Kieron Phipps Accredited as Kieron A. Phipps also, he was one half of the Second Assistant Director team with Michael Flynn on the Quadrophenia shoot. Subsequent creative success came as a first Assistant Director on Four

Weddings and A Funeral (1994) and Martha, Meet Frank, Daniel and Laurence [1998, featuring Ray Winstone]. See also: Patsy Pollock. CONTACT: Exec (Diary Service) 01753 646677.

Pie, liquor and mash *"2 & 8."* The price paid by Jimmy for his order of pie and mash located in Dalston, London. (Although a film location site lists it as being Cooke's at 48 Goldhawk road in London). During the course of enjoying his meal at an undisclosed pie and mash shop we observe Jimmy's relish at tucking in to his food [heavy on the liquor] disturbed firstly by the arrival of a leathered-up Kevin and then two Mods from the local scene. Over four hundred such establishments have existed in the last two hundred years with one located on Eel Pie Island, a venue close to Pete Townshend's and The Who's hearts, called Eel Pie House. Poor Jimmy, just as he begins to delve into his food using a Lorna Doone [cockney rhyming slang for spoon] he doesn't manage to finish. For an enjoyable account of the history of this long enjoyed delicacy, see Pie 'N' Mash: A Guide to Londoners Traditional Eating Houses [J Smith & Sons, 1995].

Oliver Pierre *"How does that feel?"* asks the tailor to stroppy young mod Dan (Daniel Peacock)

"Awful!" comes the cheeky response.

Cast as a bespoke tailor, so common in the early Sixties, he has to deal with a strident, detail-obsessed youngster whilst struggling to acknowledge the thrust of the new fashion demands implicit of youngsters. Punk Svengali and fashion guru Malcolm McLaren articulates further, "The Sixties notion of fashion primarily can be summed up by the fact that the teenager was fashion..."

[Below] extras dressed as police during the Brighton shoot of Quadrophenia.

continued the former Sex Pistols manager in the 1997 documentary Rebellion: Undressed. "This generation had a very different sens of itself." Also in the same scene, Jimmy is observed ordering his own new suit for Brighton at the same time Pierre's character finally loses patience with Dan's cheekiness.
The first waves of Mods were, as the The first waves of Mods were, as the serene George Melly explains in Revolt into Style, "...true dandies, interested in creating works of art - themselves." Moreover, to be accompanied by a male friend rather than a girlfriend, as is the case with Dan, was atypical Mod behaviour of mind. Your girlfriend's opinion, should you have even had one, was not sought. Granted that the Quadrophenia Mods are from the second wave of 1963/4 the conclusion is nonetheless apt, "The little Mods used each other as looking glasses." Concludes Melly, "They were as cool as ice-cubes." Oliver has made numerous TV appearances including an episode of Stay Lucky [a series within which Leslie Ash was to feature and he alsoa cted with her in the film, Shadey]. He portrayed a chef in The Long Good Friday (1980), Kaplan in the steamy White Mischief (1987) and in Morons From Outer Space (1986) a comedy that marked Quad actor George Innes in a minor role also. Sadly, he has since died. See also: Bibliography, Trevor Laird, P.H Moriarty.

Oliver Pierre

Pinball A major focus in The Who film of Tommy, a pinball machine can also be found in Quadrophenia; firstly at the Goldhawk, Alfredo's coffee bar and then at the Beach Café in Brighton.

Stephen Poliakoff A scriptwriter and director whose relation to Quadrophenia is indirect but nonetheless of note. Born in 1952, his screenplay of Bloody Kids (1980) gained a theatrical release and gave an early career boost to a number of Quad actors. Former crew members Ray Corbett and Brayham conclude the link with both artists involved on Century (1993) and Hidden City (1988) each directed by Poliakoff. See also: Stephen Frears, Gary Holton, P H Moriarty, Jesse Birdsall and Christian Wrangler.

Police The more that is revealed about the behaviour of the police in dealing with the bank holiday skirmishes of the Sixties, the more dubious their action becomes. Youngsters were literally arrested regardless of whether they were involved directly in any unsavoury acts. The National Council of Civil Liberties reported this kind of over-reaction at Brighton, "Over 110 arrests were made," enunciates Professor Stanley Cohen, "the vast majority of them for offences directly or indirectly provoked by the police activity i.e. obstruction or using threatening behaviour." During the Summer of 1964 a police van was stoned by youngsters when it ordered those gathered to disperse, "It was the first time I had seen policemen in England attacked like this." Reported Paul Barker in New Society magazine. "It was curiously shocking." Even bystanders watching the action barracked police when they attempted to intervene. Officers in Brighton would wear the distinctive white helmets [some are shown in Quadrophenia] in a tradition dating back to the Twenties, and a couple of horseback policemen are seen breaking up the Mods on the seafront in another historically correct piece of drama. Sixties Brighton had a famous white skinned police horse called Kim who was called in to quell the crowds for the first time.

Following the subdued August bank holiday where there was not a repeat of the Whitsun scuffles in Brighton; the chairman of the local juvenile court congratulated the police on containing the problem. The Police received donations totalling more than £100 from well wishers following the Whit sun skirmishes and were lauded for their success. Further empowerement through The Police Act (1964) meant that a maximum of £20 fines could be dished out for obstruction far easier than ever before. See also: Bibliography, Brighton, Stanley Cohen.

Patsy Pollock Unanimously well-praised casting director for Quadrophenia. She also co-produced Alan Clarke's Rita, Sue and Bob Too (1986). Patsy is included in a book that provides a very thorough account of his career with contributions from Phil Daniels, Ray Winstone and Philip Davis amongst many others. Occasionally credited as Patsy Pollock, her other film work has encompassed Restoration (1995), In The Name of the Father (1993) and Braveheart (1995). See also: Alan Clarke.

Polydor Record label that put out the Quadrophenia soundtrack album. Pete and Roger were also recorded talking about the music and the film in an exclusive release sent out to radio stations to promote the movie in 1979. Polydor released all singles by artists on The Who management's record label.

Polygram Video Along with the Feature Film Co. they were responsible for the video release of Quadrophenia.
Polytel Films Responsible for co-producing Quadrophenia with The Who Films. The only other film released by them was a 1979 TV movie titled Too Far to Go. See also: The Who Films
Pool Valley The location for what must be one of the smallest coach stations in Britain, a sign for Pool Valley can be seen in the background when Dave leads Steph away from the arrested Jimmy in East Street. Opposite the corner entrance to the cinema, the sign is behind them on the wall of the unnamed pub.
Pop Art "A fairly simple form of [Pop Art]." Pete Townshend with reference to The Who. Briefly utilised by Townshend with the band heralded as "This is Pop Art group The Who" captured for posterity during the introduction to The Good's Gone on the first-rate BBC Sessions album. By late-1965 The Who no longer continued to exploit the Pop Art or the Mod angle. In an early scene from the film Jimmy goes in to the supermarket where Steph works as a cashier and places a Pop Art style "Pow!" promotional card in to a basket before she recognises him and coincidentally, a photograph of Keith Moon exists within which he is wearing a white sweat shirt with the same word. Paul Weller, former guitarist and vocalist with The Who/ Kinks-influenced band The Jam can be seen playing a Pop Art guitar in Modernist expressionism video accompanying his single Peacock Suit.
The Pretty Things "One of the greatest R&B bands of all time." Van Morrison. First charting in June 1964 after forming the year before, their name appears on a poster in a scene outside the Goldhawk following news of the attack upon Spider. Probably best known for A House in the Country all of their singles were put out on the Fontana label. The Pretty's played Brighton in '64 but as a band they split up in 1976. See also: David Bowie, Brighton's Florida Rooms.
Serge Prokofiev A Soviet composer whose work has a tonal quality that was always changing. Born in 1891 he died in 1953. If you listen to I've Had Enough during the climactic scene on the cliff top at Beachy Head, one of his pieces is echoed through the synthesizers on the track.
Pubs Much has changed since the 1978 location filming in Brighton most

noticeably on East Street and the neighbouring seafront area of King's road. The Pickwick eatery at number seventy-seven, features in Quadrophenia when many youngsters are seen rushing past pursued by the police. The premises later became Fagin's Cocktail bar. The New Heart and Hand pub at number eighty, shown in the film is still here but now called the Prodigal, whilst the pub next to it at number seventy-four, once the Greyhound [where Dave pulls Steph away after Jimmy's arrest] is known as the Fishbowl nowadays. It can be located upon seeing the vertically positioned Bass brewers sign that sticks out above the entrance. In London, Jimmy, Dave and Spider travel to an anonymous pub to get a supply of drugs for their Brighton weekend but get conned by an unscrupulous villain called Harry North. However, looking closely at the moment that Jimmy makes the initial £10 deal, he is given a plastic bag of pills from the back of a car and in the background lettering reading 'Wellington' can just be deciphered. The exterior of the Bramley Arms, is another setting where a gang of bikers whilst on the road in front of the premises sets upon Spider and his girlfriend. Thirty years later and the premises is now used as both residential and business dwellings. Coincidentally, Franc Roddam's son now lives in a flat there!

The Punk and The Godfather Heard over this track taken from The Who's Quadrophenia is an echo of "M-m-m-my-g-g-g-generation." Most listeners fail to recognise its inclusion. Townshend's gentle vocal styling works best in evoking an empathy with Jimmy's plight. The song plays out over the closing credits of the film. See also: Drugs, gin, Levi's, Quadrophenia, Schizophrenia.

Quadrophenia Definition: A personality split into four separate facets; advanced state of schizophrenia; twice the normal accepted medical condition; inability to control which facet is foremost at any one time. Quadrophenic: an extremely volatile state of mind; a condition of today. The instrumental track Quadrophenia developed from Townshend's misinformed definition of schizophrenia.

Quadrophenia An instrumental track from The Who that is reminiscent of the Tommy period with its undulating synths evoking a sense of fluidity heard during the scene which sees Kevin beaten senseless by Jimmy and the others. Whilst later on in Brighton, its climax is segued with a moment that sees Jimmy on the beach. Reverberations of Love Reign O'er Me can be detected as well.

The 1973 Who album Pete Townshend generated idea for a mini-rock opera around the members of the group. Titled Rock is Dead - Long Live Rock, which, in unison with some elements from his then unreleased Lifehouse project, transmuted in to the Quadrophenia album. The initial idea to chronicle the early life of a Shepherd's Bush mod came from Roger Daltrey resulting in the album's conception as a soundtrack to a movie that was never going to be filmed. From fifteen hours of recorded music, Townshend initially planned on issuing a four-album set prior to some fifty songs. John Entwistle remixed the album for the 1979 film release. The double-album sold over a million copies in its first three weeks on general release on 26 October 1973 and remained on the chart for thirteen weeks, peaking at number two. Chalky, soundly portrayed by actor Phil Davis, was a fan; "I'd heard about a film of Quadrophenia being on the cards, " he told the author, "of course, we all wanted to be in it. I had the Who album and played it ovar and again. The Who never lost their credibility whatever came after, and neither did the film."

Being kept of the number one slot by David Bowie's Pin Ups album, which included his own versions of Anyway Anyhow Anywhere and I Can't Explain. Released in America 3 November 1973, it was beaten to the top spot by Elton John's Goodbye Yellow Brick Road, John went on to provide a memorable appearance in the filmed version of Tommy. The album was dedicated to a number of groupings, the youngsters of the Goldhawk Road club, Carpenders Park, Forest Hill, Stevenage New Tavern and to those that the band played to at the Marquee in London and the Brighton Aquarium in the summer of 1965. In the original album, The Rock track has Jimmy swimming out to a rock but Ken Russell had already used this imagery in the climax to Tommy.

However, Quadrophenia does start and end on a rock, or rather a rock face i.e. Beachy Head. Quadrophenia has always caused divide opinion amongst critics and fans alike and here's one taken from The Beat Goes On, "Riches and respectability are powerful antidotes to gut rebellion, Quadrophenia, Townshend's attempt to exorcise the ghost of Tommy, was a plush, smooth production, without sharp edges. The flashing, raw energy, which propelled The Who along ten years ago, has been almost entirely dissipated."

The track listing for the original album is: I Am The Sea / The Real Me / Quadrophenia / Cut My Hair / The Punk And The Godfather / I'm One / The Dirty Jobs / Helpless Dancer / Is It In My Head? / I've Had Enough / 5:15 / Sea and Sand / Drowned / Bell Boy / Dr Jimmy / The Rock / Love Reign O'er Me. Amongst the many Who bootlegs a copy of the demos exists twinned Lifehouse. An American label called King Biscuit Flower Hour made available a number of intriguing Who-related selections, a 1979 double open-reel album marking Quadrophenia played live being one.

The film "Hell on Wheels! - "The Year was 1964, and the Battle was just beginning!" "A Way of Life" 1997 re-release. Most Americans thought Quadrophenia was a concert film with little idea of it being a feature film. Polydor put out an American promotional offering in 1979 of Roger and Pete discussing the film and its music. A double CD audiophile was also released in 1991. Upon its original release Quadrophenia flopped in the States and was subject to a remix, an additional trio of new tracks Get Out And Stay Out, Four Faces and Joker James added to the original and ones included by other artists. Coupled with The Kids Are Alright documentary it was put out again. The soundtrack album made number twenty-three in October 1979 whilst the re-

mixed version peaked at forty-seven in July 1996. The 'Music from the soundtrack of The Who film' released by Polydor (3577 352) had a track listing consisting of the following:
I Am The Sea/ The Real Me/ I'm One/ 5:15/ Bell Boy/ I've Had Enough/ Helpless Dancer/ Doctor Jimmy on Side One with Side Two consisting of Zoot Suit (The High Numbers)/ Hi Heel Sneakers (Cross Section)/ Get Out And Stay Out (The Who)/ 4 Faces (The Who)/ Joker James (The Who)/ The Punk and The Godfather (The Who)/ Night Train (James Brown)/ Louie Louie (The Kingsmen)/ Green Onions (Booker T and The MG's)/ Rhythm of the Rain (The Cascades)/ He's So Fine (The Chiffons)/ Be My Baby (The Ronettes)/ Da Doo Ron Ron (The Crystals). The Real Me, 5:15, Bell Boy and Love Reign O'er Me are all collected on Thirty Years of Maximum R&B.

Films and Filming awarded Quadrophenia the accolade of the "Most distasteful film of the year" in its 1979 poll! For articles/ reviews about the film see any of the following titles: Film Review magazine: Yearbook 1997/ 8 and February 1997, Empire (February 1997), Films and Filming (September 1979), Total Film (February 1997), Sight and Sound (February 1997), Photoplay (March 1979), Time Out (August 1979), Premiere (February 1997), Monthly Film Bulletin (September 1979). The Brighton Evening Argus of 5 Oct 1978 has some photographs by David Bennett appertaining to the location shooting of the film and a 14 January 1997 headline 'Brighton rocks on for reel' is an article about the filming.

When released theatrically in 1979 the running time of Quadrophenia was given as 120 minutes but its subsequent video and DVD formats offer a figure of 114 minutes. Upon original release in cinemas across Britain the film caused quite a stir amongst young audiences often involving trouble between various factions, it was, "an exciting way to watch a movie." As music and film author Stuart Maconie related in a BBC 2 documentary commemorating the year of its issue. Of the original cast, only Toyah Willcox commented on the appeal of Quadrophenia in the programme, writing in her 1999 autobiography Living Out Loud, she talks of attending a private screening of the film given by Franc Roddam at a Piccadilly screening theatre, "It wasn't long in to the film that we realised that most of our scenes had been cut. The film had taken on a completely different flavour: it had become a story centred around Phil Daniel's character rather than about a gang of seven people." See also: Brighton, Quadrophenia alley

Quadrophenia DVD The DVD has the additional advantage of the viewing having the option to instantly select one of eighteen scenes from the film, which are listed as: 1. Titles, 2. Ambitions, 3. My Generation, 4. Party's Over, 5. Hard Work, 6. Revenge, 7. Dealing, 8. Stolen Goods, 9. The Weekend, 10. Seaside Blues, 11. Brighton Beach, 12. We are the Mods, 13. Nicked, 14. No Home Coming, 15. Not Mad, 16. Love Sick, 17. Had Enough and 20. End Credits. The most recently released 2-disc DVD features commentaries from Phil Daniels, Franc roddam and Leslie Ash also chips in. There are also lots of extras worth watching too.

Quadrophenia Posters A discrepancy exists in the group shot photograph used to promote the film; in the one used for the 1997 re-issued video and DVD Sting is looking up whereas in an earlier photo used and still available, he is seen gazing downwards. Also, Trevor Laird [Ferdy] touches his ear with his left hand rather than draping it over Toyah's shoulder as in the alternative version. Another poster, primarily for Europe and America, sees the group all wearing slightly different clothes to the more familiar 1997 picture with the image reflected beneath. Sting, for example, has a leather coat around his shoulders in a shot that was used for the cover of a subsequent video release. And again, some continental posters feature the cast in slightly different poses. 'An unforgettable journey to forbidden extremes.' Was how

American magazine New West termed the film whilst another poster had the byline, 'Quadrophenia The Movie: A trip that will wake you up and shake you up. 'Quadrophenia The Movie: A pocketful of dreams was their way of life. Quadrophenia The Movie: A condition of Today.' Whilst the Australian one, designed with a bright red background reads, 'Al ough intelligent film throbbing with action – A must-see film.' Concluding with ' Evokes the street heroics of Saturday Night Fever, Rebel without a Cause and West Side Story.'

Quadrophenia Videos At least four separate covers exist for the video release of the film with the latest one being the 1997 4Front budget label noteworthy for its group shot on the cover and target icon. Previously, another, on the Channel 5 label, uses the shot of Jimmy on his scooter at the cliff tops at Beachy Head with the name of the film printed on an angle. Whilst yet another, an American "R" rated release from RCA / Columbia, used the reflective shot of the cast as its cover with two shots of Steph and Jimmy in Brighton [smiling as they walk along the seafront a moment before Chalky instigates the attack on the Rockers café and the second being of the two lovers in the secluded alleyway.] A third shows the Ace [Sting] dancing in the ballroom. Quadrophenia is also available as one part of a budget box set with Tommy. A fourth packaging sees the scooter-seated Ace Face [Sting] dominating the frontage with the film title running vertically to the right. Its back cover has small pictures of the group cast, Jimmy and Monkey on the couch at the Party and a group shot of scooter-riders.

Deleted scenes Four segments featuring the Brighton Ace Face Sting are said to have been cut from the final film to not detract the attention away from Jimmy. Another saw a huge billboard advertising hoarding promoting the People Like You campaign featuring a close-up of a woman, cigarette in hand and a man looking at her. Jimmy is found crouching behind and in front of it, hiding as a group of Rockers pass by. Jimmy with the model – a second sequence was also dropped. Here, Jimmy is seen sharing a lift with a heavily made-up model who was probably the woman from either the photographs that he masturbates to or the actress used in the filmed agency ad. Wearing a hideous white polka dot dress and huge fake eyelashes she resembles a young Angie Dickinson. Meanwhile a happy master Cooper has his deckchair-like patterned blazer on in a scene that has survived through the eye of Frank Conor's camera.

Racism It is Jimmy that starts with the first of three dubious remarks made at, or about Ferdy when they meet outside the Goldhawk club. Ferdy groans when asked to supply Jimmy with an excessive amount of pills, claiming he had to go to south London to acquire this new batch. Jimmy retorts with a remark about him having to take a *"banana boat back to Jamaica"*. Here it appears to be a part of the banter between the two men but in the latter examples, Chalky with Jim and Dave when they look for Ferdy and Pete's crude comment at the scrap yard where Jimmy goes to seek out an alternative supplier, both leave a bitter taste. Trevor Laird did have reservations about playing the role seeing Ferdy as a Jamaican rather than Londoner. However, they are a part of the nature of those particular characters and this is exemplified with Kevin's coarseness during the chat with Jimmy at the café following their reacquaintance at the bathhouse.

Radio London *"Radio London: Whoopee!"* Found at 266 MW, the station is heard on a transistor radio situated in many a teenager's bedroom back in the Sixties, Jimmy's being no exception. The station mentions actual events occurring in Aden, then a British colony and the concerns of local shopkeepers of violence affecting their business at seaside resorts like Brighton. Such stations were significant in that they had a ready made market place of affluent young consumers who could easily listen to them by purchasing inexpensive 'trannies'. Other popular stations incl. Caroline, Luxembourg and Radio 270.

Ready Steady Go! "It's seven minutes past six – the weekend starts here!" A completely 'teen-age show' beginning off with a Mod pulling away from a set of traffic lights to the sound of the above words flying behind him. Rehearsals for three to four hours on the Friday afternoon occurred with performances that were initially mimed in preparation for the show taped later. In 1964 RSG! was playing Louie Louie by the Kingsmen and Tommy Tuckers' Hi Heel Sneakers, both to find their way onto the Quadrophenia soundtrack some years later. Filmed in a basement studio of the now defunct Redifussion television in central London, tickets for RSG! were highly sought after. Presented by 'Queen of Mods' Cathy McGowan, the set consisted of primary coloured targets and chevrons to compliment the freshness and vigour of the show's ideals. The importance of the audience, made up of many a flash mod girls and boys, to dance throughout the show, was encouraged by the programme makers. But what Go! Offered was a sanitised version of mod with no drugs or unpleasant aspect revealed.

It was here that Dusty Springfield got her big break as a solo artist with her debut hit You Don't Have to Say You Love Me. Many of the shows were directed by New York born director Michael Lindsay-Hogg who went on to helm the 1994 feature Celebration: The Music of Pete Townshend and The Who aka Celebration: The Music of The Who aka Daltrey Sings Townshend. The Ready Steady Who! A studio-recorded EP was put out on the Reaction label in November 1966 consisting of five tracks, Disguises, Circles and the Batman theme with the remainder presenting Keith Moon on lead vocals [Barbara Ann and Bucket T] and all tracks can be found on the A Quick One album. Further developing an association with the show after Anyway Anyhow Anywhere was selected on the very day it was released, to be one of the rotated theme song to the show [others included Manfred Mann's 5-4-3-2-1]. At home, an animated Jimmy Cooper watches the band perform the song on the show to the bedazzlement of his father [Michael Elphick]. An October 1966 show presented a Who 'happening' for half of its on-air time that caused a great stir amongst the public due to its provocative auto-destructive act by the band. The Who closed their association with the popular music show by playing on the last ever-recorded programme in December 1966. See also: The Kinks, Andrew Loog Oldham.

The Real Me Featured at the start of the film with a proud Jimmy winding his way down to the Goldhawk club on his scooter. Me follows immediately from I Am the Sea with its energized boom-boom-boom cemented by some great Moon drumming. Released as a single in America, Belgium, France and Japan with its U.S b-side of I Am One, it did not fair well. Its climax was altered and faded out which gave it an extra few seconds from the album version. A cover version by Fastball is featured on Substitute, a Who covers album released in 2001. See also: girlfriends, mental illness, Steph.

Melinda Rees With sole responsibility for all things do with continuity on Quadrophenia. Made more complex for it being a period film, it was not however a picture that escaped without the odd blooper or two. The disappearing windshield on the scooter that Jimmy rides along the top of Beachy Head heading the list [see goofs]. Could she be found guilty for allowing a Motorhead t-shirt to be worn by one of the grappling Rocker extras in the Brighton scenes when we learn that the group was formed in 1975 and not 1964, which is where we are meant to be? See also: Beachy Head, Brighton, extras.

Reviews I would like to take a moment to thank and acknowledge the inclusion of the following reviews gathered from various mediums. Each one has been included to provide a balanced view to demonstrate the mixed reaction that Quadrophenia received upon release and how it continues to stir mixed opinion. "Based on the Who album, the gritty youth-centric realism blends laughs with symbolism, psychology and some driving rock music." It's a tribute to helmer Franc Roddam's simple, restrained direction that the down beat ending, when the jobless, exhausted kid is left in the advanced state of schizophrenia implied by the title, succeeds in being dramatic." Variety Movie Guide [Hamlyn, 1991]. "A drama of bitter rivalry...on the beaches of Brighton in 1964. What passed for a successful musical at the end of the Seventies is typified by this violent, screaming and wholly unattractive amalgam of noise, violence, sex and profanity." Halliwell's Film and Video Guide, Leslie Halliwell [Harper Collins, 1997]. "The main thing you notice about Quadrophenia is the guts it has simply to be realistic and not compromise for the sake of political correctness. People certainly weren't prepared for this and a few even left...in the final stages as Jimmy faces his breakdown it successfully shows the isolation a man can face. The film has excitement, humour, an excellent story and, most importantly, a brilliant soundtrack by The Who without which nothing would make any sense." John Marshall, 1997 [Found at flueuropa.com/quadrophenia.com.] "This is a great teen movie...it's gritty and real and funny all at once and has some great music and clothes in it to boot. A word of warning: sometimes the Mods' accents are so thick you could spread them on toast..." Daily Pensylvanian, 1996.

Or "Quadrophenia is one of the great movies and has a real rock spirit to it. I felt, sitting in the theatre watching it, that I had gone through the experience...that was a movie I felt was very successful giving you that feelings." Writer/ Director Cameron Crowe, Rock Explosion, The British Invasion of America in Photos 1962-1967 by Harold Bronson [Blandford Press, 1984]. "Superior mix of early Sixties 'angry young man' and rock movie...a real sleeper." Leonard Maltin's TV Movies and Video Guide [Penguin, 1988]. "Despite its British setting, Quadrophenia evokes the universal feelings of teen emotions with a depth seldom captured on screen." L.A Times. "Fine as long as its sticks to recreation of period and place...but as the film progresses, it becomes bogged down in silly moralising and metaphysics, struggling to accommodate itself to the absurd story of the Who's rock opera." Geoff Andrews, Time Out Film Guide, ed.Tom Milne [Penguin, 1991].

"I've seen this film probably close to forty times. I have never grown tired of it. It's just the greatest Rock & Roll/ pop music-related drama ever made. If you hate R&R or do not know what a 'Mod' is...well, you'd hate it, probably. But if you 'understand', y'know? Or at least like gritty British working-class films, it's the Holy Grail." Coleen Toews (http://uk.imdb.com)

"Even eighteen years on it's still awesome stuff, the impressive period detailing detracting not a jot from the perennial coming-of-age drama. The action is powerful, the script streetwise, the music uplifting and pacing superb. Best of all though is the cast, almost everyone of them now a familiar face." Neil Jeffries, Empire, February 1997. "Sex and drugs and rock 'n' roll had never been portrayed like this until The Who decided to make a film out of their concept album. It turned out to be one of the most astute moves they ever made. Quadrophenia is a naturalist piece of filmmaking that captures England's working class youth culture in all its energetic, exciting, sordid glory. Still fresh, still vital, and still Brighton's finest hour apart from the FA Cup Final." Mike Dunford, Brighton Evening Argus, 30/ 1/ 1997.

"Quadrophenia is a bright, funny and thought-provoking film about Jimmy's willingness to drop old friends, habits and long term job prospects in return for the short-termism of living for the moment and having a sense of belonging. The film documents the swinging Sixties in what appears to be a true to life account of both the lighter and darker sides of youth culture – something that was still a relatively new and shocking experience for parents and society to comprehend."

"The primary plot concerns the growing alienation and eventual suicide of Jimmy, but perhaps precisely because of the film's attention to surface detail and the extent to which it looks at group activities, this is never very forcefully: the scene in which Jimmy finally rides his scooter over a cliff top proves singularly unmoving." Alan T.Sutherland, Sight and Sound, Winter 1979/ 1980. "...one of the best films about youth ever made, beautifully illustrating the frustrations of being young and bright but still having no future. Daniels gives an amazing performance...so intense and full of divergent emotions, he seems ready to explode at any moment." The Motion Picture Guide, N-R, 1927 – 1983 by Jay Robert Nash and Stanley Ralph Ross [Cine Books, 1986]. "Highly enjoyable rock musical combining the music of The Who with a nice feel for the mood of the Sixties." Elliot's Guide to Films on Video, by John Elliot [Boxtree]

The Rock A concoction of everything else on the Who album, it is nonetheless an effective piece with a discernible Tommy sound to it. You can almost visualise Robert Powell as the RAF pilot father of the young Tommy or the bubble-permed Daltrey clambering about to it. Best categorised as an aural recap of emotions.

Rockers *"All that greasy hair and dirty clobber. It's diabolical."*
This is Jimmy's summation of Rockers / Greasers up until the time that he actually meets and gets to know one of them, his old school friend Kevin. Up until the moment that Kev comes to see him whilst he is out in the shed looking at his scooter his opinions were drawn purely from appearance only. Kevin may

not be the most articulate of young men but he has something reasonable to say about identity and our perception of such in this scene. Never an exploitable consumer group in the sense that the Mod youngsters were, these young men and women developed from the Teddy Boy of the late Fifties with a favoured look of leather and denim adopted. The Leather Boys (1964), a British film, is worth seeking out as it offers an insight in to the mentality of the former 'ton-up' boys in an entertaining narrative. Get hold of a copy of Jurgen Volimer's photo book Rockers [Edition Oehrli, 2000] is equally discerning.

Franc Roddam "I consider Phil (Daniels) a partner in this movie. He helped create it with me." Franc speaking on the Quadrophenia DVD.

Born in Cleveland in April 1946 Roddam directed television features prior to, and following, Quad. He also devised the Eighties television drama series Auf Wiedersehen, Pet which gave prominent roles for Quad actors Timothy Spall (whom he brought to prominence in the Quad) and Gary Holton. Many viewers will also remember Michael Elphick's occasional role as the hard nut Magowan. Commendable in that there is widespread agreement from both critics and audiences alike, of how convincing the dynamic sequences such as the beach battles, unfold in Quadrophenia. Such is their dynamism that they retain their energy no matter how many times the viewer comes across the film. In a past-undocumented interview, when asked about the violence aspect prevalent in the movie, Pete Townshend conceded that however well received dramatically, his own focus for Jimmy's story was different. For him, the young Mod's journey was centred on a spiritual plain [a favoured Townshendism]. From the main actors down to the dressed-up extras, Roddam manipulated his cast perfectly, eliciting a suitably vexed response from Toyah and Phil Daniels in particular. As the location shooting schedule intensified, the director became to distance himself from the cast yet many extras involved in the Brighton seafront moments were still influenced, "I ran over to the Mods and told them 'those fucking policemen extras are fucking up the scene; go for them for real!'" recounts the director in a quote collected from the special photo montage include in a recent video release of the film. "And so when they mix," he adds, "these people are almost fighting for their lives." Sting met Franc Roddam at an audition for the film where the two proceeded to chat about Newcastle and a Herman Hesse novel that both had read. An hour later he offered him the role of the Brighton Ace Face. "My role was more a fantasy in an otherwise realistic film." Concludes the actor and musician in a later interview. Many will recall The Family, a Seventies 'fly on the wall' documentary which Roddam worked on back in 1974 but it would be Quadrophenia that provided the springboard to making American studio supported films. Manifesting itself in The Lords of Discipline, next came a reinterpretation of the Mary Shelley Frankenstein tale with the Ace Face, Sting, in the male lead role in The Bride (1985). Gary Shail, Phil Daniels and Timothy Spall all had supporting roles, as did Quad's Sound Editor John Ireland. Franc does not make films that receive a great deal of media spotlighting; his involvement in Aria (1987) within which he directs one of the ten collected shorts inspired by an operatic aria, being no different. His segment, Tristan und Isobel, is held as one of the stronger pieces in a collective including Ken Russell and Derek Jarman. War Party (1989) was preceded in 1991 by K2 [aka K2: The Ultimate High], a story detailing an attempt to scale the second highest peak in the world. Franc attended the 1997 Brighton premiere of the re-issued Quadrophenia so clearly it still has a place in his heart. His film and telly work continues to range from the serpentine to the ambitious; with two recent made-for-TV, Moby Dick and Cleopatra, 1998 and 1999 respectively, big stateside hits. Seeing Dummy (TV, 1977) that Pete Townshend sought out Roddam for the role of director for the Quadrophenia project. See also: Sean Barton, Films in Review (May 1983), Chris Menges, Screen International (May 1979/ November 1997), Sting, Christian Wrangler.

The Ronettes Shaped by writer/ producer Phil Spector, who eventually married and later divorced lead singer Veronica 'Ronnie' Bennett. Their track Be My Baby, heard as the lads arrive outside the house party in Quadrophenia, sold over a million copies. It was their biggest chart success.

Bill Rowe With an extensive and esteemed career in film sound, Rowe lent his skills to over a hundred films and was acknowledged by the industry by winning an Academy Award for Best Sound for The Last Emperor in 1997, adding nicely to his Bafta for The Killing Fields (1984) and a special achievement award from the British Film Institute in 1985. A consummate sound re-recordist, Bill was the Dubbing Mixer for Quadrophenia with his professional association with many of its cast and crew including: 1. Clockwise (1985) – Benjamin Whitrow aka Fulford, has a supporting role, 2. Lost Angels (1981) as Supervising Re-recording Mixer he worked with John Ireland, Sound Engineer on Quad, but here as the Dialogue Editor, 3.Give My Regards to Broad Street (1984) Gary Shail and Jeremy Child appear in this piece of Paul McCartney fluff, 4. Rosie Dixon: Night Nurse with a small role for a youthful Leslie Ash, 5. Listzomania and Tommy (both 1975) each furnishing Roger Daltrey with substantial screen roles and, incidentally, directed by Ken Russell, 6. Cal (1984) see Patsy Pollock and 7. The Mission (1986).

Andrew Sanders Assistant Art Director on Quadrophenia. It is the responsibility of the Art Director [aka Set Designer] to see that the Production Manager's vision for a scene is carried through. Andrew filled the latter role on Franc Roddam's K2 and on The Hit (1984). Other projects have included the exquisite Sheltering Sky (1990) that gave an eccentric gem of a character role for Timothy Spall. Whilst as Art Director on Privates on Parade (1982) Andrew Sanders was part of a cast and crew with Michael Elphick.

John-Paul Sartre I think against myself.
Esteemed by the original Mods Sartre advocated the philosophy of humanism; existentialism to you and me, which sought liberation from the rejection of the past. He quantified that who a person is, should be based upon what he or she does. "Freedom is not important," offers Michel Contant, a friend of Sartre's, " it is the road you take to achieve it where significance is found."

Sawdust Caesar novel / newspaper headline
"I love Brighton, beautiful Brighton, its pretty girls, the warm, London village atmosphere and tolerance."

203

Consisting as it does of fictitious names of characters but written by someone that was there and involved in incidents that occurred in 1964. Writing in the prologue, Howard Baker concurs, "This, therefore, is an entirely false yet enigmatically very real account of the Mod and Rockers days of the Sixties." Taking its title from Margate Magistrate Dr George Simpson and his bombastic 'Sawdust Caesars' speech that made the front page headline of the Daily Express on 19 May 1964, almost his entire speech is quoted verbatim in the courtroom scene from Quadrophenia. Only, the location has changed to Brighton for the sake of continuity. See also: Dr George Simpson.

Scarves Observe one of the young Mods wrapped up in a red, white and black football scarf appertaining to Manchester United in the scene where a rag bag of a marching band struts along Brighton's East Street. Jimmy and the others oddly join in the precession as it makes its way towards the seafront passing the ABC cinema and thus revealing one of the film's most prominent faux pas. See also: goofs, Grease, Heaven Can Wait.

Schizophrenia "Schizophrenic? I'm bleeding Quadrophenic."
[Jimmy in The Who's Quadrophenia album notes].
"*Bloody split personality!*" Jimmy's dad. "Four self's I want to find and I don't know which one is me." The Punk and The Godfather. Literally defined as 'split mind' resulting in a divide between the intellect and emotional facets of the personality. A loss of vivacity and drive becomes self-evident with vagueness to the thought process. Jimmy does display some signs of the illness especially in his diminishing lack of interest and capability in relating to others. Whilst in addition, his impairment of the role he has been given at the advertising agency builds to a verbal detonation of poor Mr Fulford. Consequently, Jimmy falls deeper in to isolation and a sense of eccentricity is felt by friends such as Dave and Steph [think of the tempestuous coffee bar confrontation]. His dad may not understand why he has to be a part of a gang but Jimmy embraces being a Mod not to submerge his identity but to recognise it as being what he IS. Unlike Mrs Cooper, he does acknowledge that Jimmy seems a little different to most and he does address the past family history of mental illness [on the side of his spouse] following their confrontation when Jimmy returns home late one

evening. Worthy of note in that in that the Who album lyric has his mother talking about the illness but in the film it is his father that does and how it 'runs in the family.'

Schizophrenia, as an illness, develops in adolescence or early adult life and its instigation remains illusive. The cover of the Who album shows the four mirrors of his scooter reflecting the members of the band and this is aped in the film, only replaced with multiple images of Jimmy as he tinkers with his bike in the shed. During the course of the film there are no obvious reference points to indicate such an affliction experienced by Jimmy. See also: Bibliography

Scooters *"Running about on them bikes all night. It's not normal..."* Jimmy's mum. "I ride a G.S scooter with my hair cut neat." I've Had Enough / Sea and Sand. *"Poxy hairdryer!"* Kevin remonstrating his opinion.

Scooters seen in the film: i. Lambretta LI Series 1 and 2, ii. Lambretta LI Series 3. The LI 125 Series 1 was a four-speed scooter reaching the dizzy capacity of 42/3 M.P.H., costing the Sixties Mod £155 17s 6d. The LI 150 - Series 1: retailing at £174 17s 6d the 150 was categorised as having a 'wide style' look and could reach almost 50 m.p.h. The LI 125 - Series 2:

Another four-speed, clocking in at the same maximum as its Series 1 counterpart but for £157 19s 6d. Two-grey, it was unusual in that its headlight was built-in to the handlebars so as you turned the light did likewise. It was in production from October 1959 to November 1961. LI 150 - Series 2: The most successful selling of any Lambretta model, presented from October 1959 through to November 1961 also, and costing £169 17s 6d.

Vespa GS: 'paradis per due'. The GS 160 Mark 1, first produced in 1961, is regarded as the most stylish of the Gran Sport models, who can forget the

205

Brighton Ace Face's beautiful chrome horse?
Quadrophenia scooters : "When the engine stopped, so did the music." The filmed enhancement to the basic [album] story stimulated a renewal of interest in scooters. Jimmy's scooter, with its registration number is KRU 251 is a 1962 Lambretta LI 150 model; a workhorse type of machine. In actuality, Jim's reg had an additional 'F' at the end which signified its true 1967 registration). His scooter is heavily accessorised by a body work painted in green, red and white with a spare wheel on the back next to a carrier and chequered black and white chequered mudguard on the back wheel. Some LI lettering and tassels on his handlebars are quite hard to acquire for the modern day scooterists. As the Ace Face on the Brighton scene, Sting rides a Rally 200 with panels fitted giving it a Grand Sport look. Photographs of 1964 Mods at Brighton show many with their vehicle registration positioned on the front mudguards as is the case with Ace and Jimmy. His registration number is MFG185G. Remarkably, both scooters have since resurfaced in a Portsmouth scooter shop. Allstyle Scooters in Portsmouth held the ownership of both Jimmy and the Ace Face's scooters. Said to have been fully-restored and available for hire but have since been sold on a couple of times. In late-2008, the scooter was sold at auction for 36k ($53k). According to contributors on the modculture.com site, Sting was unable to ride a geared scoot and a number of scooters were utilised on screen[3 Rally 200's and a TS 125 model]. A chap from Gloucester was said to have bought one, used in Quadrophenia, from a house clearance sale, a Rally model, and restored it. A mute point, in the Quadrophenia story presented initially on The Who's album, Jimmy says that he rides a GS Vespa scooter yet in the film he rides a Lambretta. Why? Was it because the Lambretta proved itself more popular amongst teens than Vespas? Furthermore, he steals Sting's Vespa from outside of the Grand Hotel by using his own scooter keys. How would this have been possible? Granted, the same Vespa ignition key did indeed start all other Vespas made between 1956 - 1965 but surely not those of its competitors too. He would have needed to penetrate the steering lock, pull out the choke, and check the fuel lever before locating a key that fitted! Artistic

A QUADROPHENIA ANTHOLOGY

licence prevails. Pete's scooter was a 150 GS Vespa that had been owned by enthusiast Bill Drake since 1969 and used by his father previously, "Before filming began I was asked to identify suitable scooters [for the cast]." He told me. Bill travelled with the Property Master for the film to find machines that could be used for the 1964-set story. "I rejected a Lambretta GP because of its year," he continues in a letter to the author, "The gent from the film company over-ruled me saying that the square headlight could be disguised with some fur." At this point Bill left the project but his scooter was used in Quadrophenia, "Apparently, Pete [Garry Cooper] pulled away full throttle at a set of traffic lights and turned the machine over. It took three days to persuade him to get on the bike again I am told." The scooter was returned to Bill after being resprayed. See also: Phil Davis [Chalky]. "Go Gay." Sixties ad slogan for Lambretta, "Go where the action is – go Vespa." Sixties ad slogan for Vespa. For a fifteen-year period after the Second World War, the Italian scooter was more popular than the traditional motorbike. By 1950 a little more than eight thousand scooters were sold globally rising to just over 109,000 by 1957. A real scooter mania kick started in 1959 with the sale of 160,000 in Britain alone, rising to more than sixteen million sold today worldwide. It was the early-Fifties that scooters were initially imported in to Britain for their utility use. Mods started to ride them from 1962 onwards. The GS 150 and 160, a union of performance and style, became the most popular Vespas amongst teenagers thanks to their sporting look. In 1962 the British Lambretta Owners' Association was organising runs down to Brighton but visiting rallies organised by the club date back to 1956. Clubs exist across Britain, Europe and the world with annual runs to Hastings and the Isle of Wight popular attractions still. Scooting backwards to 1960, groups of Scooter Boys were becoming common but by 1964 their semblance, boosted by the media, had turned nasty, "Scooter Gangs 'Beat Up' Clacton" screeched the Mirror following minor scuffles between Mods/ Rockers at that seaside location. Most of the scooterists and Rockers in Quadrophenia do not wear helmets, simply because the legislation making the wearing of crash helmets compulsory would not be introduced until 1972 with the Road Traffic Act.

The Italian scooter has been regarded as a working class sports car complimented by the Mod whom accessorising made their vehicle an extension of his already elegant, wardrobe.

1 VESPA / 2 LAMBRETTA : A brief history

Vespizzatevi! – Vespa Yourselves!
[Fifties Italian advertising slogan].

1. With Fascism having crumbled, Italy in 1945 was a ravenous beast but a remarkable resurgence occurred by way of an aeronautical designer called Enrico Piaggio and his entirely fresh guise for a two-wheeled, open scooter. Incorporating aesthetics and practicality with American financing, Piaggio's idea remobilised the entire country. Manufacture of the 'wasp' [Vespa in Italian] collapsed in the late-sixties but today versions continue to zoom out of factories, only from India not Italy. A staggering eighty-nine different Vespa models have been produced totalling more than fifteen million sales. Ferdinando Innocenti, its founder, died in 1966 after which time responsibility for the company passed to his son. "The World's finest scooter" [Lambretta ad]. 2. The first Lambretta came from Italy in 1947 through Ferdinando Innocenti, who commissioned his designer Corradino d'Ascanio to create what was deemed an 'exquisite social appliance' [in a company newsreel] which, in keeping with Lambretta, was also funded by the American dollar. Footage from the original newsreel is included in the meritorious documentary Classic Motorcycles - Scooter Mania [Channel 4, 1993], a real must-see if you are a scooter fan. Footage of Mods arriving in Brighton can also be enjoyed in the film. Competition between the two manufactures was intense but ironically, both went on to homogenise their identities. A distinction can be drawn in that the Lambretta has a narrower backside than the Vespa. Returning to the documentary, "The Vespa is a snail, an invertebrate, the Lambretta however has a spine."

Named after the region of Lambrate, Milan, where the scooters were built, Lambretta production ceased long ago but components continue to be made, under licence, in India. As a cheap and low-maintenance contraption both were smashingly practical for the sixties, live-at-home youngster keen to keep up with the trends. A series of models were introduced to the British market from the late-fifties LD 125 to the Li 150 [early-Sixties] to the Centro and TV 175 Series 2. In 1965 the Lambretta LI 125cc cost £129.10.0

Stylising and Fetishisation "...apparitions from sci-fi stories, like rolling technical monsters." Rock Music: Culture, Aesthetics and Sociology.

Deliciously, there was quite a number of ways to enhance upon the basic scooter frame, to have it chromed-up and mixed with dark colours or two-toned was popular due to it being a lot cheaper. Chalky and Jimmy's scooters are good examples. Front and rear luggage carriers for both types cost 59s 6d L 57 6d whilst a windshield for the Vespa cost £5 or so. Mirrors retailed at £12/6, a clear view windscreen cost £4 15/- and not forgetting your trusty foxtail and aerial. Spotlights and mirrors peaked in being added in 1963/64 the time when most photos were caught for posterity by the media. By the close of 1964 fashion had moved on from this. The primary difference between the Lambretta and Vespa being that the Vespa was added to which succeeded in enhancing its curves. As newer models came on to the market, favourite entries in the collections prior to 1962 were the Vespa GS 160cc and for Lambretta, it was the TV 200cc [reaching a speedy 75 m.p.h.]. The GS 150cc and TV Series 2 transposed those followed by the GS 160cc and TV 175 Series 3 [replaced in 1963 by the GT 200cc]. The latter taken over by the SX 200cc by 1966. Finally, the Vespa GS 160cc was deposed in 1965 by the SS 180cc however, it is commonly agreed amongst enthusiasts that the GS 160cc and GT 200cc was *the* Mod scooter model of choice.

Others included the new Lambretta 100cc Cento, 125cc slim style, 150cc Special Pacemaker, and the 200cc G.T'. New Vespas numbered the 90cc, 150cc Sportique and the 150cc S.P Supreme in 1964. By 1966 fashion add-too's include spotlights, fly screens, front bumpers, headlight grills and horn covers. Hire Purchase enabled youngsters to purchase scooters on the 'never-never' but by the mid-Sixties such items were increasingly more costly to obtain by this method. The end for the Mods came in the following year with outrageous ads for psychedelic scooters [stocked by Eddie Grimstead in London's East Ham]. Writer Umberto Eco regaled the Vespa as a 'subtle seduction of faraway places...a symbol of an unfilled desire. Vespas were even sold as 'providers of pleasure.' Lambretta and Vespa sweatshirts/ hooded tops/ watches, clocks and calendars are now purchasable. The scooters have disappeared and now it is the related-items that sell. The ease by which both the Lambretta and Vespa trademarks are available on license means that licensing anything can be considered. The Purple Hearts, a band that once supported The Jam, were a part of the brief mod revivalist groups in the late Seventies and aped the classic typeface of Lambretta for their own logo. They toured with other mod bands and put out a single called "Jimmy" in 1980. Whilst the Brighton-based Lambrettas went one step further and took the name itself.

In Quadrophenia I cannot recall seeing a single woman riding her own scooter. Nevertheless, today's machines are popular amongst the female scooterist. The small-framed Lambrettas, lower on the floor and thus easier and lighter to handle being favoured. It is said that the older and arguably better looking Vespa and Lambrettas can be especially troublesome, often proving expensive and difficult to repair if you have no knowledge of their machinations. The reliability of the Vespa is looked upon as a better first-time option due to the ease of accessibility of parts. Enthusiasts more often than not vocalise a penchance for the Lambretta, "I personally prefer its sleeker look and style." enthuses Brighton-based Leon Trigg, a Velocifero rider of the late-Nineties. It is possible to acquire a restored Lambretta Li 125 or Li 150 series II from between 2.5k- 3.8k or unrestored Lambrettas from about £800. In the 1908s, a new Vespal, the Cosa, was introduced to the market but proved not to be a success. "Vespa. An Italian idea by Piaggio" and "Make the Vespa choice" are two contemporary ads which sees the mythology of the scooter becoming the desired object. See also: bibliography, goofs.

Sea "The continuous whisper" Graham Greene, Brighton Rock.
The water at Brighton sometimes looks like fizzy lemonade, all-bubbling away

as it splashes against the shore. The Spiritual symbolism of the sea is well documented, as is its significance in relation to a spiritual and religious appropriation. In addition, to be 'all at sea' is to be lost, an idea often viewed in past centuries as a bringer of death with a strong religious undertow. Beneath it was viewed as death, silence and desolation but in actuality it is a source of creation, "beyond the memory of history" as Simon Schama elegantly put it in Seas – Landscapes and Memory. Jimmy goes to the water's edge on many occasions, repeatedly alienated both from, and by a present that will soon become a part of his past. The water literally washes all such things away leaving only the essence of himself. Now this can be deemed exacerbating, enthralling or terrifying in its devastation but for him things can now only improve. The first image in the film is of a heavy-limbed but charged Jimmy walking with some conviction away from the cliff top at Beachy Head. He has quite literally turned away from all that he had valued. In the 1973 Who album of Jimmy's journey, the young man recounts moments in his life from the vantage point of 'The Rock' but for the filmed version of Quadrophenia the imagery is still there both pre-credits where he walks away from the cliff top and the final scene where his scooter flying over the edge. Ken Russell had used a waterfall climactic scene in Tommy whereby the protagonist scales a waterfall and up to a mountaintop where the story ends with Roger Daltrey cloaked in silhouette form.
See also: Beachy Head, Bibliography
Sea and Sand The end of the Who track lifts lyrics from I'm the Face, a single put out by the band whilst known as the High Numbers, as well as from Helpless Dancer and I've Had Enough. The tentative sound of the sea and its feathered inhabitants are tied by Daltrey's high-pitched intonation concluded with a rhythm with inflection of 5:15. Closing with the line "…here by the sea and sand, nothing ever goes as planned," reminiscent of Townshend's "…out of my brain on the 5:15." See also: fashion, 5:15, girls, slang.
Sex "Sex is pleasure, marriage is virtue." Malcolm Muggeridge.
One of the most famous sex scenes in any British film has to be Jimmy and Steph's tryst during the rioting. He also gets to survive a snogging from Monkey whilst being tempted purely by her offer of drugs at the house party. Returning

after his frustration at missing Steph everybody else appears to have paired up for the evening in the bedrooms upstairs.

Initially put on limited sale in 1961, the contraceptive pill AKA "The Pill" gave women a defence against unwanted pregnancies if they could find a doctor that would prescribe it to them without their parents being informed. Still, a distinction was being drawn marking a separation of relationships and sex for reproduction. Jimmy falls for Steph after their time in Brighton but discovers that she is the one more open to the causality of the scene than he is, invariably he gets hurt. *"Fuckin' meant something to me!"* See also: Leslie Ash, bibliography.

Sex Pistols Recorded a version of The Who's Substitue as did Blur. Roadrunner also covered by the Pistols as it was earlier by The Who. Punks, like the Mods before, were consumers of amphetamines and especially in the form of speed. Pete Townshend wrote Who Are You after a drunken meeting with two members of the band in a London bar back in the late Seventies. A version of Substitute can be found on the Swedish bootleg LP Bad Boys which is an interesting album for its cover art, a pastiche of Sgt.Pepper, including Pete Townshend, Keith Moon and David Bowie. The Who appear on the soundtrack release of The Filth And The Fury (2000) a feature documentary about the Pistols. Lead singer Johnny Rotten auditioned for the part of Jimmy but was rejected by the insurarers due to the noteriety of his band at the time.

Gary Shail Just why is he nicknamed Spider and what does he do to sustain his mod life style? Could it be that his silent creeping about disturbs those around him? Probably. We know that he lives at home with his parents but what his actual name is remains a mystery. In relation to Dave his own dislike of the *"monkey brained"* Shail is glaring; think of Alfredo's cafe where Jimmy, Dave and Chalky are gathered around a pinball machine and up struts the dizzy Spider full of sickly sweet enthusiasm. Clutching a bottle of Pepsi, [very Mod] complete with stripy straw, he attempts to ingratiate himself by spouting off about the vast quantities of drugs he wants for the Brighton weekender. The others merely tolerate his presence in only Gary Shail's second on-screen appearance, bemusing the others with his desire of his *"thinking about getting a gun."* Spider is an affable chap possessing a shining sense of fashion, all shirt and tie, sharp

[Above] Scenes from Quadrophenia featuring Gary Shail. as Spider.

suit rounded off with a green raincoat and precise hair, combed and snazzy. And to cap it all, he is the only member of the crew to have a regular girlfriend, naturally a Mod too, resplendent in a red leather coat accompanied by a pixie-like haircut. We never get to know her name but her adopted look is equally as fine as her scooter-riding boyfriend is (her actual name was Tammy, off-screen). The couple heighten the distress experienced by Jimmy after a gang of Rockers sets upon the couple whilst they were on their way to the Goldhawk after stalling outside a pub. The attack seen in the film resultes in a mistaken revenge beating of Jim's newly found schoolmate Kev at Shepherd's Bush market. However, the former was shot at night and the Bramley Arms pub was kept open whilst the crew were filming there. Roddam encouraged the actors to improvise and the resulting line about Spider's scooter being a 'hairdryer' was created. Shail and Gary Holton, his rocker attacker, later became firm friends ane even acted together in a stage musical as well as both playing in a short-lived band called 'The Actors'. Gary Shail has recently returned to acting after many years away and continues to make music at home.

Shepherd's Bush "It's just basic Shepherd's Bush enjoyment."
Pete Townshend on the delights of The Who playing live.
Having as it does a heavy Irish residency, it's known for its market and as a location with a very long history as a concert venue at the Empire on the busy Shepherd's Bush Green. The Bush is recognised as significant in its vlue as a focal point in relation to The Who and its reputation as a major Mod hotspot. Its underground tube station glimpsed during this scene opened in 1900 with the Central Line including a nearby stop for Goldhawk Road. A number of scenes

213

from Quadrophenia were shot in the locality including on the Goldhawk road, Lime Grove and Richford street.

In 1995 Roger and John played a set at the Green's Bottom Line club. The Who's internet released album The Blues to the Bush was recorded partly at the Empire as well as in Chicago, Illinois. It features a rendition of Anyway Anyhow Anywhere specially recorded there in December 1999. Pete Townshend's solo album Live At the Shepherd's Bush Empire concludes the Who affiliation. See also: Alfredo's, Goldhawk Road, Irish Jack.

Shingle There is no sand visible on Brighton beach, only shingle. Hard and unfriendly, it came in useful by curbing the summertime boredom of youngsters back in 1964. Much of it was thrown at other youths and unfortunate bystanders as well as the police. The ABC cinema had the glass in its seafront entrance smashed too. Jimmy can be seen throwing stones at unseen assailants during the beach fighting but he is significantly not shown physically scrapping unlike the others [see Chalky, Dave, Spider, Dan or John for example].

Shirt and tie Why is it that Spider [Gary Shail], the Ace Face [Sting] and Jimmy [Phil Daniels] all at some time or another are seen with their tie slackened to about an inch with the top button of the shirt visible? See also: suits

Dr George Simpson A Margate magistrate forever remembered for his 'Sawdust Caesars' diatribe against the holiday-time coastal violence of 1964. Then a family GP for twenty-five years, Dr Simpson was embraced by the press of the day, which lauded his speech into front-page news [the Daily Express, opposite]. Regrettably, for those caught up in the scuffles in Margate [following on from the Easter troubles at Clacton] Simpson realised that he was dealing with what was becoming a regular occurrence and consequently a media platform to counteract the rising tide of violence was seized with some zeal.

Dishing out an excessive fine of £75 to seventeen-year-old James Brunton of whom Sting's Ace Face character returns the cheeky cheque quip, much of Simpson's original speech is used in the Brighton courtroom sequence in Quadrophenia. Incidentally, his *"long-haired louts"* line addressed whilst Brunton was up in front of the court is made even more ridiculous when it is revealed that the youngster actually had short hair! Dr Simpson's identity is not acknowledged in the scene but John Phillips portrays him on screen. "It is not likely that the air of this town had ever been polluted by the hordes of hooligans, male & female, such as we have seen this weekend and of whom you are an example. These longhaired, mentally unstable, petty little hoodlums, these sawdust Caesars who can only find courage like rats, in hunting in packs, came to Margate with the avowed intent of interfering with the life and property of its inhabitants. In so far as the law gives us power, this court will not fail to use the prescribed penalties. It will, perhaps, discourage you and others of your kidney who are infected with this vicious virus." [Special court held on Whitsun Monday to hear cases of 44 youths charged] Daily Express, 3d: Tues May 19 "Sawdust Caesars" headline.

Immediately following this, the press seized upon the imagery evoked by Simpson - the Express, Daily Sketch, London Evening Standard and Daily Telegraph all using language of a similar ilk. See also: Bibliography, Newspapers, John Phillips.

The Sixties – relevance to events occurring in the film:

1960 - Prime Minister Harold Macmillan quips, "You've never had it so good." In the late Fifties whereas now it was more a case of you've "never-never" had it so good. National Service had been abolished and a lower school leaving age introduced as Britain entered in to a bright, new decade some 5.5 million people had their own cars in comparison to 2.250 million in 1950.

The year of 1963 is noted on Bell Boy as being the year in which Jimmy joined the Brighton Ace Face and others in the trouble at the resort. 1964 'Skid lids', crash helmets, were still not yet compulsory but most youngsters would wear them. BBC 2 goes to air and Naked Lunch by William Burroughs was published. The Top 10 chart included hits by Cilla Black and The Searchers whilst The Beatles topped both the singles and albums hit parade. Easter The coldest for eighty years, chilly and wet. May saw twice the national average of rainfall whilst the temperature on the Thursday before the Whitsun weekend was 62 degrees. All police leave over the holidays was cancelled as violence erupted. The weekend of 26/7 March in Clacton saw an invasion of youngsters involved in trouble that was really a struggle between London Mods and local Rockers.This was followed by Great Yarmouth, both East Coast resorts with limited amenities. Clacton saw ninety-seven arrests with an estimated £513 caused in damages. Bournemouth saw fifty-six, [£100 estimated damages] and Margate found sixty-four, [£250 estimated damages]. In Brighton over a hundred arrests [£400 in estimated damages] was concluded with an unknown number of youths eventually charged in two special court sittings. At 7:30 pm on the last weekend evening of the holidays, police rounded up all Mods and Rockers and took them to the train station, marching them through the streets as they went, viewed by the Evening Argus as a 'sullen army'.

May Southend, Bournemouth and County Durham all reported trouble. Abuse of civil liberties by the Brighton police presented itself with youngsters put in communal, overcrowded cells. Some were held for up to three days. Scotland Yard's Flying Squad was flown down to Brighton to combat trouble. "Never before has a civilization reached such a degree of a contempt for life; never before has a generation, drowned in mortification, felt such a rage to live." Raoul Vaneigem [The Revolution of everyday life, Channel 4, 1985] With the bank holiday scuffles being exploited by the press, the authentic cognescenti distanced themselves from the hybrid definition of Mod, a move away from the 1962 period where disciples were interested in nothing but Modliness. West Ham United won the FA Cup.

August Police tipped-off that Hastings was to be invaded by waring youths rather than Brighton, consequently, all leave was again cancelled. The average weekly wage was £16 14/11. Art colleges across the country would prove to be recognised as enormously influential for music/ fashion/ creative output. A new Labour government in October resulted in Harold Wilson as the first Labour Prime Minister in 13 years.

1965 - 66 The seaside happenings were now expected and skirmishes in Brighton, Weston-super-Mare and Great Yarmouth continued with springtime visits and other seaside towns but not as serious as they had been. The popularity of The Who came in to the spotlight as The Beatles and the Rolling Stones fame reaches fever pitch.

1966 Skirmishes in Brighton and other coastal towns reoccur but nowhere near

the extent of past years as previously detailed.
The Seventies – relevance to events occurring in the film:
1978 Quadrophenia goes in to pre-production prior to its commercial release in 1979, sixty-one films were made in Britain whilst by 1979 it was down to fifty-four, with 111.90m visitors to British cinemas.
1979 The Who docu-film The Kids Are Alright and Quad are both exhibited in cinemas across Britain. An arduous twelve months saw heavy snow, strikes, petrol in short supply, the IRA on full operative mode, Nottingham Forest winning the European Cup and Arsenal the F.A Cup all rounded of with a new Conservative government with Margaret Thatcher as Prime Minister. Kramer Vs Kramer picked up an Academy Award for Best Film whilst the year also saw the release of Apocalypse Now, Alien and Manhattan. The best-selling single sing was Art Garfunkel's Bright Eyes followed by Cliff Richard's We Don't Talk Anymore, which says enough really. Sting, reaps commercial success with his band The Police scoring three Top 40 hits and by 1980 they were the top selling act in Britain. The summer saw a Mod revival led by The Jam who release their All Mod Cons album. Quadrophenia came out on 14 August with a premiere at the Plaza 1 cinema in the West End of London with cast members in attendance. The Who turn up but a bearded Pete Townshend almost fails to be allowed in by an over zealous commissionaire who doesn't recognise him! [A cutting of the incident can be seen in The Who Concert File]. An explosion of Mods on scooters made the headlines too, consequently blocking Lower Regent Street. Jimmy's story went on to be the eighth most successful picture of the year, grossing £36,472 over its first seven days in the capital. Sting attended a Who concert at Wembley a few days after the film was put on general exhibition. The band also played sold-out shows at the Brighton Conference Centre [now known as the Brighton Centre] that November, issuing a special Royal Mail 'first-day cover' to commemorate the gigs. The finger of blame pointed to the popularity of the film in igniting the gang-related scuffles that summer on Brighton seafront. The Kids Are Alright (AA) opens on 31 August in Brighton whilst Scum (X) with many Quad cast members appearing in, is released in November. Quadrophenia is presented at the ABC Brighton at 2:30 5:30 8:30.

217

Mike Shaw Besides the headlining Daltrey, Entwistle and Townshend providing a virtual Who's who of musical directors on the film, Mike brought his technical know-how as Music Co-Ordinator on a very busy soundtrack. With more than twenty tracks included, he had his work cut out. He again had a hand in the Who's album release Meaty, Beefy, Big and Bouncy and Hooligans, as well as on a subsequent Who compilation LP simply titled Greatest Hits. Mike was an old grammar school friend of Who manager Chris Stamp and brought on board as a Production Manager for the High Numbers, with a brief of shaping their live presence in to a more theatrical coherence. He later went on to be an executive at Track Records and was present at the High Number's Notting Hill rehearsal for Stamp and Lambert Shaw felt that they played even better at their gigs. With Kit Lambert, Mike made a rough 16mm promotional film of the band performing at the Railway Hotel [see the inside cover of Meaty for a photo] made to use as an aide for possible future bookings. It was a novel idea and one that had not been widely utilised before, even being played in the background at their gigs. Lambert had held the camera and Shaw managed the single light source to capture a raw but memorable slice of the band exploding in their wholly owned live domain.

Snack bars A common social gathering point for sixties teenagers, with coffee bars after youth clubs leading the way amongst many in Brighton and elsewhere. The unfortunate Rockers are set-upon by hundreds of roaring Mods in a snack bar that once stood at the top of East Street. Brighton police were not too pleased when its window was shattered during location filming there in 1978. You can see a fellow mod chuck a table through it from inside the premises just after Jimmy throws food at the agitated owner hiding behind the service bar. Metal railings attached to the building opposite [look up and you will see them] are noticeable during this moment and remain. However, looking for the snack bar today will prove a fruitless task; it has been absorbed in to the neighbouring Queens hotel to such an extent that you would hardly know it was ever there. Clearly it was, because when Chalky spots one of the Rockers that forced him off the road earlier that day pull up outside the premises, look closely as they charge across the promenade to the snack bar and a sign above the entrance

There is a great deal of slang used by many of the characters in the film and below is an explanation behind many of the terms used.

Amphetamines Prevalent with young sixties mods and known as uppers, ups, wake-ups, bennies amphetamine sulphate, dexies, black beauties, jollies or speed. See drugs for specific usage.

Bird *"Where'd the bird go?"* Jimmy to no one in particular after Steph disappears off with Pete shortly after their arrival in Brighton. ii. A young woman viewed sexually also used / recognised as pertaining to a prostitute.

Blocked/ leapers Mod term for being high on amphetamines as mentioned in Cut My Hair.

Blues A favoured mod slang to describe amphetamines.

Bollocks Profanity frequently uttered by Jimmy and Spider et al but not common usage in 1960s.

Cunt Spouted by many of the male Mods in Quadrophenia and originally developed from cunte, count[e] and the Germanic Kunton. Used in the film to describe a foolish or despicable person i.e. Pete [by Dave] who again calls Chalky this following his scooter accident and those at the advertising agency are termed as such by Jimmy.

Face Defined in Rave Off as 'A character who imposes himself by his appearance alone…keeping up the pose, nervousness, suppressed agression." The originators of fashion styles adopted by the ordinary mods who themselves wore the uniform of i.e. parka, Fred Perry, Levis. See also: Bibliography, Mods.

Fuck Quite prominent in the film especially when used by an exacerbated Jimmy following his collision with a mail van, *"Oh fuck, look what you done! You cunts. You've killed me scooter... Mr Fuckin' Postman..."*

Gaff Colloquialism with a strong cockney usage and heard in relation to a home or location. Keith Moon mentions it in the song Bell Boy.

Gollywog A racist term used in the 1960s, coming from the word golliwog. Pete labels Ferdy in this way in a brief conversation with an uncomfortable-looking Jimmy at the scrap yard owned by Fenton's uncle. Also observe the racist graffiti sprayed on to the corrugated iron gates of the entrance that reads 'NF is opium'. NF being the initials of the right wing National Front movement prevalent from the late Sixties forth.

Gordon Bennett Astonishment, a euphemism derived from James Gordon Bennett, after whom many motor and aeronautical events were named...an alternative to *"Cor blimey!"* popularised in the Carry On films by Sid James. Heard in Quadrophenia by Jimmy's father in the kitchen upon seeing his son wearing sopping wet jeans.

It Refers to the sexual attractiveness of a female as perceived by a male, in the case of Quadrophenia, Dave who defines Steph this way to Jimmy whilst seeing her at the Goldhawk dancing with Pete. Additionally spoken to indicate the act of sexual intercourse. A further adaptation, in use back in Brighton in 1964 was in a newspaper listing advertisement for the Florida Rooms eg. "Top of the It parade," as the popular venue was termed.

Leapers Terminology adopted by young Mods in the Sixties to describe the physical stimulus of amphetamines. Jimmy and his mates attempt to buy *"blues - 250 leapers"* from the crooked Harry North in a scene in the film.

Mush A man, a term of greeting.

Nig-Nog Not originally a racist term but a description for an unskilled man. Its derogatory use was widespread by the mid-1970s. However, it is not wholly authentic in its adaptation by Chalky [in the scene where he, Jimmy and Dave go in search of Ferdy] in Quadrophenia. See also: Gollywog.

Ponce To sponge, scrounge or cadge from others, disparaging inscription for a man. Used since 1915 and utilised by Chalky's Mod mates in the film.

Poof An effeminate person e.g *"Poofs wear lacquer."* Jimmy's macho rebuff whilst at the local gents barbershop wonderfully proven by fellow Mod Dan's innocent affirmation that he wears it and as funny as it reads.

Poxy Worthless. Generally a term of abuse. Utilised by a stressed-out Jimmy to inform his boss at the ad agency that he will no longer be requiring his clerk job.

Rave A common occurrence for gatherings in the late eighties and early-nineties was also used back in the sixties. A July 1961 'All-Night Rave' at the Florida Room in Brighton proving as such.
See also: Bibliography.
Tacky Herbert More of a late 1970s term rather than circa 1964 [in the film] but incorporated wittily by the designer at the ad agency following Jimmy's delayed collection of some photographs.
Ticket - 1 & 2 A Mod term used to describe a person that has not quite got the right idea on the fashion front. A follower rather than a leader or setter. The Who's as the High Numbers drop a name check in the mod homage I'm The Face as does Jimmy when taking with Kevin in his shed. *"States – third-class tickets."* defines Jimmy of Rockers to Kevin. Also a style for a Mod girl incorporating plain clothes, no make-up and distinctly male trousers.
Wanker and Cunt *"That flash cunt"* description of Pete by Dave. *"You're all wankers and cunts!"* Screams Jimmy at his former mate's outside Alfredo's after the fracas with Dave.

Wogland Used to describe any any country with a specifically non-white populace i.e. Aden, the location where Jimmy's school friend, Kevin has just returned from on a tour of duty with the Army.

reads East street. In addition, the New Heart pub, once situated across the road from here can be seen. See also: East Street, Pubs.

Snake Belts Unbelievably, one is worn by the juvenile-minded Spider you can see it during the Beach Cafe scene at Brighton where he stands in front of the table. Jimmy also wears one revealed when he goes to see Steph at the supermarket where she works. It can also be seen during the moment spent with Harry North. Produced in 2-tone colours of green/red/blue and red and recognisable for the silver "S" shaped buckle with its connected loop. Many school children had them in the 1970s, I know that I did and I bet you did too!

Timothy Spall A marvellous character actor of both film and television, who along with Ray Winstone and Phil Davis has become a top name in the British acting community since being in Quadrophenia. Tim played Harry the projectionist at the ad agency where Jimmy is employed as a mail clerk. He is in a single scene with Phil Daniels and Patrick Murray which follows on from the legendary piece of mod philosophy by Jimmy with his: *I don't wanna be like everybody else..."* speech to a bemused Kevin in the shed out back of the Cooper house. All wrapped up in a blue tank top jumper, brown striped shirt and yellow tie Spall barracks Jimmy for drugs [of which he is not at all forthcoming] all the while losing to him at cards. So engrossed in the game is Harry [Spall] his nonchalance towards his duties of projecting the commercial for a group of executives in the screening room opposite, makes him almost joyfully juvenile. Quadrophenia was Tim's first film experience that lasted for the single day that it took to shoot the scene. He has since acted in a trio of Mike Leigh films and made an endearing impression as Barry in the Franc Roddam devised Auf Wiedersehen, Pet. Written by Dick Clement and Ian Le Frenais, the team also scripted Still Crazy (1998) again starring Tim with Pet co-star Jimmy Nail and featuring a blink-and-you'll-miss-it cameo from Phil Davis. Phil Daniels puts in a very brief appearance too, although neither of the Quad actors share the screen.

Born in February 1957 and an Order of the British Empire

(Top) Alfredo's as seen in Quadrophenia and (below) as it is now, open again after some years of being derelict

holder no less, the versatile Spall gave a portrayal as Paulus in Roddam's The Bride. Tim's face has turned up in many film and telly projects numbering an episode of the Michael Elphick series Boon. His vocal dexterity enhances Chicken Run (2000) a full-length movie from the makers of Wallace and Gromit, expanding the Quadrophenia alliance next to Phil Daniels and Benjamin Whitrow. Other work incls: Harry Potter & The Goblet of Fire (2005) and Vanilla Sky (2001). See also: Mike Leigh, Patrick Murray, Franc Roddam, tank top. CONTACT: Markham and Froggatt Ltd, 4 Windmill St, London W1P.

Dusty Springfield Brought up in Hove, East Sussex, Dusty played local Brighton venue the Hippodrome on Sunday 23 August with The High Numbers part of the supporting bill. See also: Simon Napier Bell, The Who.

Christopher Stamp "One was a soft, 'Wilde-looking' man with worried eyes and pursed lips; the other good-looking wild yobbo wolf looked like his minder."
So defined Andrew Loog Oldham, the original teen-aged manager of the Rolling Stones, upon seeing the Who management team of Kit Lambert and Chris Stamp at a gig in 1964. Previously packaged by Pete Meaden as a dish to be savoured by the burgeoning teen Mod audience, the High Numbers [The Who, before and after] had steadily built up a following by mid-1964 but lacked that certain something to break commercially. Twenty-two year old Chris had met the then-twenty-nine year old Lambert whilst both working as Assistant Directors on The L-Shaped Room (1962), a film that Stamp's actor brother Terence had been up for a part in. It was after searching for a band to work with on a new project that Kit Lambert stumbled across a Numbers gig following a fruitless probing for the whereabouts of The Who by Chris Stamp. The band was at that time entering into a period of much anticipation and excitement, as was its audience. "In England," explained Rolling Stone

magazine, "Mod was like the beginning, its virtues were similar [to rock]: violent displays of unbridled joy from young, newly affluent prefabricated hoodlums. Outrage for its own sake; consumption without guilt." Perhaps a little exaggerated but partly correct in expressing its zest. Townshend had said that he had to learn to think and act like a Mod at a time when The Who were regarded as a cult within a cult. The consensus was thus this: if you were a Mod then you liked The Who, simple as that. Chris saw the band play a gig at Watford Trade Union Hall [said to be on August 1] a few days after Lambert had seen them and following a Notting Hill audition the duo set up a fresh company, New Action, to manage the band. Retitled The Who, they would remain in control of the group until 1974 since which time Bill Curbishley has managed them. Stamp, not regarded as being overtly business accumented, veering rather more to the creative side of the business, it is a credit to all concerned that through sheer hard work the band broke through to be accepted by their target audience. All the more remarkable in being one that was more preoccupied with listening to records than seeing a rough bunch like the High Numbers/ Who. "We loved the music, we loved the thing that was happening, we were dedicated to change and the bigger thing." reflects Chris in Oldham's autobiography Stoned. As a reference source of the sixties music scene it is worth a read as it contains a photograph of Chris Stamp with a drag-queen vision of Keith Moon. In addition, a b/w shot of Chris and another of Pete Townshend also grace the book. Who producer Glyn Johns is one of the key figures interviewed therein to. A genuine East Ender by birth, Chris worked on the fruit barrows in his youth whilst brother Terrence would find success as an actor. Given a Story Consultant acknowledgement on the Quadrophenia credits Stamp had completed an early draft of the script with Pete Townshend, approaching the story from a very different view from the one that has remained. Their version concentrated more directly upon the spiritual journey of Jimmy Cooper. A picture of Chris with Kit Lambert at their Track Records office can be found in Jan Olofsson's My Sixties photobook.
See also: Bibliography, scooters

Terence Stamp Glancing through the pages of Double Feature, the third part in the autobiography of this quintessential British actor, Who fans will find a number of the photographs of interest. Brothers Terence and Christopher appear together in two shots; one finding them in a chequered trousers get-up, another in crombie coats and silk scarves and a third framing Chris and Kit Lambert with their latest act, Arthur Brown [remembered for his hit Fire, covered later by The Who]. Double Feature begins with a Pete Townshend lyric and is one in a series of books written by Terence, others include Coming Attractions and Stamp Album. Born in the midst of World War II, Terry made his name during the swinging sixties London scene immortalised in the Kinks song Waterloo Sunset. Film wise, his headlining performance in Stephen Frears' The Hit (1984) co-starred Phil Daniels Meantime screen buddy Tim Roth. Poor Cow (1967) is worth a mention as it saw Stamp working with Quadrophenia cast members John Bindon and Kate Williams in a movie that was in itself to play a major role in The Limey (1999). Clips of the film were used in the latter, which again starred Stamp and features The Who track The Seeker. The song is heavily prominent in the trailer for the subsequent video release from Film 4. See also: Stephen Frears, Tim Roth.

Stardust A 1974 film that had a role for Who drummer Keith Moon accompanied by an excellent soundtrack that featured My Generation as well as tracks from the Chiffons, the Supremes and Manfred Mann.

Stars Is it merely a coincide or is there a significance in the two stars that are positioned on the light shield of his Lambretta and the necklace / ear rings worn by Monkey at the house party?

Martin Stellman "Stellman shoots from the hip." so penned Films and Filming after Martin was interviewed about his directorial and co-writing debut of For Queen and Country (1988). His was one of the three names on the Quadrophenia script after being asked to contribute to it prior to finishing his own screenplay for Defence of the Realm in 1985. Born in 1948, at the time of the original release of Quadrophenia two more of his scripts would be made; Cheap Perfume and Babylon [which saw Ferdy aka Trevor Laird in the part of Beefy]. Both films were released theatrically in 1980. He received a story credit for Nicole Kidman film The Interpreter [2005]. Stellman directed Jimmy's dad, Michael Elphick, in the early-1990s telly drama Harry.

A QUADROPHENIA ANTHOLOGY

Steph Lisa Jewell's witty tale of love between friends, Thirtynothing, [Michael Joseph, 2000] name checks the film, mentioning that one of the main characters resembled Phil Daniels, "Quadrophenia was Dig's favourite film of all time..." In the story, he falls for a girl that looks just like Leslie Ash.
Sting *"Phew...look at him!"*
Steph to Jimmy, upon first seeing the Brighton Ace Face.
Quadrophenia commenced filming in September 1978 at a time when The Police phenomenon was about to explode across Britain, America and Asia the following year. It was during filming in Brighton, he had to return to London to perform on the Old Grey Whistle Test with his band The Police. His performance was watched by cast and crew members in a local pub. With the release of the film in 1979 and thanks to three hit singles, Sting, resembling a young Malcolm Macdowall, had his newly found fame exploited in relation to his involvement in Quadrophenia by way of many magazine, television and newspaper features. There is a picture of Sting as the Ace Face from the courtroom scene in Quadrophenia found on the back of their debut album Outlandos D'Amor (1978). Despite this concentrated effort Quad was not well received upon its American release. Only after being coupled with The Kids Are Alright did it find an audience over there. Meanwhile in Britain, film magazine Sight and Sound voted Quadrophenia the worst British film of 1979! Although Sting as the Ace Face, the leading Mod on the local Brighton scene, is seen only during the seaside segments of the story, he cleverly manages to ingratiate enough kudos to be singled out in many reviews. This may appear a little unjust when compared to the performances given by Phil Davis or Mark Wingett [not to mention Mr Daniels himself]. Still, as Ace, former school teacher Gordon Sumner, Sting to you and me, makes his presence felt shortly after Jimmy and co arrive at Madeira Drive on the

227

Brighton seafront and near to the Aquarium and pier. Exuding a cocky, ceremonial confidence, the peacock-like Ace momentarily glances around at the throng of parked scooters and an excited face, then satisfied, swiftly pulls away on his chrome G.S scooter. A half-dozen others ride behind him concluding a statement of non-verbal intent. It is a key moment in the minutiae of the Mod infrastructure and Sting carries it off with the necessary aplomb. One or two scenes featuring the Ace were said to have been cut out of the final print o the film so as not to detract from the main prominence of Jimmy in the story.

Before Quadrophenia he had not been seen in any films but he had won a part in The Great Rock and Roll Swindle (1978) spotlighting Malcolm McLaren's influence on the Sex Pistols. An outrageously camp performance landed on the cutting room floor and did not feature in the finished film but it can be enjoyed in The Filth and The Fury (2000). Maintaining the Punk affiliation, John Lydon was, as has already been stated, been put up to play the Ace Face [as had Garry Cooper] in Quadrophenia but eventually lost out to Sting who would work on the shoot for six weeks. Jimmy's insecurities are exposed at the Aquarium Ballroom where a perfectly poised, [or posed] grey suited Ace absorbs the attention of the dance floor crowd. Strutting purposely to the strains of Louie, Louie, all arm and leg movements accompanied with a twist of the head; I think Gary Numan took this on for his own electro pop performances later.

Alluringly drawn to him Steph dances with, or indeed next to Sting whose presence literally lights up the floor (even though the actor is a lousy dancer). But not even the eagle-like Ace is wholly untouchable, oh no, Jimmy takes to flapping about on the edge of the balcony above and briefly manages to outshine him by diving down in to the crowd below. All this before being ejected by security as Monkey and the others look on. Clearly vexed, watch how Ace arches an eyebrow in distaste at having the focus taken away from him. Moments later everybody continues dancing to the jingle-jangle of the Philadelphia-formed Orlons crooning Wah-Watusi. On the day of the scuffles on and around the seafront we spot Sting as he and the main cast join the other Mods attached to a marching band moving down East street. Passing the ABC cinema and disappearing off towards the promenade end of the street the scene links immediately on to the beach set-to. Here, in what can only be defined as a venomous absorption of method acting, Sting assaults a couple of coppers outside the gents lavatory [still there today]. If played on video in slow mode, you will see him finish the fight and whilst turning to escape he looks directly in to the camera with a demonic, maniacal and gratuitous smile spread across his face. Little wonder that Roddam cast him as Dr Frankenstein in horror flick The Bride. On standard playback the moment passes very swiftly, and strangely, it flows as if being another take of the same scene. Check it out yourself and I guarantee you will be intrigued.

Mysteriously enough, an earlier moment has the exact same action: only this time a horse-mounted policeman comes charging at the camera [narrowly missing a petrified middle-aged female extra] and then strikes out with Henry V relish with his truncheon right at the lens. Indeed, the whole battle arrangements are beautifully choreographed. Again, watched in slow motion they illicit a ballet-like grace. Penned in amongst the other Mods collectively bouncing up and down to the chant of *"We are the Mods, we are, we are, we are the Mods..."* the evil intent in the-then twenty-seven year old Sting expresses itself when to create a diversion to allow the youngsters to disperse from the clutches of the police. By smashing a huge glass-fronted window this action leads to Jimmy and Steph dashing down an alleyway leading off the main street. It is here, behind the cramped doorway, that they indulge in a bit of highly charged erotica; the memory of which still brings fans to the spot. Unfortunately, the door is usually locked but if you do visit, you may be fortunate enough to catch a brief glimpse inside before employees of the Chinese restaurant [to whom the space once belonged] slam it closed on you. In playing Ace, Sting enjoyed his acting stature in the film and even gets to pull a police man off a horse before setting about inflicting a severe kicking, all this after pushing others aside in his relish to do so. This is not the only time that is demonstrative of the dark humour flowing through his screen persona. When Jimmy is mistakenly arrested and forced into the back of a black police van containing three Rockers and one officer he is wary of the possible problems ahead. However, seconds later the van stops and we see Ace outside furiously resisting arrest from three officers until finally, he relents; only giving in after a flurry of expletives. The younger Mod can barely believe his eyes and relaxes. Ace offers one of the Rockers a smoke from his gold cigarette case only to snap it shut at the very moment the guy reaches in to it. It is a great indication of a delightfully childish behaviour. Both Jimmy and the copper take a cigarette with the former looking as a child would do around a distant relative; furtively finding eye contact but un-nerved by the sight opposite. The actual name of the Ace Face is not revealed and his inclusion in the courtroom setting following on from their arrests further restores Jimmy's misplaced faith. The scraggy mass of bruised and battered scrappers roars in approval at his audacity to pay his hefty £75 fine by way of a cheque. *"I'll pay now if you don't mind,"* chirps Ace, immaculate in a suit and three-quarter length leather coat, *"You haven't got a pen have you, your honour?"* As has been stated, the essence of this remark came from a seventeen-year-old at Margate Magistrate Court in 1964.

Concluding his screen time by desecrating the Mod ideal so vehemently held on to by Jimmy, the vision of a still grey suited Ace is finally revealed but completed with a pill box hat tilted slightly to the left, white gloves clasped over the shoulder and brass buttoned chest defining his post as a hotel bell boy. "Ain't you the guy who used to set the paces, riding up in front of a hundred faces?" Barks Daltrey in the accompanying Bell Boy. It is the spectacle of this uniform of a different kind that leads Jimmy to steal Ace's GS Vespa scooter, parked at the side of the Grand hotel [where the real Ace is found to be employed], and speed off towards the climactic moment of the story, high above the cliffs of Beauty Head. "I think it was a good film all around," concurred Sting in Films and Filming magazine, "and that part was very useful."

Reminiscent of a young Malcolm McDonnell, only leaner, success advanced after The Police disbanded with a still flourishing solo career supplemented by an eclectic pursuit of acting parts. One of the most recent being a cameo in Lock, Stock and Two Smoking Barrels, a Brit-flick that finds Paul Moriarty amongst the cast. A memorable collaboration with Dire Straits for the single

Money for Nothing also links with Leslie Ash, who herself acted in an earlier DS video clip. Born in 1951, Sting derived his nickname from his penchant for wearing a stripy jumper that made him resemble a bee. He worked with fellow Quadrophenia actors Benjamin Whitrow in Brimstone and Treacle (1982) and again with Phil Daniels, Franc Roddam and Gary Shail on The Bride. A 1992 guest spot on The Simpson's found him in the collected company of Who dignitaries John Entwistle and Roger Daltrey, who were both featured in a later episode of the cartoon show. Finally, Sting rides a Vespa scooter with the capital letters of "GS" stuck on its body, a typical mod add-too. Peculiarly enough, his real name is, Gordon Summner...
Other work incls: The Adventures of Baron Munchausen (1988) alongside Oliver "Tommy" Reed.
See also: David Bailey, Brighton, Grand Hotel, Quadrophenia posters/ videos, Scooters. Book sources incl: Sting - Demolition Man by Christopher Sandford, (Warner Books, 1998), Sting: The Secret Life of Gordon Sumner by Wensley Clarkson, (Blake, 1996), Sting - A Biography, Robert Sellars (Omnibus, 1989), Sting by Marsha Bronson (Exley Publishing, 1993), Films and Filming (Sept 1982) interviews by Sally Hibbin and Martin Sutton. CONTACT: Markham and Frogatt, 4 Windmill St., London W1P 1HF. Website: Sting.Compaq.com or www.timepass.com.
Joyce Stoneman Wardrobe Supervisor on Quadrophenia. Joyce was the Costume Designer on the 1978 film The Class of Miss MacMichael, which gave early roles for Phil Daniels and Patrick Murray. Other work incls: Absolute Beginners (1986). See also: Ray Corbett, Patsy Pollock, Ken Wheatley.
Suicide "It's no good staying alive if you're gonna be suicidal."
Pete Townshend.
Suits 'Watch the cloth, moth!' Favoured by the Mod and adopted by characters in Quadrophenia except for John Altman who goes for a more casual, American collegic look of sports shirt and jeans. Jimmy boasts to Steph about his latest addition, ordered in advance to wear in Brighton. Dan also obsesses with a fitting at a local tailor shop. Dave has a pinstripe combo of whose stripes is thinner than those worn by Chalky or Jimmy. One male mod extra was fitted out

231

in an authentic silk suit but ruined it by jumping in the sea during the fighting scenes set on the seafront at Brighton. Two-tone mohair suits were popular amongst Mods at the same time as male pop groups in the flourishing early-sixties teen market, bands such as the Dave Clark Five, Gerry and The Pacemakers, the Kinks, The Beatles and The Merseysounds. Mainly formed from working class backgrounds and managed by middle class figures, all struggled to perform freely in the confines of shirts and ties foisted upon them by management teams packaging them up ready for consumption. In the Seventies, The Jam continued the tradition when punk was emerging and by 1979 advertisements in the pages of NME hawked "mod trousers/ 2-Tone trousers/ mohair trousers/ Stay press trousers and three-button jackets". Characters Simon and Fulford at the ad agency to the young Mods all wear them in Quadrophenia, the only difference setting them apart being in the detailing. Sting's grey silk suit cost £500 to make. See also: Fashion, Parkas, Dave Wax.

Sunglasses Jimmy and Ferdy wear the black, wrap-a-round type popularised by Two-Tone / Ska bands of the late-seventies pop scene in Britain. Ferdy wears his inside at the house party whilst Jimmy has his own on inside the Goldhawk and at Alfredo's coffee bar one evening. Pete is seen wearing a pair too but his are most unsightly in comparison to the stylish ones worn by the others.

The Supremes Formed in the late Fifties, this all-girl group scored a number of hits in both Britain and America from 1964 onwards with records like Baby Love, You Can't Hurry Love and Stop in the Name of Love. Hailed as the most commercially successful female group in the Guinness Book of Hit Singles, Baby Love can faintly be heard as the Mods arrive at the Kitchener Road house party. The record hit number one in Britain in October 1964. It was re-released in 1974, an anthology album was released on Motown records in 1970, whilst former vocalist and full-time eccentric, Diana Ross has pursued a successful solo and acting career.

Derek Suter Clapper Loader on Quadrophenia in a position sometimes called Second Assistant Camera Assistant [*sic*] which involves marking a slate recording the specific scene

about to be filmed. Derek has also been an Electrician and Focus Puller. See also: Terence Stamp. CONTACT: c/o London Management and Representation.
James Swann Given a "...without whom" thanks on the closing credits of the film. See also: Freddie Haayen.
Synthesiser The heartbeat whilst the lyrics/ vocal is the oxygen pumping it.
Shel Talmy Record Producer for The Who on My Generation, Anyway Anyhow Anywhere and I Can't Explain 1965 singles and Substitute in 1966. Talmy also worked with the Kinks.
Tampax Having been ripped off in a drugs deal with local hood Harry North, our Three Stooges, Jimmy, Dave and Chalky find themselves resorting to extreme methods to find a supply of amphetamines for their Brighton beano. And this is where a multiple display of Tampax sanitary products is at the centre of one of the funniest and most inept burglaries performed in a film. Tentatively forcing their way inside a darkened chemist shop, at which their friend Monkey works, Jimmy takes the search to find drugs seriously, whilst his mates joke. In the midst of looking around they manage to knock over a mountain of boxes on display above a set of wooden draws positioned in the middle of the store.
Tank tops Tim Spall's character wears one as does one of the youths involved in beach fighting, a lovely blue one. A 1964 Mod is seen wearing one in a photo taken during the bank holiday skirmishes in Brighton. See also: Phil Daniels.
Mike Taylor Intermittently recognised as Michael Taylor, he followed his time as Film Editor on Quad with The Long Good Friday (1980), a British underworld tale with minor roles for P H Moriarty and Trevor Laird.
Teddy Boy As a youngster Roger Daltrey was amongst the faces recognisable in what is now acknowledged as the first wholly distinguishable formation of youth identity. 'Teds' evolved from a working class background and their visual appearance frightened many by consciously drawing up on what they were wearing as a form of expression albeit misconstrued as aggression.
Teenager "The new exemplars of teen horror: Mods and Rockers." Jonathon Green writing in All Dressed Up. "Wildly-dressed teenagers" Brighton Evening Argus, May 1964. "The town was full of dirty grubby teenagers..." commented an appalled Mrs Simpson, wife of Margate Magistrate Dr George

Simpson, to The Daily Mail [19 May] about the seaside influx of teenagers during whitsun 1964. A classification coined in the Fifties, the teenager established the space between childhood and adulthood surmised Dick Hebdige and this space means money. A massive £220m was spent annually by them according to the newspaper the Daily Mail in September 1964. Phil Daniels celebrated his nineteenth birthday on set and was presented with a special Quadrophenia themed cake. See also: Youth.

This is England Director Shane Meadows feature film covers many areas seen in Quadrophenia and even its poster apes the 1979 flick.

David Gideon Thomson Executive Producer for Polytel Films. He was again involved with The Who Films production team of Roy Baird and Bill Curbishley on the gritty bio-pic McVicar, teaming up with Roger Daltrey a fellow Producer. John Peverall and John Ireland round off the Quadrophenia ensemble on a film momentous for marking the arrival of Kenney Jones as Music Consultant in unison with Pete, Roger and John. See also: Polytel Films.

Simon Thompson Hair Stylist responsible for fashioning the cool delights of Monkey and the Ace Face and the slightly dodgier mops given to Spider and Steph [said to be a hairpiece]. Simon honed the styles given to Gwyneth Paltrow in Sliding Doors (1998) and Emma (1996).

Pete Townshend Earth. "...and I saw that everything was emptiness, and chasing the wind, of no profit under the sun." [Ecclesiastics].

Pete Townshend started writing what was to become the Quadrophenia album in France during the early summer months of 1973 with its release coming that same November. He was twenty-eight at the time. At least fifty songs were written prior to reaching the demo stage where the other Who members could contribute. Put out as a double-album it peaked at number two on the UK album chart. Subsequently, the original soundtrack album to the 1979 film incorporated a dozen tracks from the 1973 Who album whilst an additional selection of artists such as James Brown and The Kingsmen pushed the later version to number twenty-two on the album charts that October. A reissued and remastered rendering of the former made the lower end of the charts in July 1996. "Quadrophenia was completely intractable." Explained Townshend in The

Guitar Greats [see bibliography] who acknowledged that the recording of the album was complicated by the need to re-record numerous sound effects in the stereo rather than mono format. The aural sounds of the sea were taken from a visit to Cornwall whilst for 5:15, a train driver at Waterloo station was bribed to sound his whistle as his train left the station so the sound effect could be recorded. Regarded as very much a Townshend masterwork with little input possible from the others in the group, it is nonetheless held by Roger Daltrey as his favourite Who album of the Seventies. Its genesis arose from an idea called Rock is Dead: Long Live Rock, back in 1972, with its simple premise defined by Pete as concerning a youngster sitting on a rock and reflecting upon his experiences gathered over the last few days. LLR, as we all know it, turned out to be a great Who single sounding not dissimilar to Johnnie Be Good and The Doors' L.A Woman. Tracks were laid down in a converted church near Battersea power Station, a useful London Who location adopted for the cover shot of their Odds and Sods compilation album in 1974.

Not overly well-received upon its initial release, Quadrophenia is an Who album that has continued to breath even up to and into the present with a theatrical tour of the music occuring in 2009. The band toured Britain, America and the world playing Jimmy's story as their theme using artists as diverse as P J Proby and the since-disgraced, Gary Glitter. In subsequent shows the highlight of which was the 1996 Hyde Park gig which had Phil Daniels playing the narrator. On tour recreating the sound of the album proved nigh on impossible. Various attempts at putting the synthesised tracks on to tape all flopped and for Keith Moon it was a maddening task to keep in time. "In many ways it was too ambitious," argue authors Nick Logan and Bob Wooffinden "both thematically and musically, and the more heavily-orchestrated style didn't suit the band..."

As the first son to a saxophonist father and singer mother Peter Dennis Blandford Townshend was born on 19 May 1945. Steadily developing a physiognomy reminiscent to that captured by Gaugin in his work Night Cafe at Arles, he was not given the most conventional of up-bringings, therefore his quest to re-explore his formative years is admissible. Taking up an editorial position at Faber and Faber, it was in 1985 that they published his collection of writings collated as Horse's Neck [the title relating to a childhood moment] much of which explores the early part of Pete's life. Both articulate and brutal in its use of imagery and language it is easily digested in a single sitting. A cluster of concise chapters flow forth and Pancho And The Baron will be of special interest to embryonic Who fans. The Who are hailed in some quarters as the first Punk band and young followers of that brief movement liked the band because it was relatively easy to play their songs. "He thinks he's past it, but he ain't" exhorted Sex Pistols drummer Paul Cook to the New Musical Express in 1977, "He's still great." Years later, Billy Idol who had started out as part of punksters Generation X went on to play the bell boy role in a stage revival of Quadrophenia. With the Sex Pistols at the peak of their fame in 1978, Pete found himself drinking with two of them in a Mayfair club. At a particularly low ebb, both professionally and personally, he mistakenly took one of them for Johnny Rotten [John Lydon] and after a fracas with a presupposing press photographer the Who man was asked to leave. Townshend was eventually awoken by a police officer telling him to go home [he was asleep by a roadside]. This humiliating experience provided the ingredient for Who Are You, the first single from The Who in two years. Coincidentally, their last single was a reissued Substitute back in 1976; a song covered by the Pistols and available on a live album called Raw. A 1977 Sex Pistols bootleg called Bad Boy pasted an image of Pete on its cover, a piss take of Sgt. Pepper's, alongside Bob Dylan, Hendrix and Jim Morrison. I think that Pete would have smiled at that at the very least. Leading agitator Rotten had been considered for the part of the Ace Face in the Who's Quadrophenia but as we know, director Roddam settled with Sting. He was also briefly thought of for the role of Jimmy. A solo album project called White City saw Pete the subject of a South Bank Show special in 1984 where he came across as bright and cohesive when speaking at length about his search to discover his roots endemic of this "upper middle-class kid - which is what I am."

Besides the album completed by 1985, an accompanying forty-five minute film was made within which Townshend acts.

Aside from his contractually obligatory Who compositions, Pete was to write a third musical work, The Iron Man, based upon a 1968 children's story by Ted

Hughes. This production manifest itself in 1993, some four years after its release as an album, and included vocals from John Lee Hooker, Nina Simone and Roger Daltrey. The Who contributed two songs; Dig and a new version of the Arthur Brown hit Fire [an interpretation not well received by critics]. An American feature length animated film called The Iron Giant was in cinemas in 1999 and Pete Townshend was credited as one of its Executive Producers. Endeavouring on, a radio script for his long-lamented Life house spectacle was finally premiered on Radio 3 later that year also. The full script and elongated introduction outlining the theme of the work which back in the early-seventies was commissioned as a film, was published by Pocket Books [1999] with Pete sharing writing credits with Jeff Young. Various CD packaging of Life house was also put out commercially initially through Townshend's official Eel Pie website. Two biographies worth seeking out are Townshend - A Career Biography written by Chris Charlesworth and published in 1984 by Proteus. A former NME journalist, Chris also wrote The Who: The Illustrated Biography [Omnibus, 1981]. A third, Behind Blue Eyes - A Life of Pete Townshend is well researched but a regurgitation of many gathered interviews. Its made useful by its author's personal relation to its subject. Written by Geoffery Giuliano, it came out in 1996 through Coronet Books [Hodder and Stroughton]. Pete Townshend Live (1993, MCPS / Polygram) is worth a look if you want to hear some solo and Who tracks played live from a gig in America. See also: Adolescence, My Generation, Quadrophenia, The Who. CONTACT: Eel Pie Publishing, The Boathouse, Ranelagh Drive, Twickenham TW1 1QZ. Good websites to visit include: www.petetownshend.com or ww.mrshowbiz.go.com/people/petetownshend/
Toyah "All the time I couldn't bear to talk about the making of Quadrophenia and in more recent years I still couldn't bear to talk about it. I was angry at the end result, and I was angry at the way [the cast] were treated while making it." Toyah writing in her autobiography, Living Out Loud.
Sometimes credited as Toyah Willcox [as she was in Quadrophenia] or Toyah Wilcox, she was born in 1958 Toyah was the ideal age to be cast as mod girl Monkey in Quadrophenia, and she looked right to; with bleached blond hair covering the tips off her ears rounded off with a low fringe.

Apart from Leslie Ash, Monkey is the only female in the film however, not a great deal is revealed about her. What for example is her actual name? We know that she works in a chemist shop that Jimmy and his mates break-in to for drugs and that she has a passion for him but little else is sketched out. Although in saying that it curiously fits in well enough.

Her character in the Alan Fletcher novelisation of Quadrophenia shows Monkey accommodating with her sexual favours amongst the male Mods yet on screen this is only hinted at. I am thinking of Dave's lackluster advances at the house party as an example [or is he simply after her drugs?] Whilst there that she implements a premeditated attack upon the real object of her desire: one Jimmy Cooper. It is impossible not to empathise with Monkey as she is pushed away when he sees Steph dancing closely with Pete to the mellow sounds of the Cascades' Rhythm of the Rain.

Toyah's character smothers Daniels with genuine affection whilst he merely struggles to free himself from her and the confines of the sofa. Ms. Willcox won the part of Monkey after Franc Roddam had goaded her in to proving her dramatic prowess by giving Phil Daniels 'The snog of his life.' as she put it. Jimmy becomes more embroiled in his quest for Steph as the film progresses whilst Monkey continues to be seen around the Mod group up to their final scene together at Alfredo's coffee bar. The day after Jimmy returns to London from his court date in Brighton and the final straw comes from, of all sources, his best mate Dave. His sexual crudities prove too much for the dishevelled Jimmy as Monkey watches his attack upon his former friend outside the cafe. *"You're all wankers and cunts!"* spits the fleeing Cooper in this the last scene we see with Toyah in it. Throughout the film she is often affected by his actions and behaviour yet, he shows scant interest in her. In the plentiful dance hall sequences Toyah giggles a lot and generally enjoys herself and I defy anyone not to linger upon seeing either her or Phil Daniels dancing away to Hi Heel Sneekers the next time you play it at home. In a slice of normal Mod behaviour she mainly dances alone or with a girlfriend, never together with Jimmy. Mod dancing was very much an integral part of the lifestyle, the sounds favoured were no longer those suited to couples; you could groove alone, with a girl or in

'We knew we were in the "In" picture of the year as soon as we started shooting it.' Toyah, speaking in the documentary '1979'. (Above) as she looked in Quadrophenia.

a group but most were interested in what the others were doing. When Chalky informs everyone that Spider [no mention of his girlfriend being there too] has been attacked the boys jump on to their horses, I mean scooters, to wreak revenge. The girls in the basement club continue dancing with scarcely a boy now in sight. One of them resembles Sharon Watts from Eastenders: all brassy blond bigness. Monkey dons three-quarter length skirts [as does Steph] and there is a lot of variety in their clothing, although it is not all necessarily appealing. Take the sleeveless grey dress worn by Monkey with its v-shaped front. Yuk. "The guys were the focus of attention and the girls took a back seat." recounts a former Mod eloquently in You'll Never be Sixteen Again, "We orbited really. We orbited round their stars. It was as if the roles were reversed...the boys were getting prettier and the girls were getting plainer." Silver cross earrings are also seen on Monkey and is it wholly coincidental that she exhibits a star shaped necklace whilst Jimmy has the same icon on the windshield of his Lambretta? Accidental or not, it is a shrewd touch. As the seafront battle betwixt

239

chasing the wind   A TO Z ANTHOLOGY

the young Mods and Rockers climaxes Toyah can be spotted cursing those jostling her in what transcends realism for authenticity on the beach. Allegedly, she was said to have broken her arm during the filming. The atmosphere on set was to be a little stifling with the arrival of the film's three Executive Producers and not one the Birmingham-born actor/musician found comfortable. In 1985 she and Roger Daltrey met again with their casting in Murder: Ultimate Grounds for Divorce. Highlighted in books by photographer David Bailey an expressive and dynamic Toyah is shown and two others featuring Pete Townshend [one with the band and another individual shot from 1985] endow If We Shadows [Thames and Hudson, 1990] as does the Ace Face himself, Sting, in the same collection. Bailey's Archive 1957 - 1969 displays a group shot of an extremely young and moody looking Who in a second anthology published in 1999.

Both before and after Quadrophenia Toyah had, and has continued acting supplemented by a successful music career peaking in 1981 with four hit singles. For some, Toyah remains that exquisite pop pixie creature of the early-Eighties, divinely made-up in what resembled ancient Japanese warrior wear [all curves and big shoulders]. This looks to be true for her fans today, check www.juniornet.de for website and fan club information to catch my drift. Notable film parts have embodied direction by the late Derek Jarman in the punk-fuelled Jubilee (1978) and The Tempest (1979). Some may recall her in The Ebony Tower (1984) co-starring with Laurence Olivier and Greta Scacchi in which a scene where the girls' bottoms are revealed seems to have stayed with me. Children's telly has embraced a contrasting Toyah in such late-nineties shows Toyah!, Toyah and Chase, Brum! and lately My Barmy Aunt Boomerang all fitted in with the periodical theatrical performance. Presenting has also featured in her repertoire, helming a music video show on VH1. Possibly her most infamous credit is as one of the voice artists for the BBC 2 Teletubbies phenomenon [she can be heard over the opening credits of each show!] Her long-delayed autobiography Living Out Loud was published by Hodder and Stoughton in August 2000 however, there are no photos of her part in Quadrophenia. Much has been made of her very public plastic surgery and she continues to tour and make new music whilst also acting. There are plentiful websites dedicated to her on the

Internet and I would direct you to any of those listed below [it has to be said that scant mention of her Quadrophenia role can be found here]: or www.toyah.com
Trains Jimmy is seen swigging back the pills with his trusty bottle of gin prior to climbing aboard the 5:15 back to Brighton but why is that Fulford [Ben Whitrow] is seen sitting in one of the compartments? Observe the look on the faces of the two city gentlemen commuters as a stoned, eyelinered Cooper sits between them. A photo of Jimmy heading into Waterloo station is featured in the Who album booklet but, trains to Brighton actually run from Victoria and not Waterloo.
Train tracks Incorporated as a metaphor in Quadrophenia that suggests a possible means of escape for Jimmy. Note how its proximity becomes even more closer in the morning following his refuge in the back garden shed after falling out with his mother. The tracks are used as a cipher to visually move the story back to Brighton which shows itself as a ghost town for him upon his ill-fated return.
Transistor Radios The availability of cheap radios such as the portable, battery powered type was significant in that pop music was made available to a fresh consumer group: the teenager. Electrical retailers like Currys sold pocket-sized ones and the larger transistor type ranging in price from £7.19/6 to 17 gns for a Decca Debonaire model 'finished in mushroom pigskin or blue'.
Brian Tufano Delivering a splendid visual complexion to Quadrophenia as its Director of Photography [sometimes known as the DP or Cinematographer] his work can be seen in a number of mainly British film and television series. War Party (1989) directed by Franc Roddam and Tube Tales (1999) within which Ray Winstone aka Kevin has a part concludes the Mod mash connection. Brian was responsible for cleaning-up the film prints of Quadrophenia in readiness for its 1997 cinema re-issue. Franc roddam rememebers that he was very impressed with the film upon becoming involved with its editing.
CONTACT: McKinney Macartney Mgt Ltd.
Ken Tuohy Acknowledged on the credits as Production Assistant on Quadrophenia. See also: Caroline Hagen.
Uniformity Jimmy finds himself beating up Kevin, albeit without initially realising his identity, purely because he is

dressed in the wrong clothes: greasy black leathers.

Universal Their famous logo is shown prior to the opening scene of the film.

Uniforms G.P.O workers wear what resemble Salvation Army style uniforms in the two vastly different instances that Jimmy comes in to contact with them, the first at a record store and the other during the scooter accident. The scruffiest sea cadets ever are seen to be outfitted in all kinds of uniforms whilst parading down East Street on the day of rioting at Brighton (not meant to be in the film).

Union Jack flag The royal flag that should in fact be called the Union flag and not the Union Jack. Various theories about its coming in to the vernacular but generally held to date back to the reign of Queen Anne. Made up from components of St George [white background], St Andrew [blue background] and St Patrick [its red cross] whilst Wales is not represented.

[I] Connections – The Who: These have been numerous and stretch throughout the career of the band: Pete Townshend had a huge Union Jack on his wall whilst staying at Kit Lambert's place above the Who HQ office in Belgravia. For Mods and Pop Art artists, the Union flag was grasped to represent a rejection and reinterpretation of patriotism. "He turned our national symbol into an abstraction far more effectively than Jasper Johns...whether or not Pete Townshend fully realised the nature of his abstraction is not the question; he was impelled to do it by the pressures of the times." Angela Carter, New Society 1967 and collected in the Faber Book of Pop. The flag was no longer seen as representative of the Queen but realignment to youth. A Union Jack can be seen in the background and Townshend is wearing his own jacket in a Pop Art styled group shot for their important magazine spread for The Observer. The original album cover for The Kids Are Alright finds the band feigning sleep wrapped in the Union flag in a shoot for Life magazine but in fact, they were asleep after having been ejected late in the evening from a hotel the night before. The video to promote the single of the same name sees Keith Moon wearing a Union Jack shirt. To publicise their The Kids Are Alright American tour, their first since 1982, the three remaining members of The Who made the cover of Rolling Stone on 13 July 1989 with a photo inside finding them wrapped in the American Stars and Stripes. John Entwistle paid £30 for a

Union Jack jacket to be made and also had others made in the form of the Welsh/ Scots and Irish flags. Irish Republicans who demanded that they not wear the jackets at a Dublin gig in 1966 threatened the band. Entwistle eventually played the gig in an Eire tricolour ensemble! Both John and Pete can be seen wearing Union jackets in numerous photo shoots through their career. Album cover art wise, the story is similar, 1.The Who's Last compilation album cover, 2.Join Together single promo film finds Roger Daltrey with a Union Jack on his back coupled with a bulldog in the middle of it. 3.The Who's Greatest Hits – an American compilation from MCA in 1983 has a jacket on its cover made up of the Union flag. 4.The BBC Sessions album used the same Kids group photo wrapped in the flag.The flag can be spotted on the wall of Jimmy's bedroom in the Quadrophenia photo booklet from The Who album.

Film usage: 1. A Union Jack is seen as part of a design on a scooter next to Jimmy's as he pulls up outside the Goldhawk at the start of film. 2.The industrial digger at the council tip where Dave works has a flag attached. 3. Seen on the back of a scooter driven by one of the Mods that beat up Kevin after chasing him from outside Shepherd's Bush market. 4. Sewn on the backs of fighting, Parka-clad Mods on Brighton's East Street. 5. A Union Jack is seen on the Palace Pier at Brighton and viewed in the film when Jimmy walks on the beach following his return. A group shot The Who was taken there in 1965 with John Entwistle wearing his UJ blazer. 6. A Mod girl wears a blazer with a Union Jack pattern upon its sleeves is glimpsed as the crowd get corralled together by the police on East Street. 7. Another lad, spotted standing next to the Ace Face in the seconds before Steph, Jimmy and the others break loose following Ace's smashing of a shop window, has a patch with the insignia upon it. 8. An additional youngster, resembling more a skinhead than Mod, has a Union t-shirt.

Contemporary usage: Punks would subvert its significance, again in the way that The Who used it as an anti-establishment symbol. The Spice Girls, Eurythmics, Oasis all borrowed the motif of cool Britannia / Brit Pop in Nineties. David Bowie wears an Alexander McQueen-designed Union Jack coat made up of the emblem on the Earthling (1997) album cover. Rick Buckler, former drummer of The Jam has a Union Jack badge on his shirt for the cover photo of their This is the Modern World album. Weller's Style Council swapped the UJ for the European Union a modern mod band. Weller's band The Jam popularised the Union Jack blazer so much so that by 1980 they [and UJ ties] could be bought mail order for £55 / £65. Carnaby Street clothes shop and its "London, England" coarseness of today rely heavily on its imagery. A track of the same name is included on the 1977 Jam album In The City. See also: Flags.

Gene Vincent 'Sweet Gene Vincent' Ian Dury. Ray Winstone sings one of Gene's hits, Be Bop A Lula, in that revealing bathing scene towards the start of the film. Lula, with its simple guitar solo, was a hit three times in 1956 and Vincent was the first singer to make the leather look his trademark. Often dressed in black from head-to-toe, Gene was termed by his record label Capitol as their Elvis. He survived the plane crash that included Eddie Cochran amongst its fatalities sometime after both artists had appeared in The Girl Can't Help It (1956). His music can also be heard in Ring-A-Ding-Rhythm (1962) and in David Lynch's Wild at Heart, whose main female protagonist is called Lula. This bad boy of Rock and Roll died in 1971 aged thirty-six. See also: The Black Leather Jacket by Mick Farren [Abbeville Press, 1985].

Wah-Wahtusi Recorded by the Isley Brothers, it is the version from The Orlons that features in the Brighton ballroom scene. See also: The Orlons

Gilli Wakeford As Make-Up Artist on Quad it was Miss Wakeford who stuck the eye shadow on Gary Shail's Spider Mod boy and the eye liner on to the face of a stoned Jimmy whilst on his way back down to Brighton on the celebrated 5:15.

Waterloo train station Seen briefly as Jimmy sets off on his way back to Brighton. Services no longer leave from the station today favouring Victoria instead. A photograph of the exterior of this ornate station is included in the booklet of images included in The Who's 1973 Quadrophenia album. A train driver at the station there had to be persuaded to sound his whistle so that it could be recorded for inclusion on the album, by way of a sweetener.

Dave Wax Presently situated on the Hammersmith Road in west London, Dave Wax & Sons continue the bespoke tailoring business patronaged by Jimmy and his Mod acquaintances in the film. The name "Dave Wax" is clearly visible on the top of the box containing his new thirty-shilling suit that Jimmy opens up in his bedroom in anticipation of the Brighton trip. See also: suits

We Close Tonight Included on the re-mastered 1998 Who compilation album Odds and Sods this John Entwistle composition was originally meant for Quadrophenia. Often credited incorrectly to Pete Townshend.

Dave Wedgbury In-house photographer for Decca Records and the man responsible for taking what has been recognised as one of the seminal band shots of the Sixties, the famed Big Ben photo. Curiously, the reality for its inspiration was more logistical, as with most things, with the record company's office situated near to the London landmark and hence the composition. The 1965 image captures a fresh-faced bunch of men packaged up and ready for consumption. A second picture made the cover of the My Generation album interesting in that I was shot from above using a technique copied much later especially during the punk era. He also snapped leading modsters The Small Faces. To see the picture have a look at The British Century by Brian Moynahan [Weidenfeld and Nicolson, 1997].

Paul Weller Mod meister whose singles whilst he was with The Jam were released on Polydor label, the same as The Who, following signing to them in 1977. Whilst in The Jam he can be seen sporting a Who badge and home-made vertical arrows upon his chest ala Roger Daltrey on the cover of their This is the Modern World (1977) album. Weller met up with his former hero Pete Townshend for an interview that appeared in the now defunct Melody Maker in January 1981. Paul appeared with The Who and others at a special charity gig at the Royal Albert Hall in November 1999. Weller had previously played the venue as a solo artist. On the Paul Weller Live album (1994) his Bull-Rush track segways in to The Who's Magic Bus. Whilst his interpretation of The Who's Circles is included on Substitute: The songs of The Who covers album. After the demise of The Jam following an ill-received final gig at the Brighton Centre in 1982 he formed The Style Council with ex-Merton Parkas member Mick Talbot who had also played on some later Jam tracks. A worthy solo career has since seen Ray Winstone, Kevin from Quadrophenia, make a guest appearance in Weller's promotional video for the single Sweet Pea, My Sweet Pea single. Paul's track Everything has a Price to Pay was used on soundtrack of

Winstone's film Face. His Stanley Road album features a Mod on a scooter amongst the favourite things artwork that was designed by Pop Art artist Peter Blake. Weller devised the format of The Soul Stylists – 40 Years of Modernism [with Paolo Hewitt, Mainstream, 2000]. Check out The Complete Guide to the Music of Paul Weller and The Jam by John Reed [Omnibus Press, 1999]. See also: Philip Davis, The Jam, Pop Art, Sex Pistols, Union Jack, Ray Winstone.

Wellington public house The name of the public house which is the focus of Jim and his pals being turned over in a drugs deal with local villain Harry North.

Terry Wells Property Master on the Quadrophenia shoot. Terry Wells Senior, as he has sometimes been titled, worked with Quad casting Director Patsy Pollock on both Braveheart and In The Name of the Father over the course of a career that began in the 1970s. Other work incls: The Elephant Man (1980).

Westminster A man at the baths where Kevin and Jimmy meet up after some years is wearing a towel around his waist which reads "Westminster" which is odd in that Jimmy is a local of Shepherd's Bush.

Kevin Wheatley Set Director [aka Art Director] on Quadrophenia. Kevin's association with fellow crew members is demonstrated on Babylon (1980) where he worked alongside Ray Corbett and scriptwriter Martin Stellman. Absolute Beginners (1986) found Joyce Stoneman as Wardrobe Supervisor and again, Ray Corbett. See also: Stephen Frears, Trevor Laird.

Benjamin Whitrow Pictured below, he contributed his plumy vocals next to the ubiquitous Tim Spall in the Claymation feature Chicken Run (2000) which marked the third occasion that they had worked together; Quadrophenia was succeeded by Ben's role in an episode of Frank Stubbs Promotes, a television drama series spotlighting Spall. Ben was fittingly cast as Simon Fulford ['Mr' to the likes of Jimmy] a figure of some responsibility at the ad agency where the young 'Cooper' is employed in the mailroom. Whitrow plays the be suited, middle-class figure of authority [Headmaster/ Chairman/ Businessman etc] often challenged by others such as Jimmy in the case of Quadrophenia. The two come head-to-head following the latter's delayed return to work following his court appearance in Brighton. However condescending in manner [he addresses Jimmy by his surname and does not offer him a seat when summoning the youngster to his office], he does attempt to placate the Mod. Fatefully, Jimmy explodes after hearing how fortunate he is to have the much sought after mailroom job, *"Oh yeah,"* snarls Daniels in one of the most celebrated moments in the film, signing his own dismissal, *"well find one then..."* Poor Fulford gasps in disbelief at his outburst as both actors frown madly at each other. The scene concludes with Jimmy quitting in the manner of which many would applaud. Intermittently billed as Ben Whitrow, this experienced Royal Shakespeare Company actor can be seen in Chaplin (1992) as indeed can Paul Moriarty. In addition to Restoration, with its casting organised by Patsy Pollock and Hawks (1989). Clockwise (1986) finds Ben again suited-up only this time as a public school headmaster; Bill Rowe was the Sound Re-recording Mixer and closing the Quadrophenia amplification, in 1982 Benjamin acted in Brimstone and Treacle which starred the Ace face, Sting. See also: Jeremy Child, Phil Daniels. CONTACT: Lowe Coulston, 37 Berwick St, London.

The Who "Ladies & gentlemen, a nice little band from Shepherd's Bush – The 'OO." [Jeff Dexter introducing The Who at the Isle of Wight gig, August 1970].
In 1964, The Who were regularly having to spend several hundred pounds in replacing guitars and mics destroyed during live performances. Even then Pete Townshend was encouraged to annihilate his guitar by Kit Lambert if a member of the press was in the audience. Embracing elements of the Auto-Destructive art philosophy practised by Gustav Metzke, the truthful origins of this on-stage phenomenon are less exotic. Metzke had presented a lecture at the Ealing School of Art in 1962 at a time when Pete was there as a graphic design student. Most would agree that evidence of his influence upon the nineteen-year-old would harness itself in the novel use of feedback rather than anything else. Remembered as one of the first to explore this new ethos involving painting with hydrochloric acid, Metzger subsequently devised lighting projection effects used at Who shows at the Roundhouse in Camden in 1966.
A 1964 gig at the Bluesday Club at the Railway Hotel in Harrow saw Pete accidentally crack the neck of his guitar and not wanting to lose face he proceeded

to smash it to pieces. The excited crowd at the cramped, low-ceilinged venue lapped this up thinking it a part of the show. Consequently Mr Townshend had set himself an expensive precedent. With the popularity of the band growing word soon spread and audiences would be disappointed if this particular kink was not demonstrated for their delectation. A fire hit the now derelict Railway, situated next to Harrow & Wealdstone station on the Bakerloo Line, in May 2000 and its future at the time of writing was in doubt. The beginnings of the band that combusted in to The Who, via The High Numbers and almost The Hair [Pete's idea], dates back to the teenage years of the four boys each heading towards their collected state of 'Maximum R'n'B'. John Entwistle and Pete Townshend had played together in trad jazz combo called The Confederates until 1960 when a second band found John switching from the trumpet to bass guitar and Pete from banjo to guitar. All the while pugnacious Teddy Boy Roger Daltrey was doing very nicely as lead guitarist in his semi-professional band the 'Dazzling' Detours. Entwistle was invited to join by Roger and Pete came aboard thanks to the recommendation given by his old mate. It was agreed that their progressive future lay in the shape of a four-piece and from there on in Roger took on vocal duties. The Detours played many local gigs including the Goldhawk Road Social Club in Shepherd's Bush, the venue that Jimmy heads towards at the start of Quadrophenia. Wearing purple jackets, white shirts and bow ties what a giddy sight they must have once looked! An alternative name was sought after another band with the same name had been seen on telly and thus The High Numbers were born. They reverted to The Who by mid-1964 but what would always remain from those times was the arrow logo devised by Pete that was painted on to the side of their battered tour van. The search for a new drummer was imperative following the departure of their previous one, Doug Sandler, and concluded in '64 with the auditioning of a seventeen-year-old trainee electrician at his local pub, the Oldfield. Dressed entirely in orange, including his hair, Keith Moon demolished a drum kit [not even his own] and was given the job. Moon was then playing in surf band The Beachcombers and drumming like a demented Thunderbirds puppet he contrasted bizarrely with the circumspect Entwistle, the aggressive Townshend and casual Daltrey strutting, each contributing to the dynamic that was The Who. Their professional fate was sealed following Lambert's attendance at an other Railway gig as has been recorded elsewhere. It was as Kit defined perfectly, "A moment of certainty." Chris Stamp saw their next gig and all plans of furthering their film careers was shelved in favour of co-managing the band. Pete Meaden, their then manager of sorts, was given a golden handshake and success soon arrived with the release of their debut single I Can't Explain, a Townshend ditty recorded in two hours. It went on to sell a healthy 104,000 copies sending it up to number nine on the charts. Debut album My Generation, itself completed in two x 4-hour sessions, was put out on Christmas day 1965. Esteemed music writer and author Nik Cohn may not have been a fan of the Mod movement *per se*, but he could still reconcile the sheer tenacity of The Who as performers. "They made the kind of noise that makes your eyes blur," he commented [see bibliography], "that hits you and hits you, that half way destroys you." The Who were the sum of their parts: Roger's gravel yet often emotive voice, Pete's gentle lilt and strained aggression, John holding it all together, the frame around the image if you will and Keith brought his mad drumming energy. Watch The Kids Are Alright and nothing more need be added.

Hailed in some quarters as the first Punk band members of which liked the Who's music because it was relatively easy to play. Songs recorded by The Who continue to find a contemporary audience through insertion on film soundtracks such as Almost Famous (2000), The Limey, Summer of Sam, Austin Powers 2 and American Beauty (all 1999), Rushmore (1998) to Fever Pitch (1997), Grosse Point Blank (1997) as well as in Goodfellas (1990). Over the years magazine coverage of the group has been considerable, of especial interest is Rolling Stone: The Complete Covers 1967 – 1997 printed by Harry N Abrahams Publishers in 1998. As a group they made its cover in October 1978, June 1982 [showing a bearded Pete and John next to a curly premed Roger Daltrey] and July 1989. Individually, Keith Moon got the December 1972 cover, Roger made it that April but it has been Pete Townshend that has had the closest relationship with the American music publication. He has both written for, and been interviewed in the magazine initiated in October 1971 then November 1977, June 1980 and again in June 1982. Book wise, seek out The Who: Teenaged Wasteland – The Early Years by Chris Welch and Richard Barnes' Maximum R&B or any of those recorded in the bibliography. Websites are collected below but I would have to say that I much prefer the linked sites that are available; those up kept and maintained by fans. Again, I would refer you to the bibliography for a full list.

To conclude, for some bizarre reason, the powers-that-be in Brighton has a policy of naming the buses after personalities with a link to the town and thus The Who have their own! It is a single-decker one running on the Marina route. Both Dusty Springfield and Annie Nightingale, each former residents, are also included. See also: Bill Curbishley, Roger Daltrey, John Entwistle, Kit Lambert, Pete Meaden, Keith Moon, Chris Stamp, Pete Townshend, Toyah Willcox.

Kate Williams Having acted in film and television since the sixties Kate has portrayed characters in productions written and created by such diverse talents as Dickens, Ken Loach and Johnny Speight. As Mrs Cooper, she is very much out-of-touch with the kind of lifestyle that her teen-aged son is living but unlike Jimmy's father [Michael Elphick], her fear for his well being manifests itself through oppression. After progressively questioning his erratic behaviour her despair peaks during the scene where Jimmy returns home from Brighton following his court appearance. With her pale complexion heightened by red hair and a burgundy dress, she literally pounces upon him the very moment that he enters the hallway. See how the rage intensifies as the camera closes in upon her face virtually filling the screen as she harrangs him about his drug taking and weekend activities. Brandishing the Daily Mail, with its headline of 'The Reckoning' as documentary proof of his likely involvement in the scuffles, Kate smothers the entire scene. It's almost comical to see Jimmy shrinking away from her assault both verbally and physically. "Due to technicalities to do with filming I started work on the film the day after I had the interview and I had no script as there was insufficient time to get one to me," reiterates Ms Williams in a letter to the author. "So the director talked Phil [Daniels] and I through the scene, explaining what he wanted and we improvised it. I was very impressed that Phil, a young actor, should be that trusting with someone he had just met." This is her definitive moment in the film and one for which her mannerisms remind one of the green-faced wicked witch from The Wizard of Oz. Seeing that movie as a child for the first time, it is never forgotten and Kate is similarly notable in the above scene. It has since been revealed that former Coronation Street star Amanda Barrie rejected the role of Jimmy's mum in the film. But it's is impossible to think of anybody but Kate in the role. "That scene was done in one take, a tracking shot down the hall." Concludes the actress via a correspondence with the author.

How vastly conflicting from her earlier incarnation as a saucy holiday camp nurse in Holiday On The Buses (1973), a big-screen foray from the popular telly series. Some 13.7 million viewers tuned-in to watch its eventual small screen premiere in 1979, the same year that Quadrophenia was on general cinema release. Her link with Quadrophenia was to be enhanced in 1983 with a role in a film comedy written by and starring Daniel Peacock called Party, Party. Mr & Mrs Cooper, Kate and Michael Elphick, acted together in a stage play after making the film. Kate appeared in an episode the classic Minder series, in the same one that featured a young Ray Winstone and Gary Holton too. She was also in C.A.T.S. Eyes, the Leslie Ash drama series and did a stint in Eastenders.

See also: David Anderson, Michael Elphick. Other work incls: Poor Cow (1967), What's Up Nurse? (1977).

CONTACT: Gavin Barker Associates, 45 South Molton Sreet, Mayfair, London W1.

Wimpy Bar During the Brighton rioting much of which occurs on East Street, customers inside the Wimpy bar at number 65 look on bemused as the scuffles between mods and police take place outside the restaurant. In Brighton there was once a Wimpy on the nearby Western Road [above which Pete Townshend had a discothèque called The Box] which made the news with residents complaining about the late-night noise generated by youngsters gathered there.

Mark Wingett went on to become a regular face amongst the cast of police drama The Bill since its small-screen inception back in 1984. However, it is as Jimmy's roguish best mate that is to be our focal point, shimmering as he does as the sartorial Modernist Dave. His fresh-faced role in Quadrophenia offers a great deal of reassurance towards Jimmy, often asking of his well being over the course of their adventures around the Mod haunts of local dance clubs, pubs and cafes. Consistent in their concern for each other, the pals come to blows over of all things, a woman. Steph [Leslie Ash] may not be anything extraordinary but her effect upon them both proves fatal. The reason given as to why Dave and the others abandon Jimmy down in Brighton [he does at least shield Steph after his mate was grabbed by the police] was of the necessity to return to work the day following the weekend. Their once obligatory boyish revelry, full as it was of eager rumbustuous relish, collapses in a final dénouement generated by a crude insinuation none to subtlety delivered by Dave. Little wonder that Wingett's character is head-butted by Daniels outside Alfredo's.

"I fancied you and we had it off..." as Steph so eloquently summarised.

Dave works at the council tip in a nod to the sentiments of the original Who album whereby Jimmy gets a job as a dustman. Similarly, one of the characters in the similar coming-of-age films, The Leather Boys, also works at a tip. In many ways Steph is more suited to somebody like Dave [we never get to know his surname] rather than to one with such fragility as Jimmy. The coffee bar scene is the last moment that they share and puts a full stop on their relationship. Before such an extreme conclusion the two had been the closest in the group, even at times synchronising in wearing similar v neck jumpers, Dave in red and Jimmy in blue. They also wear boating-style jackets seen much later on in many a Paul Weller/ Style Council pop promo whilst the customary dark blue Levi's are another shared favourite. Jim had freely transported his friend around and about on the back of his scooter up until Dave's is repaired in time for the Brighton jaunt. It would be a fair assumption that the two would not have ordinarily fallen out over a girl but the attitude of both Steph and Dave is so appalling that it disappoints both Jimmy and the viewer. In fact, Daniles loses a whole lot more than a friendship and a girlfriend; his entire 'way of life' is transposed. Even more, he is led to see his Lambretta destroyed before his very eyes whilst involved in a road accident, symbolising his castration from everything Mod.

From the off Dave positively encourages a fully blocked Jimmy in his pursuit of Steph whom they first see dancing with boyfriend Pete [Garry Cooper] at the Goldhawk. Away from this their relationship is shown to be one of great warmth and sheer unadulterated joy of the moment, each jigging away to the sound of Cross Section's covers of Hi Heel Sneakers and Dimples tracks. Spontaneously giggling together, Dave wears a mustard-coloured jacket, shirt, tie and trousers topped off with personally omnipresent pork pie hat alongside his equally smart associate. The morning after Jimmy was ejected from the Aquarium ballroom and his disappearance in to the Sussex night; many of the Mods meet up at a seafront café. Chalky and Dave arrive together and regale the others with their tale of sharing the archway under the pier with a trio of fornicating Rockers, whilst Jimmy sits alone nearby. Dave approaches and playfully ruffles his friend's hair. *"Leave me hair alone will you Dave!"* he barks. *"You're fucking mad you are..."* continues Dave whilst taking the seat opposite. Eagerly devouring a dribbling egg sarnie, all coughing and spluttering [to his mate's and our displeasure] he asks how he has been doing. A second before, a female café assistant had ordered Dave to take his feet off the benches to which he replied *"Piss off!"* before complying and grinning ruefully. The atmosphere is lightened somewhat when Jimmy hears of a lost opportunity of finding Steph away from Pete the previous evening. Now joined by Chalky, Spider and Ferdy who come over once Dave has eased the way, Wingett articulates his lust towards Steph only being curtailed because of his mate's interest, of course. *"You animal!"* snarls a placated Daniels as the gang all snigger.

Down at Brighton both Dave and Chalky prove themselves wickedly adept at fighting, with Dave beating up an older Rocker who resembles a reject from the Village People; all leather cap and moustache. Amidst the pulsating adrenaline on the beach they meet up again with Monkey, Steph and Jimmy. *"What's that?"* gasps Steph upon seeing Dave's knuckle-dusters belying his previously deferential nature. Throughout the film his look is crisp; cloaked in Levi's, white jeans [eminently Mod], v necks, parka, suits and hat and next to Jimmy is he the major character? Well, not quite. As becomes clear upon watching Quadrophenia, each character is important in making the film what it is: flawed and contrived at times maybe, but a fine and dandy example of an all too brief period of genuine idealism.

Away from the film, Mark was heavily identified as PC Carver from telly's The Bill although he has in fact acted in a couple of films away from his telly work. Breaking Glass (1980) is as has already been acknowledged elsewhere, a film starring Phil Daniels, saw Wingett cast as a band member of the group managed by the former. Patrick Murray and Gary Holton are in addition glimpsed in smaller roles. The Production Assistant on that picture was Caroline Hagen a crew member from Quadrophenia. In the spring of 2000 Mark was the recipient of a This is Your Life show with guest appearances from Daniels, Phil Davis, Trevor Laird and John Altman. Also had a stint in EastEnders just like Jimmy (Phil Daniels) and many other Quad actors.

See also: Goofs, hats, Trevor Laird and Gary Shail.

Ray Winstone *"Well, Ray is a bit tough, isn't he? Good as gold, though."*

Phil Daniels, Ray's Quadrophenia / Scum co-star and off-screen friend. Arguably the biggest star to come out of Quadrophenia, the Hackney-born Raymond [as he is credited in Quadrophenia] could have pursued a career as a professional boxer or footballer having gathered experience in both disciplines at amateur and schoolboy levels. As an actor his vocation had reached its nadir following a term of inactivity prior to a stream of powerful character parts in Nil By Mouth (1997) and The War Zone (1999). Helmed by actors and first-time directors Gary Oldman and Tim Roth respectively both had been cast with Phil Daniels in the Mike Leigh film Meantime. Ray's interpretation of Jimmy Cooper's school days friend Kevin [Kev] marked the third occasion that they had appeared together on film. Both had acted in the original TV version of Scum as well as its re-shot big screen version put out in cinemas two years later in 1979. In the mid-Eighties Ray and Phil were cast in Les Blair's Number One (1984), as was P H Moriarty.

It was as Carlin in Scum that Winstone batters Phil Daniels with some snooker balls packed inside a sock that produced one of the many set pieces in a story set in a young offenders centre. *"I'm the daddy now!"* snarls Winstone after rising to the top of the pecking order in a snippet of dialogue as renowned as any cult film. The two actors held its director Alan Clarke in high regard, as did Roth and Oldman. Winstone even went as far as acknowledging Clarke as the driving force behind his Scum performance. Read the film biography by Richard Kelly for a fuller account of the significance of Clarke's influence upon all the above actors. Such is the other worldliness of the acting world in that the violence of Scum is juxtaposed in Quadrophenia with the mistaken Winstone taking a drubbing from Jimmy and the other Mods in revenge for an earlier attack on Spider [Gary Shail]. In what is a lame looking crash watch the moment Ray comes off his motorbike and falls or flops onto a mass of cardboard boxes when pursued by a dozen or so scootered Mods. [The scene was Ray's first time on a motorbike]. Chalky and Dave lead the others as they wade in to the outnumbered Kev only for it to suddenly dawn upon Jimmy that he is attacking his own friend, none of the others realising the irony. In an extremely intense few moments he freaks out and screams at them to stop before zooming off.

Their reacquaintance had shown the possibility that they could renew their friendship even after Jimmy shows his shock at seeing Kevin dressed in a black leather jacket, thick lumberjack shirt, greased-back hair and plodding, calf-length biker boots. The young Mod is not the only one perturbed by his 'Liberace' quiff (as ray termed it in a 2009 television interview); the leathers might be practical for riding his motorbike but off it he truly is *'diabolical'* as Jimmy terms him. Matters are made untenable for Jimmy by the arrival of John Altman and a fellow Mod at the café where the two old friends had been chatting, causing the former to beat a hasty retreat. Kevin is a person who speaks his mind however crudely, take for example his dismay at Jimmy's flap in seeing him in his Rocker gear, *"Whassa matter, am I black or summit?"* He is a rough lad and none-too-bright after informing Jim that he had joined the Army to be 'different' but could not deal with the disciplinarian air. A line delivered without a trace of irony and revered as much as Chalky's quip about Ferdy. His introduction into the film is all revealing: in fact the full 'meat and two veg' are shown as he and Phil Daniels antagonise one another without realising each others identity whilst at the local bath house. Ray sings Gene Vincent and Daniels the Kinks, *"What do you think this is,"* yells the burly male attendant quieting them down with a bash on their cubicle doors, *"..the bloody Eurovision Song Contest!"* From the very off the diversity between the two old mates is obvious. Yet Winstone's character shows a naive tolerance to the fact that he is first a bike enthusiast and has no issue with Mods as a perceived enemy. Quite a remarkable viewpoint considering the reality. In a moment of insight he offers the view that to him people are all the same. Jimmy however, disagrees. *"It isn't about the bikes, is it? It's the people and I don't wanna be the same as everybody else. That's why I'm a Mod, see?"* After Kevin's bloody assault from the hands of the Mods at Shepherd's Bush, Ray is not seen in the film again.

Elsewhere, his film and television portfolio has shown a Quadrophenia symmetry with a working relationship with Phil Daniels already demonstrated. Meanwhile Ray and Phil Davis both starred in the 1999 BBC telly drama Births, Marriages and Deaths following their earlier association on the British crime caper Face (1997). Tank Malling (1989) found Ray Winstone in the title role and its credit details list Peter Brayham as the Stunt Arranger, the same duty that he performed on Quadrophenia. Additional TV work would see Ray in episodes of The Bill, Boon, CATS Eyes and Auf Wiedersehen, Pet each with Quad cast members involved. Interviewed in 2009, Ray squirmed as he watched himself in a scene from Quad with Phil Daniels, embarrassed about his 'Liberace' style quiff! See also: Bibliography, Les Blair, Blur, Alan Clarke, Phil Daniels, Phil Davis, Rockers, Paul Weller. CONTACT: CAM London, 19 Denmark St, London WC2H 8NA.

Work Ethic Mods all had to work, many in mundane office / clerical positions which meant that all of them had a disposable income to spend for the upkeep of all things Mod. At the work place they were always neatly turned out but their obsession to detail often went undetected by their co-workers and it really set them aside. There was a big difference between the daytime and night-time existence, the former occupied by work whilst the latter was playtime.

Christian Wrangler Recognised as the Sound Recordist [elsewhere as Sound Mixer] on Quadrophenia. One of his most recent films has been the Bafta-winning East is East (1999) whilst his Quadrophenia connections flourished on Bloody Kids. Also known by its alternate title of Red Saturday, Christian had earlier worked with its director Stephen Frears on Gumshoe (1971) and The Hit (1984). He was employed a further time in the sound department for the Franc Roddam directed docu-drama Dummy. See also: John Bindon, George Innes, Brian Tufano.

Wrestling A poster for this popular Saturday afternoon television feast in the 1960s & 1970s can be observed in Alfredo's café where the Mods hang out.

The Yardbirds An art school-formed band which at one point or another had members including Jimmy Paige and Eric Clapton. Paige himself was used as a session musician playing on the High Numbers single. As a part of their first studio demo recording the group did cover versions of John Lee Hooker's Boom Boom and Dimples. The modly Yardbirds first attained chart success in August 1964 and are remembered for the excellent For Your Love single. After filling the resident band role at The Crawdaddy club, by 1965 the 'birds were touring with the Kinks and Manfred Mann. Their name can be seen on a poster advertising a gig at the Marquee club whilst Jimmy and the others check on Spider outside the Goldhawk. They also recorded an album live at the Marquee, a venue for whom its gig-goers of 1965 were given a dedication on the original 1973 Quadrophenia album. Managed by Simon Napier-Bell, they bowed out in October 1966.

You Really Got Me Allegedly said to be a re-write of Louie, Louie that is featured along with Me in an esteemed version by the Kingsmen. In May 1963 the group did an entire 45-minute set based around this single song. The lyrics have a sexual dimension in the mumbled 'bone' line said to relate to the male member. Comedy actor John Belushi did his own version of LL for Animal House (1978).
See also: The Kingsmen

Youth Culture "Youth is only present when its presence is a problem or is regarded as a problem." Dick Hebdige, Subculture book.
"Youth culture is notoriously difficult to convey, but Roddam gets it note perfect." Hot Dog, Feb 2001 [now defunct film magazine which vited Quadrophenia its seventh best British film ever].
In the Seventies the youth audience was still regarded as substantial and films like Quadrophenia, Stardust and That'll Be The Day explored the history of popular culture. Back in 1963 the Mod and Rocker were the dominant cultures with girls in dresses, knitted twin-sets, ski pants and suits with even skirts flowing at least three inches below the knee. The Ted or Teddy Boy was the first really new youth fashion trend that confidently articulated the generation gap. Also relevant in its linkage with the Mod in so much as that the Ted actively enjoyed courting his vanity, a shocking realisation to the older gentlemen of that period. See also: Teenager

Zoot Money Led by charismatic front man GB [George Bruno] Money, a poster advertising one of his gigs at the Marquee club can be seen on the wall above the entrance to the Goldhawk club in Quadrophenia. You will find it during the scene where Jimmy and the other Mods comfort a dishevelled Spider, after his beating from a bunch of bikers.

Money formed his Big Roll Band in 1961 and was popular amongst mod audiences for their James Brown medley during the regular All-Nighters at clubs like the Flamingo. Zoot joined the New Animals in 1968 and is better known as an actor nowadays. He can be seen in Breaking Glass (1980) next to a host of Quadrophenia cast members. Money's only dalliance with the commercial charts came in August 1966 with the Top 30 hit Big Time Operator.

Zoot Suit "I wear Zoot Suit jackets with side-vents five inches long…"
Zoot Suit by The High Numbers (later to become The Who).

The only single put out by The High Numbers was scrabbled together by Pete Meaden whom, as we know already, briefly managed the band in 1964. Mentioned as sounding like Country Fool, a 45 rpm by New Orleans R&B outfit The Snowmen.

scene by scene brief description:

1.Beachy Head clifftop.
Sunrise. Jimmy walks away from a cliff-top and towards 1.
1.BEACHY HEAD cliffs.
Sunrise. Jimmy walks away from the cliff-top and towards the camera. The roar of the sea is a dominant factor interspersed with the introduction of the Real Me and Jimmy's multi-personality through the snippet of lyrics relating to the four facets of his personality: "Is it me for a moment? Love Reign O'er Me...Bell Boy...Can You See the RealMe.."
2.OPENING TITLES.
Jimmy on his scooter merrily riding towards the Goldhawk club. A posse of leather-clad bikers harass him, questioning his mode of transport but he retains his contentment at being a Mod, continuing with his head held high.
3.GOLDHAWK CLUB. Ext. Parking up in amongst an ocean of similar scooters Jimmy barters with Ferdy, the local supplier, for some pills.

4. GOLDHAWK CLUB. Int.
Entering the club Jimmy displays his treasure to a fellow mod and we see all the gang dancing about to Hi Heel Sneakers and then Dimples, two covers performed by Cross Section. Jimmy spots Steph dancing with boyfriend Pete as Dave, Jim's best mate, approaches and encourages him to pursue her.

5. THE COOPER HOUSE.
Jimmy returns home, steering his scooter through the narrow alleyway at the side of the house. Introduction to the family – mum and dad arguing in their darkened bedroom about sex whilst Jimmy creeps up the stairs and in to his sister Yvonne's room. Has a bit of fun winding her up then goes to his drab room.

6. JIMMY'S BEDROOM.
Cut My Hair kicks in whilst he smiles happily to himself cutting out and adding the latest bank holiday violence reports involving mods alongside the others on his wall. Satisfied with the pleasantries of the evening he relaxes on his bed whilst a portrait of a Union Jacketed Pete Townshend peers over his shoulder.

7. PUBLIC BATHS. INT.
Not certain as to what this place is, however, Jimmy is enjoying a bath in one of the cubicles until the noise from the neighbouring one disturbs him. Confronting each other, it turns out to be his old school pal Kevin.

8. CAFÉ.
Following on from baths, Jimmy is seen about to eat his pie and mash laced with liquor. Kevin comes in dressed in full Rocker leathers causing Jimmy to do a double take. Moments later, two Mod friends arrive and Jim beats a hasty retreat from the dejected Kevin.

9. TAILORS.
Jimmy pays cash in advance for his new suit in preparation for the Brighton trip. Meanwhile fellow Mods Dan and Lou struggle to be accommodated by a tailor confounded by the former's finicky demands.

10. SUPERMARKET WHERE STEPH WORKS.
Jimmy pays a brief visit to see Steph whilst she is working on one of the tills. He enthuses about his new 'whistle' and they chat about the up-and-coming Brighton beano.

11. JIMMY'S BEDROOM. P.M.
We see Jim preparing himself to go out and hear Zoot Suit playing.

12. PUB TOILET. P.M.

Our introduction to Dave, Chalky and Spider, the main cliché of male Mods. Dan informs them of a house party which they all plan on going to. Jimmy and John joke about Steph before the former asks if she wants to go with him. Pete returns and his plans are thwarted.

13. HOUSEPARTY. Ext.
The lads boisterously arrive but have their admittance prevented. Eventually John leads the way and manages to blag their way inside following this cluttered doorstep confrontation.

14. HOUSEPARTY. Int.
Be My Baby plays as the lads separate and look around the place. In the packed lounge, Monkey spots Jimmy and tempts him with her supply of drugs in exchange for a snog! The soft tones of Rhythm of the Rain whisper as he sees Steph dancing closely with Pete. Pulling away from the grasp of Monkey, Jimmy abruptly puts on My Generation causing the lads to jump about: Steph and Pete leave.

15. HOUSEPARTY. Ext.
Jim's frustration is not tempered by seeing Steph scoot off into the night on the back of Pete's scooter.

SCENE BY SCENE   A QUADROPHENIA ANTHOLOGY

trivia:
Two locations were used to represent Jimmy's house in Quadrophenia: Kate Williams details one and the other can be found at 75 Wells House road, north London.

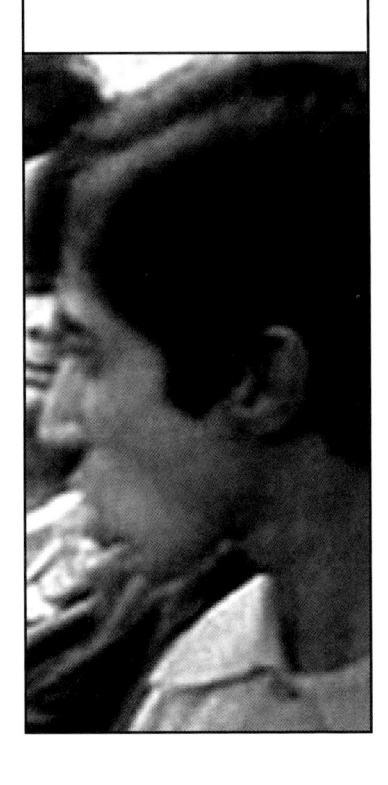

16. HOUSEPARTY. Int.
Jimmy returns inside where everyone seems to have paired off in one of the upstairs bedrooms. John and Dave are seen enjoying themselves as he passes through.

17. HOUSEPARTY. Ext.
The sound of Jimmy's scooter takes Dave away from the crowded bedroom, opening the window he spots him circling the garden on his bike. As he zooms off, smashing the white picket fence, and to the alarm of his naked pal, Jimmy just misses colliding with the expensive-looking car containing the returning parents.

18. CANALSIDE. P.M.
Jimmy skulking on his scooter. Townshend's I'm One builds on the gloom of the youngster's mood. Seeing a middle-aged couple canoodling under a nearby bridge, he vindictively shows his envy by riding straight at them and off into the night.

19. AD AGENCY. Int.
Jimmy at work, the morning following his night before. He delivers the internal mail with a lethargic exterior.

20. AD AGENCY TOILETS.
The two upper middle-class company executives, played by Benjamin Whitrow and Jeremy Child, discuss

263

chasing the wind   SCENE BY SCENE

the latest ad campaign and related health issues concerning the Private Blend commercial whilst spuccing themselves up. Jimmy coughs and splutters into a sink between them, he ignores them and they do likewise. Great humour and one of the funniest scenes in the film.

21. HOME. Int. P.M.
Mum and Dad watching telly, mum is transfixed whilst Dad snoozes with bottle of beer in hand and clad in his trusty white vest. She challenges Jimmy's behaviour and they debate the subject of 'normality.'

22. JIMMY'S SHED. P.M.
Jimmy seen tinkering with his scooter as the roar of motorbike is heard outside. He relaxes when Kevin appears. They discuss the differences between their choice of transport and Jimmy gives his *"I don't wanna be like everybody else..."* speech.

23. AD AGENCY - PROJECTION BOOTH.
Jimmy with fellow work mates Timothy Spall and Patrick Murray playing cards and laughing. The ad campaign for "People Like You" is screened and noticeably, the foreign model catches his eye.

24. AD AGENCY. Int.

Chastised for being late, Jimmy collects a portfolio of photos of the said model, which he is supposed to convey to another department a.s.a.p. He delivers his sharp *"Watch the cloth, moth!"* line.

25. RECORD STORE LISTENING BOOTH.

Anyway, Anyhow, Anywhere is heard as Jimmy takes refuge in a listening booth at a record shop to look at the said photos, one of which shows the model in a bikini. Wishin' And Hopin' plays from the box next to him with a young GPO worker eyeing the saucy pictures too.

26. SUPERMARKET. Ext.

Jimmy sits on his parked scooter waiting for Steph to finish there.

27. ROAD.

She accepts his offer of a lift home and they flirt whilst discussing her involvement with Pete.

28. ALFREDO'S CAFÉ. Int. P.M.

Night Train by James Brown plays on an unseen jukebox as Chalky, Dave, Spider and a black sunglasses-wearing Jimmy discuss their proposed Brighton escapades.

whilst gathered around a pinball table.

29. ALFREDO'S CAFE. Ext.
Noisily, but without malice, the boys leave the café after being kicked-out by the owner. Jumping onto their scooters parked outside, their next destination is revealed as being the Goldhawk club.

30. ROAD TOWARDS THE GOLDHAWK.
Spider has engine problems with his scooter and motions to the others that he and his girlfriend will catch up with everyone inside the club.

31. SPIDER & GIRLFRIEND STRANDED OUTSIDE PUB.
Having stalled in the middle of a road opposite The Bramley Arms pub, the couple grumble to each other about the technical difficulties.

32. GOLDHAWK. Int. Da Doo Ron Ron bounces around the club as Jimmy and Dave sit together to the side of those dancing.

33. ATTACK ON SPIDER & HIS GIRLFRIEND. Ext.
Tinkering away with the scooter, Spider curses his luck as a motley crew of leathered bikers abuses him and his girlfriend. Violence ensues and he takes a beating.

34.GOLDHAWK. Int
Chalky rushes in to tell Dave and Jimmy of the attack.
35.GOLDHAWK. Ext.
The boys chat to Spider and his girlfriend on the steps outside before dashing off on their scooters in pursuit of those responsible.
36.GOLDHAWK. Int.
Monkey and John continue dancing in amongst a mainly female crowd.
37.SHEPHERD'S BUSH. Ext.
A group of 8 scootered Mods cruise the streets passing Shepherd's Bush tube station and the market where they spot two Rockers at a nearby mobile snack bar.
38.SHEPHERD'S BUSH. Ext. The outnumbered duo are chased nearby where one of them falls from his motorbike and is set upon by the Mods. To his horror, Jimmy discovers that he and his mates are giving a hiding to his school friend Kevin. Still unaware of his identity, as Jimmy screams at them to stop, they continue the beating all the while he zooms away on his scooter.
39.SHEPHERD'S BUSH. Ext.
The Mods, having finished their mistaken attack, beat a hasty retreat whilst the listless and bloodied Kevin

lies amongst the market debris.

40. ALLEYWAY LEADING TO REAR OF JIMMY'S HOUSE. P.M.
A distraught Jimmy vents his anger on his bike and snaps his shades.

41. HALLWAY / STAIRS & LOUNGE.
Coming in through the front door a vexed Jimmy moves into the hallway and up the stairs where his inebriated father confronts him. Accidentally knocking his son back down the barren-looking stairwell the two square up to each other in the lounge. His dad reiterates the mental health problems of the Cooper family to a confused Jimmy.

42. JIMMY'S BEDROOM.
Following directly on from the tête-à-tête with his father Jimmy finds a moment's pleasure from masturbating whilst looking at the model photographs which he was supposed to have delivered.

43. JIMMY'S BEDROOM. 8:45 a.m.
Mrs Cooper barges in only to discover her son fully-clothed on top of the bed. He pleads sickness whilst she barracks him about obtaining a medical note from the doctor.

44. COUNCIL TIP. Ext. A.M.
A scruffy-looking Jimmy discusses a possible source of drugs needed for

Brighton with his mate Dave who works at the council tip. The latter mentions going to ask Steph's boyfriend Pete for a contact.

45.SCRAPYARD. Ext. A.M.
Jimmy turns off the main road and drives in through the main entrance. Pete soon spots him after his two guard dogs, Butch and Jenny, bark away at the anxious Mod. Pete fails to offer any help in locating a supply. and he leaves frustrated.

46.FERDY'S HOUSE. Ext. P.M.
Jimmy, Chalky and Dave gather below the steps of Ferdy's house but fail to locate his whereabouts. Derek Morgan's Burnin' Fire features as background music. The property is situated at the top of Portobello road in the fashionable Notting Hill area of London.

47.PUB LOUNGE. Int. P.M.
Pete is called to the bar phone where a belligerent Dave demands a dealers name for their Brighton trip.

48.PHONEBOX. P.M.
Chalky, Jimmy and Dave squeeze into an old red box with Dave's aggressive manner towards Pete succeeding in obtaining a contact.

49.BRIDGE. P.M.
The trio scoot towards their pick-up

destination for the drugs.
50. VILLAINS PUB. Ext.
Jimmy takes off his parka coat before heading inside whilst the ohers wait next to their scooters.
51. BAR AT VILLAINS PUB. Int.
Looking ill-at-ease, Jimmy asks the barman if he can see Harry North. Moments later he is led behind the scenes and through a sliding door, which opens up to reveal a boxing ring and gymnasium.
52. GYM IN REAR OF PUB. Int.
Jimmy mistakenly gives North the impression that he is the nephew of Charlie Fenton [Pete's uncle] before asking him for a tenner's worth of amphetamines.
53. VILLAINS PUB. Ext.
Passing his mates, Jimmy follows Harry's honcho to the back of a Jag where the Mod is handed a plastic bag in exchange for his banknote. Rejoining the others, Chalky is the first to discover that they have been conned and the trio move to attack the car in revenge.
54. CHEMIST SHOP. Ext. P.M.
The scene is set for the robbery at the chemist where Monkey (Toyah) works as the camera pans across the deserted high street entrance.

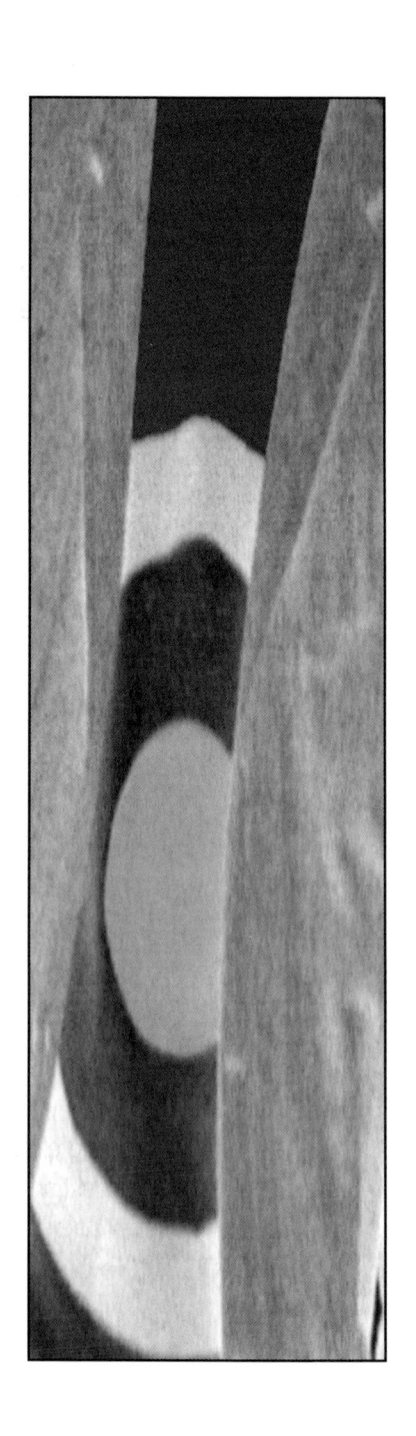

55. CHEMIST SHOP. Int.
Jimmy, Chalky and Dave break open the barred back shop window, crawl inside and look for the legally prescribed drugs. Comedy ensues as Jimmy remains serious whilst the others mess about. A telephone rings causing them to panic and flee but not before locating some Blues.

56. ALFREDO'S CAFÉ. P.M.
They join some of the others inside where they tell everyone about the robbery where one of them, Monkey, works. Jimmy offers Steph some of his cache and she asks him to see her home later that evening.

57. STEPH'S HOUSE. Ext. P.M.
They kiss and agree to see each other. Steph tells Jimmy not to tell anyone yet.

58. AD AGENCY MAILROOM. Int.
A joyful Jimmy sings You Really Got Me to the rhythm of the mail franking machine on what is pay day.

59. GENTS BARBERS. DAY BEFORE BRIGHTON. Int.
He finishes his turn following a trim, refusing the barber's suggestion of using lacquer. Dan takes his seat.

60. JIMMY'S KITCHEN. A.M.
Mr Cooper sits reading a newspaper, which forewarns of the possible weekend violence at seaside resorts. Jimmy wears a pair of wet Levi's, which he is shrinking to fit. Ready Steady Go! Is heard on the television in the background.

61. LOUNGE. Int.
Jimmy sits captivated by the Who performing the Pop Art explosion that is Anyway, Anyhow, Anywhere. His father joins him and teases his young son about their general appearance and level of noise generated.

62. JIMMY'S BEDROOM. A.M.
Revealing his newly purchased suit Jimmy prepares for the visit to Brighton. A transistor radio echoes the shopkeepers fears.

63. ROAD TO BRIGHTON. A.M.
Jimmy & Co. are seen in a battalion-like formation juxtaposed with a similar group of bikers also on their way to the coast.

64. CHALKY'S ACCIDENT.
Chalky rides on ahead of the others but is cut off the road by the oncoming bikers. He crashes whilst Jimmy and Dave catch up and check to see if he is hurt. Discovering that he is not they go on ahead without him. Get Out And Stay Out plays.

65. BRIGHTON BEACH. A.M.
The seafront starts to come to life

with deckchairs being set out and the first mod arrivals spotted on the water's edge set off with the pier in the background.

66. FIRST SIGHTING OF BRIGHTON.
Jimmy halts the posse to inform them of the distant view of Brighton (it is in reality, Eastbourne)

67. MADEIRA DRIVE, BRIGHTON.
Ext. A.M. A sea of parked scooters are presented in advance of our initial sight of Jimmy.

68. JIMMY & CO. ARRIVE. Ext. A.M.
Jimmy and Dave walk along the pathway behind surveying the crowd.

69. STEPH ARRIVES WITH PETE.
Ext. Jimmy briefly greets her before the timely sight of the local Brighton Ace Face.

70. THE ACE FACE. Ext.
Sting arrives on his scooter with a troop of a half-dozen others, briefly glancing around before pulling away off towards the pier. A battered Chalky turns up too.

71. BRIGHTON BALLROOM. Int. PM
Green Onions fills the dance floor as we see Chalky, Spider, Dave and Jimmy. Pete chats with an American girl whilst Ace dominates with his robotic dancing. Jimmy and Steph

fall out as she seeks to dance nearby. Moment's later Jim is spotted jigging away on the edge of the balcony above, egged on by the others, he dives in to the crowd below as bouncers grab him and kick him out of the place. The Southgate Royalty was the actual location used, doubling for the Brighton one.

72.BRIGHTON BALLROOM. Ext. P.M.
Jimmy is ejected from the venue and wanders off under the walkway next to the Aquarium, towards the seafront.

73.BRIGHTON BALLROOM. Int.
Wah Whatusi plays on the sound system where we see Steph dancing with the local 'Ace Face' [as portrayed by Sting].

74.BEACH. P.M. A solitary Jimmy stares out at the sea.

75.BRIGHTON BALLROOM. Ext.
The Mods begin to leave, pairing off together; Spider and his mate, Dave with Chalky and Steph with a female friend. Dave and Chalky walk through the tunnel leading under the pier that Jimmy had earlier passed through on his own.

76.CHALKY & DAVE AT THE

PIER. Ext. P.M.
Here the two debate sleeping in an unlocked storeroom where they are startled to hear unseen voices demanding that they make up their minds:they stay.
77.BEACH. P.M.
Jimmy again seen alone.
78.MADEIRA DRIVE. AMUSEMENT PARK. P.M.
The Brighton Ace Face and his posse complete a loop formation before slowly driving away on their scooters in the semi-darkness.
79.BEACH. A.M.
The paltry-sized figure of Jimmy is set against the forceful sea as the vastness of the beach reveals the sight of the pier in the distance.
80.STOREROOM UNDER THE PIER. A.M.
Chalky and Dave's rude awakening in a space shared with three fawnicating Rockers!
81.BEACH CAFÉ. A.M.
They arrive together with a tale to tell the others gathered inside the café. Jimmy sits alone until Dave and then the other Mods join him.
82.EAST STREET / SEAFRONT.
83.MARCHING BAND. Chalky and the others mingle in with the

shoddy-looking band of sea cadets as it passes down East Street and opposite the cinema.
84.PROMENADE OPP. MADEIRA DRIVE.
Jimmy and Co. come together. Steph surprises him by her appearance and they strut their stuff along the seafront. A press photographer takes their picture as Spider instigates a unified *"We are the mods, we are the mods, we are, we are, we are the mods..."* chant.
85.SEA FRONT. OPPOSITE THE MODS.
In a slight motion blur, a Rocker and pillion passenger zoom past the seafront entrance of the ABC cinema, opposite the marching Mods, just as they pass the pier.
86.CHALKY SPOTS THE ROCKER. PROMENADE. Chaos ensues as he thinks that he recognizes the passing Rocker as one of those involved with running him off the road earlier.
87.CAFÉ ON EAST STREET. Int.
The same biker then parks up alongside a half-dozen similar bikes, oblivious to the sight of the incoming throng of Mods.
88.MADEIRA DRIVE.

Let's fuckin' have 'em!" screeches Chalky as the Mods dash across the prom towards the café.

89. CAFÉ. Int / Ext.

In a poor piece of non-acting, one of the black leather and white scarf-wearing lads gurning as he makes a feeble attempt to close one half of the wooden doors to prevent the attack. With the camera P.O.V taken from inside looking out, the little café is attacked by marauding Mods forcing their way inside and whacking its horrendously outnumbered occupants to the mantra of *"Mods! Mods! Mods!"* Whilst the others scramble inside, one lad tries to escape by running through the clusters of Mods but is spotted by Dave and Chalky.

90. MADEIRA DRIVE PROMENADE. Pete in his sunglasses and ox blood leather jacket blocks the escape route of a rocker, inflicting a severe kicking for his troubles.

91. CAFÉ. Int.

The distressed café proprietor makes a frantic phone call to the police whilst Jim dives out of the way of a flying table!

92. MADEIRA DRIVE

PROMENADE. Pete and the others force a beaten Rocker to scramble over the terrace edge whilst Dave smacks a deckchair over his back for good measure.

93. CAFÉ. Int / Ext.
Many Mods dash out of the café and gather just outside its entrance. Steph grabs a hold of a exhilarated Jimmy as he tells her about his involvement inside. A final glimpse back reveals bruised and battered bodies sprawled about. The siren from a police vehicle seen immediately behind them causes the group to disperse by running back across the prom towards the beach.

94. PROMENADE DOWN TO BEACH.
Jimmy and Steph are spotted amongst the others hastily sprinting down the walkway leading on to the beach.

95. BEACH IN FRONT NEAR TO PIER.
A couple sitting on deckchairs gets knocked over by the force of the youngsters as they rush on to the beach. However, just like the Rockers beaten and forced over the terrace earlier, the woman knocked over was said to have been a stunt performer. The chanting continues a pace as the youngsters stand off from the many white-helmeted police officers.

96. AQUARIUM STEPS.
The Mods dash down the steps here, at which point, Pete grabs a nearby flowerpot and lobs it through a window. He and the others move past and take a right heading underneath the road above through a tunnel that flows out to the Beach café and the underside of the Palace Pier. It is the very same place where Jimmy, Steph and her friend and Chalky and Dave pass through following their evening at the ballroom at the Aquarium.

97. BEACH.
Chalky and Dave chat to Monkey, Jimmy and Steph amongst the throng of waiting youngsters.

98. ARRIVAL OF ROCKERS FROM PROMENADE ABOVE.
A small group of Rockers dash onto the beach where the Mods are.

99. BEACH FIGHTS.
The stunningly choreographed chaos of battling youngsters commences with aplomb.

100. POLICE VEHICLES ON A ROAD NEAR TO THE BATTLE.

chasing the wind   SCENE BY SCENE

Attention turns to a pool of police vehicles, sirens wailing, travelling along towards the trouble spot. An old, black Mariah van is recognizable amongst them.

101. THE ACE FACE IN ACTION. BEACH.

Sting, a star as the Brighton Ace Face, assaults two policemen using the fractured remains of a deckchair .Wearing an elegant three-quarter length leathercoat and charcoal grey trousers the look of glee on his face seems beyond acting.

102. MASS MOD DASH OVER PROMENADE TO EAST STREET.

An ocean of parka and blue jeaned youngsters dash back up from the beach after being corralled by horse riding police in a successful attempt to break up the fighting. They dash up and out onto King's Road making a beeline for the nearby East Street.

103. RUSH ALONG EAST STREET & BACK UP AGAIN.

Starting with a long shot of hundreds of Mods sprinting along their roar is the only sound heard as they head towards the Wimpy bar before hastily turning on their heels and sprinting back as the police cut off

Quadrophenia alleyway entrance

their path.

104. JIMMY / STEPH / ACE.
Jimmy, Steph and the Ace are spotted in amongst the sardine crowd.

105. ACE SMASHES THE WINDOW. The Mods scatter following the window being smashed in frustration by Ace.

106. JIMMY & STEPH BREAK AWAY UP ALLEYWAY. Steph and Jimmy split from the others by sprinting down the narrow alleyway leading off East Street. He pulls her inside an unlocked doorway as the sound of an angry, unseen police dog rushes past. This 'object of lust' as Toyah described Steph (Ash) is soon to become his...

107. YOUNGSTERS SCUFFLES WITH POLICE ON EAST STREET. Amidst a high decibel count of noise, parka-clad Mods resist containment from the police around the exterior of the Wimpy burger bar.

108. JIMMY & STEPH
Steph pulls Jimmy towards her and they begin to kiss. She sits on the floor in the corner immediately behind the door. There is no sound of the rioting in East Street.

109. ACE PULLS THE COPPER FROM A HORSE.
Ace pulls a copper down as kicks reigning in on the solitary officer from all around him.

110. JIMMY & STEPH.

111. FIGHTING CONTINUES.
The violence storms on a pace in front of the Wimpy burger bar, a bookshop next to it and by the cinema.

112. JIMMY & STEPH.

113. EAST STREET AGAIN.
An unseen voice amplified through a loud hailer orders the police to *"get in there – turn them over!"* along with a *"Control those Kids!"*

114. JIMMY & STEPH.

115. FIGHTING CONTINUES.
The presence of a horse-mounted police officer is seen in amongst the chaos. Dan, one of the Londoners, is also spotted. The battle between the uniformed blackness of the police and the greenness of the Modly parkas keeps on.

116. JIMMY & STEPH FINISH!
In the through the aftermath of violence, a perplexed Jimmy is forced in to the back of a police van by two officers. Meanwhile Dave pulls Steph away from the incident.

118. POLICE VAN. Int.

Jimmy's anxiety is increased after accidentally being bolted forward on to the lap of one of the others, all Rockers, seated around him.

119. BRILL'S LANE. Ext.
The reason as to why the police van shunted to a halt a moment earlier is revealed as being to accommodate one more occupant: the Brighton Ace Face. All kicking and cursing, he struggles furiously with a trio of officers outside the vehicle before relenting and taking his place in the back of the van. The arrival of the Ace lifts Jimmy's spirits.

120. POLICE VAN. Int.
Seated opposite, the young Mr Cooper looks overwhelmed by his presence, the two both smoke a cigarette and even the police officer next to them gets offered one.

121. EAST STREET AFTERMATH.
A view of a number of Mods arm-locked to the ground by police officers or else standing around in a state of suspended animation, almost as if none of them know what happens next. Ferdy and Chalky are highlighted in amongst the war-torn.

122. POLICE VAN'S DEPARTURE.
Briefly seen driving along streets with an unseen Jimmy and Ace contained within it.

123. ROAD BACK TO LONDON.
Those of the London Mods lucky enough not to be nabbed by the police head back home along the coastal road seen earlier. Jimmy is not in amongst them. Steph travels on the back of Dave's scooter in what looks like the start of a fledgling relationship.

124. BRIGHTON COURTROOM. Int.
We see the Ace Face, Jimmy, and John in amongst a motley crew of battered Rockers in their leather jackets, many with the awful complimentary white scarves. After the frivolity of the comments made by the Ace, the colour in Jimmy's face soon drains as the ominous formality of his full name, *"James Michael Cooper"* is called.

125. JIMMY'S HALLWAY. Int. A.M.
Armed with a newspaper reporting on the seaside violence and Jimmy's hidden stash of amphetamines found in his bedroom as evidence, his mother rips in to him with venom.

126. BACKYARD. A.M.
A distraught and dishevelled Jimmy hastily parks his scooter inside the shed in a clever scene that appears to present him as if he is inside a

train compartment as a loco passes along the tracks at the bottom of the family garden.

127.DENOUMENT: AD AGENCY. Int.
It is here that Jimmy delivers his supreme resignation speech to a bemused looking Mr Fulford.

128.ALFREDO'S CAFÉ. Int. P.M.
This is the last time that we see Ferdy, Dave, Chalky and Monkey. Flourishing his £5 'golden handshake' pay, Jimmy spends a fiver on a big bag of amphetamine courtesy of Ferdy, both Dave and Steph look on very disinterested.

129.ALFREDO'S CAFÉ. Ext.
A scuffle between Jimmy and Dave, as they make their way out at closing time. Chalky and Ferdy come between the two warring Mods, as Monkey looks on concerned. Jimmy finally roars away in to the darkness, out of their lives and the mod cliche.

130.JIMMY'S HOUSE. Ext. P.M.
He returns late one evening after already being told to get out by his irate mother earlier but only succeeds in being chased away by his father.

131.CANALSIDE. P.M.
Jimmy sits alone on his scooter with a barge passing background as the rain lashes down.

132.BACKYARD. A.M.
Mr Cooper Snr, enveloped in a black donkey jacket, collects his pushbike next to the shed. The sight of rail tracks in the distance becomes heightened in its adoption as a cipher suggesting an escape route to take Jimmy back to Brighton. Following his father's departure a wet and damp-looking Jimmy surfaces from having slept in the shed and opens the back door to the house. Grabbing a tie from its resting place on top of his mirrored chest of drawers, he puts it in his bag which does not appear to have much else contained within it other than a spare shirt.

133.JIMMY'S BEDROOM. A.M.
Visiting his room for the last time Jimmy silently takes a bag, rips down the newspaper articles and glamour model photos.

134.JIMMY WAITING FOR STEPH. Ext. day.
A haggard-looking Jimmy in black v neck jumper, blue jeans and unkempt hair, tries to talk to Steph after last seeing her at Alfredo's. She is in no mood for reconciliation and

is both hostile and defensive.

135. ACCIDENT WITH THE GPO VAN.

Jimmy furiously zooms off and collides with the van. The events prove too much; symbolizing his castration from all things Mod. All that remains with him are the clothes he is wearing as he abandons the scooter. The scene was improvised by Danels and the grey-haired postie was acually a stunt man!

136. WATERLOO TRAIN STATION. Int. Day.

The solitary Mod pops some more pills, washed down with a swig from a bottle of gin as Pete Townshend's gentle tones introduce the Who track 5:15.

137. TRAIN TOILET. Int.

To the sound of Roger Daltrey's gruff vocals at the start of 5:15, a middle-aged woman walks along the carriageway opening the toilet door to discover a startled-looking Jimmy in the midst of applying some eyeliner. He stares at her before barging past and again pushing past two men standing in the narrow walkway.

138. TRAIN CARRIAGE. Int.

Jimmy throws his bag out of a window much to the delight of two pretty, uniformed public school girls. One of them is Caroline Embling who also acted in Bloody Kids.

139. SITTING BETWEEN THE TWO CITY GENTS. Int.

Sliding open one of the glass-panelled doors in the confines of First Class, Jimmy sits in an empty seat between them. Their look is one of disdain whilst Jim's is of a vacated premises; so high is he.

140. VIEW OF RAILTRACKS.

141. VIEW OF THE SEA.

The waves break onto the shore as 5:15 concludes its melody.

142. BRIGHTON BEACH CAFÉ. Int.

Jimmy sits at the window seat at the cafe that the London Mods had visited during their Brighton weekend. Popping more pills, the Palace pier is seen opposite.

143. SEA.

A lone male swimmer is seen exercising in the water.

144. BEACH.

A very sharp cut now finds Jimmy crouching on the shingle as the beauty of Townshend's lyric and Daltrey's voice combine to enrich the moment with "Only love can make it reign…" The incoming tide laps at his shoes and dangling parka, motioning to hisfeet he heads away. The Palace Pier with its signage and Union Jack beneath it are observed in the distance.

145. PROMENADE.
Jimmy walks along the prom towards East Street.

146. RETURN TO EAST STREET ALLEYWAY.
A smile of recognition makes way for his lament as he kicks the locked doorway behind which he and Steph had enjoyed themselves on that fateful, sunny day.

147. GRAND HOTEL. Ext.
Sting's chrome Vespa scooter glistens in the sunlight, parked as it is along the side of the hotel. Jimmy greets its appearance as if it were an old friend, until the sight of the Ace Face destroys any hope of deliverance.

148. GRAND HOTEL. Int.
Uniformed in an embarrassingly juvenile-looking bellboy outfit, think Jerry Lewis in one of his old comedies, Sting follows a male guest into the lobby of the hotel after picking up his three suitcases outside with a barely disguised disdain of the moneyed guest. A seething Jimmy cannot believe his eyes as he rushes up the steps after the Ace screaming out with a clenched fist, *"Bell boy! Bell boy!"*

149. GRAND HOTEL ENTRANCE.
Running back down the steps of the hotel and away towards the scooter he somehow manages to start its ignition with the key to his Lambretta and speeds away, narrowly missing two passing men.

150. ROAD TO BEACHY HEAD.
We next see Jimmy bumps up off the road on the stolen scooter.

151. BEACHY HEAD CLIFFS.
Exhausted, he rides the scooter along the billiard table clifftops and along the pathway for a considerable distance before stopping. He turns the bike around, drives away only to turn back, revealing that he is about to ride towards the cliff edge.

152. CLOSING CREDITS.
With the remains of the battered chrome Vespa resting on the rocks below, Dr Jimmy plays over the closing credits.

chasing the wind BIBLIOGRAPHY

bibliography: Some texts referenced for this book have been acknowledged where used other sources include:
Richard Barnes, The Who: Maximum R&B (Plexus, 2000) George Tremlett, The Who (Furtura, 1975). Gary Herman, The Who (Studio Vista, 1975). Rolling Stone Magazine, The Who - Ten Great Years (1981, ORIG.1975) Chris Welch, The Who: Teenaged Wasteland - The Early Years (Castle, 1996) Joe McMichael and 'Irish' Jack Lyons, The Who Concert File (Omnibus Press, 1997)Comp. by Ross Hifin foreword by Pete Townshend. The Who Live (Genesis, Ltd Ed.2000). Tony Fletcher, Dear Boy: The Life of Keith Moon (Omnibus Press, 1998). Philip French and Karl French, Cult Movies (Virgin, 1997). Hanif Kureishi & Jon Savage (eds), The Faber Book of Pop (Faber and Faber, 1995). Andrew Loog Oldham, Stoned (Secker & Warburg, 2000). Stephen Maycock, Miller's Rock and Pop Memorabilia (Miller's, 1994). Peter Everett, You'll Never Be Sixteen Again (BBC Publications, 1986). International Who's Who, 63rd edition, (Europa Publications). Oxford Dictionary of Quotations, 4th edition, ed. Angela Partington (Oxford University Press, 1996). Guinness Book of Classic British TV, ed. Anne Marshall, (Guinness, 1996). Chronicle of Britain and Ireland, ed. Henrietta Heald (Chronicle Comm, 1992). Dick Hebdige, Subculture: The Meaning of Style (Routledge, 1979) & Hiding in the Light – On Images and Things (Routledge, 1988). Colin Larkin, Virgin Encyclopaedia of Sixties Music (Virgin, 1997). Dave McAleer, Beat Boom! Pop Goes the Sixties (Reed International, 1994). Joe Smith, Off the Record - An Oral History of Popular Music (Sidgwick and Jackson, 1989). Steve Humphries and John Taylor, The Making of Modern London 1945 - 85, Arthur Marwick, The Sixties Cultural Revolution in Britain, France, Italy and the U.S, Canada 1958 - 1974, (Oxford University Press, 1998). Paul Weller - In His Own Words, compiled by Michael Heatley (Omnibus, 1996). Steve Malins, Paul Weller - The Unauthorized Biography (Virgin, 1997). Mods! Compiled by Richard

284

Barnes (Eel Pie Publishing, 1979) Terry Rawlings and Keith Badman, Empire Made - The Handy Guide to all things Mod! (Complete Music, 1997). The Sharper World - A Mod Anthology, ed. Paolo Hewitt (Helter Skelter, 1999). Stanley Cohen, Folk Devils and Moral Panic (Basil Blackwell, 1972). Dave Wedgbury, Icons of Pop (Booth Clibborn, 1999). 14:24 British Youth Culture (Conran Foundation, 1986). The Subcultures Reader, ed. Ken Gelder and Sarah Thornton (Routledge, 1997). Retro Hell: Life in the Seventies and Eighties (Little, Brown and Co). Michael Bracewell, England is Mine - Pop Life in Albion from Wilde to Goldie (1997, Harper Collins). George Melly, Revolt into Style - The Pop Arts in Britain (Penguin Press, 1970) Kevin Davey, English Imaginaries : Six studies in Anglo-British Modernity (Lawrence and Wishart, 1999). Tony Thorne, Fads, Fashions and Cults (Bloomsbury, 1993). Amy De La Haye, Fashion Source Book - A Visual Reference to 20th Century Fashion (Macdonald Orbis, 1988). Paul Friedlander, Rock and Roll - A Social History (Westview Press, 1996). Linda McCartney's Sixties, (1992, Bulfish Press). The End of Innocence: Photos from the decade that defined Pop: the Fifties to Seventies (Scalo, 1997). Nik Cohn, Pop from the Beginning (Weidenfeld and Nicolson, 1969) & Today there are no Gentlemen: The Changes in Englishmen's Clothing since the War (Willmer Bros, 1971) Jonathon Green, All Dressed Up - The Sixties and the Counterculture (Pimlico, 1979) & Days in the Life - Voices from the England Underground 1961-71 (Heinemann, 1988). The Beat Goes On – The Rockfile Reader, ed. Charlie Gillet and Simon Frith (Pluto Press, 1996). Simon Frith and Howard Horne, Art into Pop (Methuen, 1987) Simon Firth, The Sociology of Rock (Constable, 1978). Nick Logan and Bob Wooffinden, The Illustrated Encyclopaedia of Rock (Salamander, 1982). Charlie Gillett, The Sound of the City - Rock and Roll (Souvenir Press, 1970/ 1983) Peter Wicke trans. Rachel Fogg, Rock Music - Culture, Aesthetics and Sociology (Cambridge Uni Press, 1987). Jim Curtis, Rock Eros Interpretations of Music and Society 1954-84 (Bowling

Green State Univ. Press, 1987). Jan Olofsson, My Sixties (Taschen, 1994). Alain Dister, The Story of Rock, Smash Hits and Superstars (Thames and Hudson, 1992). Rolling Stone: The Complete Covers 1967-1997 (Harry N Abrahams Pbs, 1998). Twenty Years of Rolling Stone: What a long, strange trip it's been, ed. Jann. S. Wenner (Ebury Press, 1987). Ted Polhemus and Lynn Procter, Pop Styles (Vermilion, 1984). Yvonne Connike, Fashions of a Decade - The Sixties (BT Batsford, 1990). Chic Thrills - A Fashion Reader, ed. Juliet Ash and Elizabeth Wilson (Pandora, 1992). Howard Baker, Sawdust Caesar - a novel of youth rebellion (Mainstream, 1999). John Tobler and Stuart Grundy, The Guitar Greats (BBC publications, 1983). Alan Clarke, ed. by Richard Kelly (Faber & Faber, 1998). Francis Wheen, The Sixties - A fresh look at the decade of change (Century Publishing, 1982). Andrew Motion, The Lamberts: George, Constant and Kit (Chatto and Windus, 1986). Nigel Cox, Lambretta Innocenti (Foulis / Haynes, 1996). The Cult of Vespa, various contributors (Piaggio, 1997). Eric Brockway, Vespa: An Illustrated History (Haynes, 1999). Eric Dregni, Scooter Mania! (Motorbooks Int., 1998). Annie Nightingale, Chase the Fade (Blandford Press, 1981) & Wicked Speed (Sidgwick and Jackson, 1999). Terence Stamp, Double Feature (Bloomsbury, 1989). Michael Brake, Comparative Youth Culture - The Sociology of Youth Sub-Cultures in America, Britain & Canada (Routledge, 1985) Rave Off - Politics and Deviance in Contemporary Youth Culture, ed. Steve Redhead (Avebury, 1995). As Years Go By- The Sixties Revolution at British Decca, by John Tracey, (Pavilion, 1993) Jonathon Green, The Cassell Dictionary of Slang (Cassell, 1998). Shorter Slang Dictionary, Compiled by Rosalind Fergusson (Routledge, 1994). The Oxford Companion to the Mind, ed. Richard L.Gregory (Oxford Union Press, 1998) Neville Marten and Jeffrey Hudson, The Kinks - Well Respected Men (Castle Comm., 1996). Dave Davies, Kink (Pan Books, 1997). Stuart Maconie, Blur 3862 Days - The Official History (Virgin, 1999). John Lancaster, Introducing Op Art (BT Batsford, 1973). A Decade of The Who (available via Pete Townshend's commercial website). Richard Rudgley, The Encyclopaedia of Psychoactive Substances (Little, Brown and Co, 1998). Paul Barker, 'Brighton Battleground', New Society magazine (21 May, 1964). Alan Clayson, Beat Merchants – The Origins, History, Impact and Legacy of the 1960s British Pop Groups (Blandford, 1995). Ali Catterall & Simon Wells, British Cult Movies Since the Sixties – Your Face Here (Fourth Estate, 2001). Kenneth Leech, Youthquake – Spirituality and the growth of a counter-culture (Abacus, 1976). Tom Wolfe, The Pump House Gang, (1992, Black Swan, 1st pub 1969), Bill Osgerby, Youth in Britain Since 1945 (Blackwell, 1998). S R Gibbons, Britain 1945 – 1985 (Blackie) Rock Docs - 2nd House: The Who (BBC2, 1993) After the Fire, South Bank Show (ITV, 1984) The Sixties, The Late Show (BBC 2, 1993) Design Classics: Fred Perry Shirt (BBC 2, 1990) Objects of Desire: 501s, (Discovery Channel, 1999) Rebellion: "Undressed -Fashion in the 20th Century" (Channel 4, 1997) Classic Motorcycles: Scooter Mania (Channel 4, 1993) Sartre: Road to Freedom. "Human, all too human..." (BBC2, 1999) Seas – 'Landscape and Memory', presented by Simon Schama (1995), Family Life (1971, directed by Ken Loach). I Love 1979, (BBC, 2000)

Locations info:
www.reelstreets.com
www.movie-locations.com

There are so many websites and search engines to choose and explore that I would recommend looking in the various Who webrings or try Google or Yahoo.

Thanks to Jezz the taxi driver for London location updates and to everyone who has taken the time to correct details.

Keep in touch:
quadmodbook@yahoo.co.uk